THE SUN CLIMBS SLOW

Erna Paris

The Sun
Climbs Slow

JUSTICE IN THE AGE
OF IMPERIAL AMERICA

Alfred A. Knopf Canada

PUBLISHED BY ALFRED A. KNOPF CANADA

Copyright © 2008 Erna Paris

Library and Archives Canada Cataloguing in Publication
Paris, Erna
The sun climbs slow : justice in the age of imperial America / Erna Paris.

ISBN 978-0-676-97744-8

1. International criminal courts. 2. International offenses.
3. International criminal courts—Government policy—United States.
I. Title.

KZ6314.P37 2007   345'.0235   C2007-902473-4

Text design: CS Richardson

First Edition

Printed and bound in the United States of America

2 4 6 8 9 7 5 3 1

To my mother, Chris Newman,
for her unwavering love and support

And to my grandchildren
Julia, Simon and Jacqueline

Inheritors of the twenty-first century

The world is sustained by three things
By justice, by truth, and by peace
—RABBAN SHIMON BEN GAMLIEL, TANNAIST SAGE
AND JEWISH LEADER, CIRCA 40 CE

These three things are actually one.
When justice is done, truth is served and peace is achieved
—RAV MUNA, THE JERUSALEM TALMUD, CIRCA 350 CE

The United States was the first nation founded on the bedrock
principle of justice and equality for all before the law. It is wrong
for us now to insist that this principle cannot be applied to all
inhabitants of this earth. Just as our forbearers did, we should
build institutions that will serve as a haven for all against the
arbitrary exercise of power.
—JIMMY CARTER,
THIRTY-NINTH PRESIDENT OF THE UNITED STATES

In the prospect of an international criminal court lies the promise
of universal justice. That is the simple and soaring hope of this
vision. We are close to its realization. We will do our part to see it
through till the end. We ask you . . . to do yours in our struggle to
ensure that no ruler, no State, no junta and no army anywhere can
abuse human rights with impunity. Only then will the innocents
of distant wars and conflicts know that they, too, may sleep under
the cover of justice; that they, too, have rights, and that those who
violate those rights will be punished.
—KOFI ANNAN, UNITED NATIONS SECRETARY-GENERAL

CONTENTS

—

ACKNOWLEDGMENTS

—

This book could not have been written without the help of key people in the field of international humanitarian law, who were willing to
answer my questions about the often arcane details of their profession. Among them, I owe special thanks to Ewen Allison, an attorney
in Washington, DC with a special interest in international humanitarian and criminal law, William Schabas, a Canadian legal scholar
and the director of the Irish Centre for Human Rights at the
National University of Ireland and Richard Goldstone, a distinguished justice (emeritus) of the South Africa Constitutional Court
and the first prosecutor-in-chief of the UN Criminal Tribunals for
the former Yugoslavia and Rwanda. All three kindly explained complex elements of the law I was unsure of and generously took time
from their busy lives to read the text for legal errors. Their help was
critical, but I hasten to add that all remaining factual errors are mine
alone. I have also benefited from my long-time membership in the
high-level Internet discussion group, International Justice Watch,
moderated by András J. Riedlmayer, Fine Arts Library, Harvard
University and Thomas Keenan, the director of the Human Rights
Project at Bard College.

In addition to those whose names appear frequently in the text,
and are therefore a part of the story, I wish to thank the following
individuals for their special contribution to this work. Richard
Dicker, the director of the International Justice Program at the

non-governmental organization Human Rights Watch kept me informed about the background to contemporary events and always made himself available to answer questions. Nidžara Ahmetasević, a journalist with *Slobodna Bosna* in Sarajevo, researched and guided my visit to Bosnia. My friend Robert Kellermann thoughtfully provided important documents concerning the use of torture in Guantánamo Bay and elsewhere after September 11, 2001. Cherif Bassiouni, one of the world's most knowledgable experts on the history of international humanitarian law and the Rome Statute of the International Criminal Court, provided me with texts on these subjects and was kind enough to read an early draft of Chapter Eleven on the creation of the ICC. Judge Hans-Peter Kaul of the ICC made it easier for me to gain access to important interviewees, and Luis Moreno-Ocampo, the prosecutor of the International Criminal Court, thoughtfully sent me updates on his work long after our formal meeting took place. Jon Allen, formerly minister for political affairs at the Canadian Embassy in Washington, worked persistently to get me an interview with John Bolton. Frank Cunningham patiently explained the thinking of the eighteenth-century German philosopher, Immanuel Kant, whose ideas about cosmopolitanism inform the raison d'être of new international criminal courts. The Canadian author and poet Anne Michaels generously granted me permission to quote from her lovely work, *The Weight of Oranges*; and the estate of the late Anglo-American poet T. S. Eliot, and Eliot's publisher, Faber and Faber Limited, kindly granted permission to quote from Eliot's poem, "The Four Quartets." Maxine Sidran read the manuscript for (non-legal) factual errors; and my agent, Michael Levine, negotiated the publication of *The Sun Climbs Slow* with my favourite Canadian publisher, Knopf Canada.

Louise Dennys, the Executive Vice-President of Random House of Canada and the Executive Publisher of Knopf Canada, took time from her formidably busy life to read the manuscript and offer invaluable editorial advice, as did Michael Schellenberg, the senior editor on the book. Michael's close reading of the text became central to my thinking. Alison Reid and Doris Cowan jointly copyedited the text and Scott Richardson designed the cover. I am also grateful to the Canada Council for the Arts for providing me with a generous stipend to help defray continental and trans-continental travel costs associated with my research.

As always, I reserve my deepest gratitude for my loyal friends and family, all of whom have encouraged me with their sustained interest in my work. My children, Michelle Paris, and Roland and Katie Paris, offered ongoing moral support during the years I spent writing this complex book. Roland, who is now an award-winning author in his own right, thoughtfully sent me dozens of articles he thought might be useful.

My mother, Chris Newman, continued to ask pertinent questions about my work, in spite of the difficulties presented by her great age. *The Sun Climbs Slow* is dedicated, in part, to her—in gratitude for the enduring love she has shown me throughout my life.

Finally, there is Tom Robinson—my husband and closest friend. Tom's professional expertise in the early Greek philosophers made him the perfect reader for Chapter Two. He also suggested the title, proofread the text and created the index. Beyond this material help, his continuing support and unfailing love lie, unseen, at the root of this book—as well as those that preceded it.

The Sun Climbs Slow

On April 27, 1941, the British prime minister Winston Churchill addressed his people in a nationwide radio broadcast. The world was at war, and the war was going badly for the Allies. That very day Greece had surrendered to the Nazis and Yugoslavia had done the same just ten days earlier. Britain itself had been under air attack for almost a year. Not that Sir Winston would ever allow such discouraging thoughts to cross his lips, at least in public; his voice, on the contrary, was inspirational, a rallying call to the beleaguered. It was also a voice of thanks to America for its recent decision to patrol the Atlantic, where German U-boats were preventing supply ships from delivering their cargo. The "action of the United States . . . will be dictated not by methodical calculations of profit and loss, but by moral sentiment," testified Churchill with a flourish of appreciation. "Never, never in our history, have we been held in such admiration and regard across the Atlantic Ocean."

Churchill maintained (rightly as it turned out) that America's participation in the war for what he believed were moral as well as strategic reasons would mark a decisive turning point in the conflict. And to emphasize this point he quoted directly from the greatly loved poem "Say Not The Struggle Naught Availeth," by the Victorian poet Arthur Hugh Clough. Clough's language may sound overly romantic to contemporary ears, but Churchill inspired the British by pointing to America's new resolve. Over the BBC airwaves came these words:

> For while the tired waves, vainly breaking,
> Seem here no painful inch to gain,
> Far back, through creeks and inlets making,
> Comes silent, flooding in, the main.
> And not by eastern windows only,
> When daylight comes, comes in the light;
> In front, the sun climbs slow, how slowly,
> But westward, look, the land is bright.

I have chosen Clough's phrase, "the sun climbs slow," as the title of my book for two reasons. First, because it is a fitting metaphor for the concerted effort that has riveted the eyes of the world over the past decade and a half and still bedevils us today: bringing criminal justice and accountability to the international sphere, where politics too often trumps law. Second, because, seventy years on, a sad irony surrounds Churchill's earnest assurances about America's commitments. The United States did help to divert and destroy the seeming relentless sweep of the Nazi war machine; and in the immediate postwar years America was an ardent supporter of international cooperation, justice and human rights. But that has changed. When the International Criminal Court—the world's first permanent tribunal of international criminal justice—came into being in the late 1990s, the subsequent Republican government of George W. Bush tried to destroy it with every means at its disposal.

—

During the last decade of the twentieth century, two remarkable, almost simultaneous, events occurred, both of them precipitated by the end of the Cold War. In 1991, the implosion of the Soviet Union opened the door to the emergence of a single, unchallenged superstate—the United States—and like all unimpeded world powers, past and present, the newly enhanced American empire soon buttressed its weight with the age-old claim that might makes right.

The second extraordinary event of the era was the creation of new international courts of international criminal justice. Fifty years after the Nuremberg trials condemned the leaders of the Nazi enterprise, the International Criminal Tribunal for the Former Yugoslavia and the International Criminal Tribunal for Rwanda were empowered to prosecute individuals for the worst offences ever codified in law, including crimes against humanity and genocide. During the Cold War, earlier judicial initiatives of this sort had been suspended in aspic. These two new courts, and several others that followed, were universally supported because they were limited to trying suspected perpetrators from specifically designated conflicts. However, when global justice assumed a permanent mien, as it did with the emergence of the simply named International Criminal Court in 1998, the United States grew wary. National sovereignty was under siege, it protested: an ongoing court mandated to try the world's worst perpetrators would challenge the rules that had underpinned the international order for hundreds of years. This was at least partly true. But a new international order favouring justice and accountability was quietly seeding itself regardless, with the support of more than half the countries in the world, especially Canada. Lloyd Axworthy, who was the foreign minister at the time, was the world's leading advocate of human security and "soft power," the use of diplomacy and persuasion in international affairs in lieu of military might.

The Sun Climbs Slow is the harrowing story of the battle waged by the administration of President George W. Bush against the International Criminal Court. It is a story about the bedrock rule of law, and what happens when national leaders subvert or ignore foundational global agreements, which have been hard won over centuries, to suit their own purposes. It is about the striking ease with which the consensus regarding fundamentals such as the abhorrence of torture and the presumption of innocence can be eroded when influential people claim that it is right to abandon long-standing laws and values, even in well-established democracies. It is about deeply rooted disagreements over the conduct of the powerful and the rights and duties of citizens, that have never ceased to demand resolution.

At the end of the most violent century ever recorded, humanity reached a major crossroads in the endemic conflict between two opposing realities: the determination of superpowers to impose their will, and the effort on the part of thousands of people across centuries to ensure that leaders who commit major crimes are held accountable before the world community. As I write these words, the neo-conservatives who achieved prominence in the United States with the election of George W. Bush in 2000 are jumping, or being pushed, off a sinking ship. Their departure makes it easier to understand their influence on early twenty-first century America and the world at large from a historical perspective.

My interest in this subject goes back to my undergraduate studies, to the then-startling recognition that differing ideas about how to live and govern justly were being debated thousands of years ago. What brought me to write this work was the realization that in an increasingly dark world where ordinary civilians are often directly targeted by enemy armies, the rule of law, alone, can offer hope for protection and deterrence; and that large-scale crimes must be elucidated and judged in order to restore social balance.

Although I have long been interested in the Nuremberg trials of the chief Nazi perpetrators at the end of the Second World War because they blazed a new trail of accountability, I may have begun this work back in 1983, while I was researching a book about France's landmark trial of the Nazi war criminal, Klaus Barbie. I became fascinated by the implications of bringing war criminals to justice. France had not recovered from the cracks in its social fabric that had emerged during the bitter wartime Nazi occupation, nor had the French seriously confronted their buried past. The Barbie trial provoked a public cataclysm, one that was repeated again and again during the decades of the 1980s and the 1990s, as the French government insistently pursued other perpetrators for crimes that were committed during that era. I came to see that, in addition to ending the impunity of high-placed criminals, the evidence presented in an open, transparent court can expose the factual truth about what occurred during a conflict; and that, if handled properly, such trials may eventually play a role in reconciling divided populations.

The writing of *The Sun Climbs Slow* has been a compelling personal experience involving four years of on-the-ground research on two continents. And throughout, I have held an indelible picture in my mind—a fleeting image of a small girl in a refugee camp somewhere in Darfur whose little form once caught the eye of a television camera. She is two, perhaps three, years old; she is standing beside her mother, who is seated on the ground. Her lower lip shoots forward in that unhappy, defiant pout every parent will immediately recognize, as if to say *"Why* am I in this strange place? I want to go *home!"* She is too young to understand anything except that her life has been interrupted. She is healthy. Her wide eyes look directly at the camera.

I want to whisk her away. Save her.

Is she still alive? She haunts me still when sleep refuses to come.

This book was written for her and for the millions like her, for international criminal justice, should it succeed, is both promise and possible antidote. We are at the cusp of something so new that it can properly be called untried.

The debate over power versus law may be as old as humanity itself. But the "winning side" in this latest eruption of an ancient dispute will help shape the course of the twenty-first century.

ONE

The Inauguration

I t is March 11, 2003, and close to a thousand dignitaries, human rights activists and representatives of eighty-nine states from around the world have arrived in The Hague, Holland—a city that has been celebrated since the seventeenth century as a centre of international diplomacy and a refuge for persecuted minorities. At one o'clock in the afternoon they begin to assemble in the ancient Ridderzaal, or "Hall of Knights," the medieval parliament of the Netherlands. Except for the modern luxuries of central heating and the small electric bulbs that illuminate a dozen chandeliers where once tapers flickered, the palatial interior of this building has changed little, I suspect, since it was constructed in the mid-thirteenth century to mark the ascension of Count William of Holland to the universal throne of the Holy Roman Empire. Two regal chairs decorated with ornate crowns and gold velvet canopies sit together on a raised dais, backed by a red velvet curtain. On the walls are the coats of arms of the former Dutch, Bavarian, Burgundian and Habsburg rulers of the country, as well as the banners of the provinces and the former overseas possessions of the kingdom. Holland has a multi-layered history of commercial sea trade and colonial territorialism.

The excitement in the room is palpable as the invited guests parade down the centre aisle to their velvet-covered seats. The world's first permanent international criminal court, the result of a 1998 treaty that came into force on July 1, 2002, is about to be formally inaugurated. Representatives from more than half the countries in the world have come to mark the birth of the most important institution to penetrate the global sphere since the creation of the United Nations in 1945. They all believe that the appalling crimes that have tainted, and continue to taint, our era simply must be addressed.

The legacy of the twentieth century is one of unsurpassed brutality. Within the span of one century we have witnessed the genocide of Armenian civilians by the Turks in 1915; the murderous Japanese assault on Nanjing, China, in 1937; the Nazi Holocaust against the Jews in mid-century; the special horror of Josef Stalin's crimes against his own people; apartheid in South Africa; the annihilation of millions of Cambodians by their fellow countryman Pol Pot; the grotesque cruelties of Idi Amin in Uganda; vicious genocides in both Yugoslavia and Rwanda; and the ongoing shame of Darfur, the Congo and the other warring regions of the African continent. The International Criminal Court was born of this history as the embodiment of a simple, powerful idea: the need for a permanent tribunal to prosecute the perpetrators of genocide, crimes against humanity and war crimes,[1] the most serious offences ever codified. It is a newborn with enough potential muscle to influence the way nations, and especially their leaders, consider their choices. Its mandate is to mount an assault on the age-old scourge of criminal impunity, on behalf of the peoples of the world.

—

We rise as Queen Beatrix of the Netherlands is escorted down the aisle by Jan Peter Balkenende, the country's prime minister. United Nations Secretary-General Kofi Annan also takes his seat in the front row. The new court is the creation of global multilateralism, and Mr. Annan has been a strong supporter. This is fortunate, for although the UN will not control the workings of the International Criminal Court, the tribunal will need its backing. With no police force or other such operational support, the ICC will depend entirely on the moral, tactical and financial support of the international community.

Also seating themselves in the front rows are the eighteen newly elected judges of the court, representing eighteen countries across the globe. One month earlier it took thirty-three rounds of ballots for the nations that had signed on to the Rome Statute, the treaty that established and underpins the ICC, to elect these men and women. Prominent among them is Philippe Kirsch, a Canadian, who is about to be chosen by his peers as president of the tribunal. It was he who headed the remarkable negotiations in Rome, in June 1998, that made this moment possible. This day is a triumph, and not merely because a criminal justice court that has been dreamed of for centuries is being ushered into the world. Before the ICC could become a reality, a minimum of sixty nations had to ratify the Rome Statute, but eighty-nine countries have already made this formal commitment. This has happened far sooner than anyone expected.

One country is conspicuously not represented in this room. The absence of the United States is glaring. "The American ambassador to The Hague wrote to say he would not attend," a spokesman for the court announced earlier to the assembled media. The brittleness in his voice was unmistakable.

Prime Minister Balkenende, a dark-haired man in his forties, moves to the podium to open the event. He looks slightly nervous as he speaks about the long history of The Hague as a locus for international justice. The International Court of Justice, which settles disputes between states, is already located here—as is the International Tribunal for the former Yugoslavia, which, as this gathering is taking place, is conducting the war crimes trial of the former Serb president, Slobodan Milošević. Appeals from the International Criminal Tribunal for Rwanda now are being heard here as well. In an emotional voice, the prime minister proudly invokes the seventeenth-century Dutch legal thinker, Hugo Grotius, whose prescient book, *On the Law of War and Peace*, published in 1625, was the first to set out a system of international law based on clear agreements between nations. Balkenende notes tellingly that Grotius was once imprisoned for his far-reaching ideals.

Now Prince Zeid Ra'ad Zeid Al-Hussein, Jordan's representative to the United Nations, approaches the podium. He is thin, balding and intense. His country's record on human rights is less than sterling; Jordanians are still subject to arbitrary arrest and detention, and journalists have been prosecuted. But his own commitment to the rule of law and to the ICC is passionate and personal. He is the current president of the Assembly of States Parties, made up of the eighty-nine countries that have ratified the Rome Statute.

He alludes almost immediately to the impending war in Iraq—the other event on everyone's mind. "At the very moment when our planet lives with the very grave challenges threatening international peace and security, we assemble here to confirm once again our commitment to the international rule of law. . . . It is an occasion the root of which is to be found in the first flickerings of human common sense. . . .

Yet, as humanity [progressed] toward the achievement we celebrate today, people throughout the world continued to suffer horrifyingly from genocide, war crimes and crimes against humanity—a constant reminder of what needed to be done."

What needed—or needs—to be done? In a few simple words, Prince Zeid has articulated the sense of urgency that characterizes this historic event, and the high expectations for the court. These include the hope that the tribunal will help to deter future genocides and related crimes, that it will be fair and transparent in all its dealings, that it will create an accurate historical record of the cases it tries and that it will formally acknowledge the civilian victims who have survived the crimes.

Those who did not survive are invisible, but conspicuously present in this room. They are the millions whose lives were shattered across the violent timescape of the twentieth century: the women, men and countless numbers of their hapless children in whose names this concerted struggle against the age-old impunity of the venal and the powerful is being launched. As Prince Zeid's words fall away, a stillness suffused with grief blankets the ancient hall, a thick quietude that stifles the well-meaning phrases.

Then, from a far corner, emerge the hesitant notes of a string ensemble—the poignant sounds of the Nocturne from Alexander Borodin's String Quartet No. 2. The partnered voices of violin and cello caress the silence, restoring dignity and grace. The universal language of music succeeds where words have failed.

Sitting high in the press section of the balcony, I acknowledge the presence of the dead. I think about the husbands, fathers and sons who were slaughtered by the thousands in Srebrenica, Bosnia, then dumped like animals into crudely dug pits; about the young woman I met in a small Sarajevo hotel two years after the massacre, who was still hoping that her father would return. I think about the loyal mothers of the Plaza de Mayo in Buenos Aires, Argentina, who paraded on the same day every week, for twenty years, holding aloft the pictures of their "disappeared" children, needing to know their fate. I remember the dignified woman I watched testify at a session of the South African Truth and Reconciliation Commission who asked the commissioner to return "the bones" of her nineteen-year-old son: he had been arrested one day many years before and had never been seen again. I remember the terrified men, women and children who thought they were safe because they took refuge in the historic sanctuary of a Rwandan church— until the minister betrayed them to their machete-wielding countrymen. And a photograph I once saw in Yad Vashem, the memorial museum to the Holocaust in Jerusalem: the scene was Babi Yar, a ravine on the outskirts of Kiev where more than thirty-three thousand Jews were shot on a clear, sunlit day in September 1941. The photographer had captured the last terror-filled moment in the lives of an entire family of women as the gun barrels pointed at their heads: an old mother, two adult daughters, a small granddaughter of four or five, and a baby, huddled together at the edge of a pit, naked, gripping one another by the arms.

Prince Zeid is speaking again. "The wrongs which we seek to condemn and punish have been so calculated, so malignant and so devastating that civilization cannot tolerate their being ignored, because it cannot survive their being repeated." He is quoting Robert H. Jackson, the former United States Supreme Court justice who became the American chief prosecutor at the International Military Tribunal in Nuremberg, where the leaders of the Nazi enterprise were prosecuted after the Second World War. Jackson's words resonate as powerfully today as they did sixty years ago.

One by one, the ICC judges are called on to take the oath of office; it is a secular oath, I note, without reference to anything beyond the integrity of their personal undertaking to perform their duties impartially and with honour. They speak English or French in accents that reflect the global spectrum. One of them is Claude Jorda of France, a country whose commendable (if belated) legal efforts to confront war crimes committed on its territory during the Nazi occupation heralded the arrival of the ICC. Hans-Peter Kaul of Germany takes his oath in English. Nothing speaks more directly to the birth of this new international institution than Germany's central presence here today. Kaul has been one of the world's most tireless promoters of the ICC.

Navanethem Pillay of South Africa steps forward. Slim and composed, she is a woman of Indian background who rose to the top of the legal profession in spite of the hurdles placed in her way.

When all the judges of the court have been sworn in, Kofi Annan moves slowly toward the podium. The secretary-general recently presided over a serious crisis in the United Nations, and the danger has not abated. The division in the Security Council over America's determination to take pre-emptive military action against the Iraqi dictator Saddam Hussein exposed a fissure in ideologies and national interests, and Annan has been unable to heal the rift. Some Americans, led by their president, have been writing bitter epitaphs for the UN. Mr. Annan's own prestige has been damaged.

He shuffles his notes for a moment, then looks up. His expression is calm, as usual. Speaking in a slow voice, he articulates the meaning of the ceremony we have witnessed. "It has taken mankind years to reach this moment," he says. " . . . These eighteen judges . . . from all regions of the world and many different cultures and legal traditions, have made themselves the embodiment of our collective conscience."

Then he addresses what may be the most difficult problem the new court will face: the inherent tension between the pursuit of justice, including accountability and possible reconciliation, and the political exigencies of brokering peace when a conflict ends. "There are times when we are told that justice must be set aside in the interest of peace," he says. "It is true that justice can only be dispensed when the peaceful order of society is secure, but we have come to understand that the reverse is also true. Without justice there can be no lasting peace."

The word "lasting" resonates through the hall. The dustbin of history overflows with examples of craven amnesties extended to criminals in the name of peace, some of which barely survived the signing ceremony, as in Sierra Leone. Sometimes they appear to hold for decades, as in postwar France—until the victims, or their descendants, screw their courage to the sticking place and demand a true accounting.

"All your work must shine with moral and legal clarity," continues the secretary-general. If he sounds a little like a Sunday preacher, no one seems to mind. The implications of the new court are far-reaching. By insisting that no person, nation or government is immune, and that justice must be done where crimes against humanity, genocide and war crimes have been committed, the International Criminal Court has effectively challenged the world of politics as usual.

As Annan finishes, my neighbour wonders aloud what will happen once this emotional ceremony is over. Her question hangs in the air: will the great dream of the International Criminal Court fall victim to power politics? Not even the most stalwart optimist would dare to argue that the absence of the world's most muscular country is anything less than ominous. Will the United States succeed in blocking this drive toward criminal accountability in global affairs? There are signs of just such a campaign.

At the crowded reception that follows the ceremony, the queen circulates among her guests. Waiters offer champagne and canapés of smoked salmon and Dutch cheeses to the foreign diplomats and the members of the new court, and to the dozens of people who have attended as representatives of international non-governmental organizations from around the world. Some of these have famous names such as Amnesty International, Human Rights Watch, the International Commission of Jurists and the French Fédération internationale des ligues des Droits de l'Homme, born a century ago during the Dreyfus Affair. These are the men and women who lobbied for almost a decade to make today's inauguration a reality—since the mid-1990s, to be exact, when the horrors of the Balkan wars reawakened the conscience of the West. They helped to organize the 1998 Rome Conference, where the court's founding document was noisily debated and finally agreed to; they disseminated information about the ICC and agitated tirelessly for the acceptance and ratification of the Rome Statute by countries around the world. The role of these NGOs in the birth of the world's newest international institution was unprecedented in global affairs, and the seriousness with which they are regarded is evidenced by the list of their funders: the European Union and the governments of Canada, Denmark, Finland, Germany, the Netherlands, Norway, Portugal, Switzerland, Sweden and the United Kingdom.

NGOs notoriously battle and bicker with one another, but in this urgent quest hundreds of such groups came together to form the Coalition for an International Criminal Court. Later in the day, when Queen Beatrix's reception has drawn to a close, the coalition holds its own celebration in the nearby Peace Palace of The Hague. A long table occupies the centre of a small room where portraits of dour-looking men stare down from the walls in perpetual disapproval. Eighteen places have been set for the newly minted judges, each setting showcasing two books: *The Key to My Neighbour's House: Seeking Justice in Bosnia and Rwanda*, by Elizabeth Neuffer, and *The ICC: The Making of the Rome Statute*, by Roy S. Lee.

The judges enter in procession to sustained applause. In return they applaud about one hundred members of the coalition. William Pace, chairman of the coalition, singles out two men from the audience. Both are in their eighties and both were prosecutors at the 1946–49 Nuremburg Trials. Benjamin Ferencz—small, energetic, white-haired—receives a tumultuous ovation. As a young American prosecutor he tried twenty-two leading members of the infamous Einsatzgruppen "elimination units," the SS death squads that followed the Wehrmacht into Eastern Europe, where they rounded up and murdered more than a million Jews. That indelible experience convinced Ferencz that the missing link in the international system was a permanent criminal court to deter and punish the most serious crimes. For more than half a century he lobbied ceaselessly, getting nowhere—until the Cold War came to an abrupt end and the agonies of Bosnia and Rwanda broke through the thin veneer of peace. If it can be said that one living person started the long process that led to this day, it is he.

His surviving Nuremberg colleague, Henry T. King, also is honoured with sustained applause. King has had a distinguished legal career since his days as a prosecutor at that International Military Tribunal. He was general counsel of the US Foreign Economic Aid Program, US director of the Canada–US Law Institute, a long-time professor at Case Western Reserve University School of Law in Cleveland, Ohio, and most recently a member of the American Bar Association Task Force on War Crimes in the former Yugoslavia. Later he will tell me that he, like Ferencz, was inspired by his experience at Nuremburg. It was his father, he confided, who had first opened his mind to the ideal of international justice. The King family held regular Sunday night "discussion sessions" around the dinner table, where they talked about world events. One Sunday in 1935 King's father challenged his young son and daughter with an important question: "What can we do about war?"

"My sister and I didn't know how to reply, so my father told us," he recalled. "He said, 'Ordinary people don't want war: it's their leaders. To stop war from recurring, we must punish the leaders who foment it.'" That lesson became etched in his memory.

Two other acknowledged leaders of the movement to create a permanent international criminal court also address the gathering. One is Arthur Robinson, the former prime minister of Trinidad and Tobago, a frail man in his late seventies. The link between peace and justice has been on his mind for decades, he says in a short speech: more than thirty years ago he created a foundation to establish just such a tribunal. He was a member of the United Nations Expert Group on Crime and the Abuse of Power, and vice-chairman of the International Council of Parliamentarians for Global Action. In 1989, when he was prime minister of his country, he asked the UN General Assembly to think seriously about an international criminal court to deal with drug running.

The last speaker is William Pace. "The ICC was born of a century of brutal wars characterized by overwhelming violence against civilians and compounded by a lack of accountability for those responsible," he says quietly, his voice breaking with emotion. "The resulting impunity furthered the cycle of violence, drove neighbour to fear neighbour, destroyed the social fabric and placed long-term peace and security impossibly beyond reach. The birth of the International Criminal Court marks a shared recognition . . . that international mechanisms can provide a forum for accountability when the national systems fail, and give new hope for justice and long-term peace."

Everything about this inauguration has been choreographed to be understood as a single narrative: the International Criminal Court is the most dramatic marker yet in the long human struggle for accountability. Every symbol folded into this pageant, from the presence of Queen Beatrix to the moving music played in memory of the millions of victims, has contained one simple, hopeful message: wars will come and go, but the global court being inaugurated today has the potential to deter crime, challenge the impunity of the powerful and add a permanent legal and moral component to the world order.

On that March day it was comforting to imagine that Idi Amin, Pol Pot and Josef Stalin—just three of history's unpunished tyrants—might have turned uncomfortably in their graves.

TWO

Roots and Tendrils

———

E veryone present in the Hall of Knights the day of the inauguration knew that the International Criminal Court would be seriously weakened without the support of the most powerful nation on earth. John R. Bolton, then the United States undersecretary of state for arms control and international security, had called the ICC "an organization that runs contrary to fundamental American precepts and basic constitutional principles of popular sovereignty, checks and balances and national independence." Had he searched the entirety of *Webster's* dictionary, he could scarcely have found stronger language with which to damn the new institution. The charge was exceptionally serious. He was suggesting that the ICC was insufficiently democratic, even illegitimate.

Bolton and other members of the George W. Bush administration also claimed that American soldiers would be in the
firing line of ICC prosecutions. This was a puzzling allegation,
since there were layers of protective safeguards in the Rome
Statute, providing for consultations and permissions before a
case could be triggered. Additionally, an article in the Rome
Statute spelled out a new concept called "complementarity,"
which meant that the ICC was prohibited from initiating an
investigation unless the country where the suspected perpetrator held citizenship either refused to hold its own trial or was
unable to hold one as a result of failed domestic institutions
and infrastructure. The latter situation would clearly never
occur in the United States, although the willingness to try a
person accused of the crimes over which the ICC held jurisdiction would always be a political choice.

Why was the government of the United States so viscerally
opposed to an international court that was mandated to prosecute the worst crimes known to humanity? Over the course of
the twentieth century, the US had been a major player in
advancing human rights, global institutions and international
law, starting with President Woodrow Wilson's call at the Paris
Peace Conference in September 1919 for a League of Nations,
an international body to promote peace through collective
security and diplomacy. And the United States had assumed a
leading role before and during the Nuremberg Trials. An
American, Robert H. Jackson, had been the chief prosecutor at
that groundbreaking series of trials. After the death of
President Franklin Delano Roosevelt on April 12, 1945, his
widow, Eleanor, had worked tirelessly to oversee the birth of
the United Nations. The United States continued to support
the ad hoc international courts that operated under the auspices of the UN, including those that were currently trying
perpetrators from the Yugoslav and Rwandan genocides.

Did a tribunal mandated to combat criminal impunity by

confronting genocide, crimes against humanity and war crimes really run "contrary to fundamental American precepts," as Bolton claimed? Given America's twentieth-century history, this was unlikely; in fact, his words ran contrary to deeply rooted commitments within American society that were central to the founding of the nation. No. It was the existence of *this* court that angered the world's remaining superpower, especially after the election of George W. Bush to the White House, and even more so at a time when America was tightening its military fist after the terrorist attacks of September 11, 2001. The reason was not hard to fathom. Unlike the ad hoc tribunals, the International Criminal Court was not temporary and short-term. It was a permanent new fixture in the galaxy of global institutions. Most important, it was structured to be independent of politics, including Security Council vetoes on its prosecutions. The ICC would be overseen uniquely by the collectivity of states that had signed on as members—the States Parties, as they were termed. The chief prosecutor and the judges would choose their cases as they saw fit, according to the court's own established criteria.

No longer tempered by the wary standoff of the Cold War, the United States was newly predominant in the world. Unlike less powerful nations, America did not need to subject itself to other people's rules—and certainly not those of Europe or Canada, for example, or their favourite new institution, the ICC. In the White House of George W. Bush, any threat to the ancient "might makes right" doctrine underpinning the world order needed to be disabled without delay. The US invasion of Iraq was born of the opium of uncontested power, just as the unprecedented creation of a permanent international criminal court was born of the need to make world leaders accountable for their deeds.

We will learn more about John Bolton's battle to maim the tribunal in another chapter. But to understand the struggle between the United States and the International Criminal Court being played out on the contemporary world stage, we must first look to the past, follow tendrils that trail back through millennia. For the quarrel between the US and the ICC was merely the most recent outbreak of an endemic dispute whose roots can be traced to the origins of human societies: to the enduring struggle between the interests of the powerful and the rule of law, to the continuing clash between the politics of power and the moral constraints of justice. The hyperpower and the tribunal had emerged in a single historical moment at the end of the twentieth century. Like boxers in a ring, each had much to gain over the long term should the match go their way, and much to lose should it not.

—

In an imagined picture in my mind stands an ancient library containing the story of civilizations past. I open the door and step inside. On dusty shelves moulder time-worn chronicles of empires at their height and musty tomes that recount the long battle to temper power with justice. The clash between those who believe that political life must be governed by universally binding norms and those who insist that the might of an all-powerful state is sufficient to justify the pursuit of its interests is as old as recorded history. It is a controversy that has been addressed by monarchs, philosophers, authors, historians, judges and policy-makers—because it speaks to the need to live in an ordered world.

Niccolò Machiavelli's famous opus, *The Prince*, may be the most widely known literary root of the theory that "might makes right." The shrewd sixteenth-century Florentine argued that morality has no place in politics (an idea that became a staple of "realist" thinking in post–Second World War international relations, especially in the United States).

Such thinking starts with the "reality" that the strong will pursue their interests when they can (interests that they frequently rationalize as benefiting others).

Two hundred years later, the eighteenth-century German philosopher Immanuel Kant articulated an influential argument on the other side of the enduring debate. Kant believed that universal norms are the indispensable backbone of peace. His cosmopolitan vision of the future predicted a globalized world in which justice—a practical as well as a moral component of peace—would transcend political borders.

Although the foreign policies of most contemporary Western nations are a mix of sovereign, interests-based realism and Kant's vision of cosmopolitanism (known today as multilateralism), the roots of the standoff between the United States and the International Criminal Court are buried deep in the foundations of this history. But behind Machiavelli and Kant, who may be best known to modern readers, stands the man who first articulated both these ideas: the notion that power trumps morality *and* that justice lies at the root of peaceful relations—the great Athenian historian Thucydides.

No one has ever communicated the tension between power politics and the ideal of universal justice more vividly than Thucydides. His subject was the thirty-year conflict between Athens and Sparta, fought in his time, more than two thousand years ago. The *History of the Peloponnesian War* has endured as the first great recounting of historical fact, as distinguished from other ancient historians' blending of fact and myth.

Thucydides was an Athenian of the famed fifth century BCE—that era of intellectual awakening in reasoning, law, democratic government, education and the dramatic arts that continues to astonish us today. Perhaps it was his physical distance from the battlefields of the Peloponnesian War, and from Athens itself, that allowed him to study the interior psychology of the campaign. Whatever lay behind his razor-sharp observations about human nature (which he believed to be immutable), his book has astounded and influenced readers across the centuries. The first published work by the seventeenth-century British philosopher Thomas Hobbes (he who concluded that human life was "nasty, brutish and short," a situation to be rectified only by submission to an all-powerful leader) was a translation of Thucydides' *History*. Mid-twentieth-century American foreign policy was also seeded by his work, as we shall see. Remarkably, Thucydides anticipated his own enduring fame: "It will be enough for me if these words of mine are judged useful by those who want to understand clearly the events which happened in the past and which (human nature being what it is) will, at some time or other and in much the same ways, be repeated in the future," he wrote. "My work is not . . . designed to meet the needs of an immediate public, but was written to last forever."

Although Thucydides was known to be dour of character and chary with his approval, he was inspired by the charismatic leader Pericles; and his reconstruction of Pericles' funeral oration to the fallen Athenian soldiers, which was delivered in the winter of 431 BCE, at the end of the first year of the war, opens a window into the civic values of Athens at the zenith of its empire.

According to the *History*, it is a day of national mourning in Athens. The citizens of the metropolis have formed a funeral procession that winds its way to the beautifully landscaped public burial grounds just outside the city walls. Wagons carry coffins made of cypress wood, each holding the remains of fallen soldiers. One wagon carries a decorated, symbolically empty, bier to honour the warriors whose unrecoverable bodies have remained on the field of battle.

Pericles speaks to the assembled people. He invokes the patriotic pride and shared values that characterize the powerful city-state, including the central idea of a common good. "Here each individual is interested not only in his own affairs but in the affairs of the state as well. . . . This is a peculiarity of ours; we do not say that a man who takes no interest in politics is a man who minds his own business; we say that he has no business here at all."[1] It follows, he continues, that the husbands, sons and brothers whose bones are being honoured on this day did not die in vain. (A theme reprised over the centuries when leaders make consolation speeches to grieving families.)

But Pericles wants to communicate something more to the mourners who stand before him. Patriotism, pride and sacrifice for the sake of the collectivity are supreme values, he says, but every public act, in war and in peace, must be subject to the laws of Athens. "We are free and tolerant in our private lives, but in public affairs we keep to the law," he tells his rapt audience. " . . . We give our obedience to those whom we put in positions of authority, and we obey the laws themselves, especially those which are for the protection of the oppressed, and *those unwritten laws which it is an acknowledged shame to break*"[2] (italics mine).

Everyone listening on that winter day of sorrow knew what was meant by "those unwritten laws which it is an acknowledged shame to break." They were the laws of universal justice that determined the ethics of human intercourse. Such rules were breached at great peril, for hubris incurred disastrous consequences that reached down through the generations, as the great tragedies of Aeschylus, Sophocles and Euripides communicated to their knowing audiences.

But the ensuing decades of the Peloponnesian War dulled the edge of Pericles' inspiring admonitions. Thucydides conveys the shifting parameters of wartime psychology as he retails the gripping negotiations that preceded each successive battle. Sea and land forces might be waiting in tense anticipation, ready to lurch into combat, but the melee needed to be justified in advance as rational policy. With Thucydides as our guide, we are transported into the company of easily recognizable human beings who debate the universal laws of justice versus the rights that are allegedly conferred on the powerful by virtue of their strength alone.

No interchange in the *History* is sharper, more aggressive or more disturbing than the dramatic re-enactment of the debate between mighty Athens and the threatened inhabitants of Melos, whom Athens is challenging to join them in the war against Sparta.

It is 416 BCE, and the war is already in its fifteenth year. The Melians are far too independent for the Athenians' liking; they brazenly insist on remaining neutral in the conflict. This is intolerable. A great fleet of thirty-eight ships carrying twenty-seven hundred hoplites (heavily armoured infantrymen), twenty mounted archers and three hundred foot archers sets sail from Athens for the island.

They anchor in a small harbour and send their representatives to negotiate, but the Melians receive them warily. They worry (rightly, as it turns out) that the "conversation" in which they are about to engage has foregone conclusions: either war or enslavement. But their anxiety merely annoys the Athenians.

"If you are going to spend the time enumerating your suspicions about the future, or if you have met here for any other reason except to look the facts in the face and think about how you can save your city from destruction, there is no point in our going on with this discussion," the Athenians warn ominously. "If, however, you will do as we suggest, then we will speak on."

When the Melians (lacking all leverage) agree to talk, the Athenians do not mince words. "We on our side will use no fine phrases saying . . . that we have a right to our empire because we defeated the Persians, or that we have come against you now because of the injuries you have done us—a great

mass of words that nobody would believe. . . . Instead we recommend that you try to get what it is possible for you to get . . .
since you know as well as we do that justice depends on the
quality of power to compel, and that the strong do what they
have the power to do and the weak accept what they must."

Against this statement of raw intent, the Melians counter
with the laws of justice: "Our view is that it is . . . useful that
you not destroy a principle that is to the general good of all
men—namely, that in the case of all who fall into danger there
should be such a thing as fair play and just dealing. . . . And this
is a principle which affects you as much as anybody, since your
own fall would be visited by the most terrible vengeance and
would be an example to the world."

"Leave it to us to face the risks," retort the Athenians
impatiently. "We shall show you that it is for the good of our
own empire that we are here, and that it is for the preservation
of your city. . . ."

"How could it be just as good for us to be the slaves as for
you to be the masters?"

"You, by giving in, would save yourselves from disaster; we,
by not destroying you, would be able to profit from you. . . .
Our opinion of the gods and of men leads us to conclude that
it is a general and necessary law of nature to rule wherever one
can. This is not a law that we made ourselves, nor were the first
to act upon it. We found it already in existence, and we shall
leave it to exist forever among those who come after us."

By suggesting that the imminent defeat of the Melians is in
everyone's best interests, the Athenians slyly apply Pericles'
famed principle of the "common good" to both parties, stating
that master and slave will both benefit from the slave's submission. The Melians see through the sophistry. They do not concede. And when they insist that they will remain neutral in the
battle against Sparta, they are lost. As Thucydides reports, the
Athenians first starved the population, after which they swept

in under the command of Philocrates, the son of Demeas, and "put to death all the men of military age whom they took, and sold the women and children as slaves." Then they colonized the island with five hundred settlers of their own.

The Athenians were not unduly troubled by the massacre of the Melians; in fact, barely a year later, the comic writer Aristophanes included a joke about "Melian starvation" in his play *The Birds*. Only when the news of Sparta's final victory at Aegospotami reached the city in 404, and the once-proud populace cringed before the likely retribution coming their way, might they have recalled Pericles' famous words about the "unwritten laws of gods and men which it is an acknowledged shame to break" that allegedly transcended human society. In the end, they were lucky: Sparta chose not to destroy them. But the once-great empire of Athens—materially ruined and spiritually exhausted—was lost, never to be revived.

———

The struggle to live in harmony with the justice of the gods preoccupied Pericles the statesman, but it was his contemporary, Socrates the philosopher, who exposed the confrontation between power and justice with an analytic rigour that has never been equalled. In the relative coolness of the late Athenian afternoon Socrates met his students at the shop of his friend Simon the leather tanner to parse the moral dilemmas that increasingly perturbed thoughtful people as the interminable conflict with Sparta dragged on. At first, his challenges and provocations were tolerated by the masses. But when Athens began to lose the war, the public turned on him. In 399 he was executed for "irreligion" and "corrupting the youth" of Athens: in other words, for encouraging them to question the received opinions of the day. In the aftermath, one devastated student, the young Plato, determined to reconstruct the conversations Socrates had held with the young men who gathered on an afternoon to talk with him—and spent the rest of his long life doing so.

In Plato's most famous work, *The Republic*, Socrates and an otherwise unknown sophist, Thrasymachus, sharply (and amusingly) debate the merits of the "might makes right" thesis versus universal standards of justice. Thrasymachus is annoyed at Socrates for insisting that it is morally wrong to harm others, and for his claim that the worst evil one can do to another human being is to make him a less worthy person by undermining his inherent goodness.

"What a lot of drivel!" retorts Thrasymachus. "Morality is nothing more than the advantage of the stronger party.... You must look at it this way, my most simple Socrates. A just man always gets less than an unjust one.... Those who reproach injustice do so because they are afraid not of *doing* it, but of suffering it.... Injustice, if it is on a large enough scale, is stronger, freer and more masterly than justice...."

" ... [Do you say then] that justice is a vice?" inquires Socrates.

"No, just very high-minded simplicity."

" ... You consider unjust people, then, to be clever and good?"

"Yes, those who are completely unjust, who can bring cities and whole communities under their power...."

Through a series of subtly crafted examples, Socrates leads Thrasymachus to agree that the society he is promoting would be anarchic and dysfunctional. "Enjoy your banquet of words," Thrasymachus hisses helplessly.

Plato makes sure his beloved Socrates wins the debate by arguing that because justice is the supreme virtue, and a manifestation of reason, which is the essence of what makes us human, moral goodness is the starting point of both individual and collective well-being. But the discussion was far from over—then or now. Thrasymachus was an obvious prototype for Machiavelli's cynical prince, whose pursuit of power is devoid of moral constraints; and more than two thousand years later, he continues to be an articulate spokesperson for the blunter-edged expressions of political realism.

Athenians were exposed to other probings of power and morality, for the famous playwrights of the day also articulated the enduring dilemmas. Antigone, for example, the timeless creation of the great fifth-century dramatist Sophocles, aggressively pushes her audience to confront a conflict they might otherwise have avoided: the rights of an earthbound ruler versus the universal laws of the gods.

Here too we can imagine the scene. It is 441 BCE, forty-nine years after the Athenian victory over the Persians at the battle of Marathon but still a decade before the start of the Peloponnesian War. Athens is a superpower in full control of the region.

The yearly drama festival has begun. The morning light illuminates a gigantic outdoor theatre as Athenians wait to see the first performance of Sophocles' new play. It is considered a civic duty to attend the theatre: seventeen thousand spectators are seated on a steep rise of stone benches that curve in a half-circle embrace around the stage below.

The actors are masked to exaggerate their character: Creon, king of Thebes; Haemon, his son; and Antigone, betrothed to Haemon. Antigone is the daughter of the former king, Oedipus, who is now blinded, exiled and disgraced after the revelation that he (unknowingly) killed his father, then married and had children with Jocasta, his own mother.

The storyline is simple: Antigone's brother Polynices has died during a rebellion against King Creon, who has decided to make an example of this treason by denying the young man the customary burial rites. Polynices' body and those of his fellow warriors will remain exposed on the battlefield, prey to crows and vultures. Distraught at her brother's fate, Antigone disobeys the royal edict and boldly —rashly—attempts to bury Polynices with her own hands; but she is caught in the act by a sentry who brings her before the appalled Creon. "I found her screaming . . . crying and cursing the ones that had done it," the sentry reports to the king.

"Did you know the order forbidding such an act?" Creon asks.

"It was plain enough," replies Antigone, " . . . for it was not Zeus who commanded me to do this, nor did [the goddess] Justice, who dwells with the gods below, ordain such laws for humankind.[3] I did not think your edicts strong enough to over-rule the unwritten, unshakeable laws of gods, you being only a man. They are not of yesterday or today, but undying, though where they came from, none of us can tell. . . ."[4]

"This girl's proud spirit was first in evidence when she broke the law; and now, to add insult to her injury, she gloats over her deed!" cries Creon. "But as I live, she shall not flout my orders with impunity!"

Whose orders should be obeyed? Sophocles is pointedly asking—the earthly edicts of an acknowledged king or the "unwritten unshakeable laws," the divine rules of unknown origin that prohibit the desecration of a body? Where does "justice" lie?

Creon's death sentence for "flouting his orders" seems not to matter to Antigone. Each believes he is behaving honourably and that the larger community agrees.

CREON: *You are wrong. None of my subjects thinks as you do.*
ANTIGONE: *Yes, they do, sir, but dare not tell you.*
CREON: *You are not only alone, but unashamed. . . . [Polynices attacked] his country.*
ANTIGONE: *Even so, we have a duty to the dead.*

Antigone is entombed alive beneath a stone, as the king has commanded. And as the gods have decreed, Creon will pay for his transgression. The prophet Teresias warns him:

Ere the chariot of the sun
Has rounded once or twice his wheeling way,
You shall have given a son of your loins
To death, in payment for death—two debts to pay:
One for the life that you have sent to death,
The life you have abominably entombed;
One for the dead still lying above ground
Unburied, unhonoured, unblessed by the gods below.
You cannot alter this. The gods themselves cannot undo it.
It follows of necessity from what you have done.
Even now the avenging Furies, the hunters of Hell
that follow and destroy,
Are lying in wait for you, and will have their prey.

Creon learns that his beloved son Haemon chose to die with his Antigone. He is transformed by his suffering; he understands that he has broken the "unspoken law." He asks to die:

I am nothing. I have no life.
Lead me away . . .

Sophocles allows the chorus the last word, which is a confirmation of "universal justice" over the laws of earthly kings.

Of happiness the crown
And chiefest part
Is wisdom, and to hold
The gods in awe.
This is the law
That, seeing the stricken heart

Of pride brought down
We learn when we are old.

As he was close to sixty when he wrote *Antigone* (the first play in his Oedipus trilogy), it is possible that Sophocles' defence of "wisdom" in the last lines of the play reflected his own thinking about the rule of law and its presumed hierarchies as he entered his last decades. We cannot know how the Athenian spectators who were seated in the outdoor amphitheatre responded. What we do know is that Sophocles and the other dramatists of his day invited their audiences to reflect with empathy on the layered complexities of moral dilemmas—and that *Antigone* took first prize at the festival that year.

Thucydides, Sophocles, Plato. Their masterworks from an incomparable era were the first enduring statements on the philosophical clash between power and justice in Western history. Their greatness illuminated the conversation. All that has followed is commentary.

—

We no longer talk about the laws of the gods, natural law or even God's law. So-called positive law is the secular currency of contemporary legal practice. It holds that law and morality may overlap but are fundamentally different. Decisions are based on legislation, treaty making and the precedents of previous cases that shed light on the issue at hand. But the ancient idea that there are underlying rules to the conduct of human affairs has never disappeared. Today it is known as *jus cogens*, meaning "compelling law." It points to fundamental norms that lie deep within the collective conscience of humanity. *Jus cogens* is the law to which there can be no exception.

Jus cogens informed the offence defined as "crimes against humanity," a felony created by the Allied founders of the

International Military Tribunal at Nuremburg in order to confront the unprecedented moral transgression of the Nazis during the Second World War. In 1946, the judges of that famous court delivered an explanation of this momentous advance in international criminal law. "The law of war is to be found not only in treaties but in the customs and practices of states, which gradually obtain universal recognition, and from the general principles of justice," they wrote. Two years later, the Genocide Convention (adopted by the United Nations in December 1948) was even more specific. The convention was created, wrote the framers, "in order to liberate mankind from . . . an odious scourge" that is "condemned by the civilized world."

The signatories to the charter that created the Nuremberg Tribunal, and the founding members of the new United Nations, recognized that crimes against humanity, including genocide, constituted a universal peril. So did the men and women who negotiated the statute of the International Criminal Court a half century later.

In the blood-red dusk of Hitler's genocide, they resurrected the ancient Greeks, legislating the "unwritten laws" of Pericles and Antigone for a new age.

THREE

The New World Order

When the American ambassador to The Hague wrote to the organizers of the International Criminal Court inauguration to say he would not attend, he was reflecting an administration policy that John Bolton had shaped, and delivered to his president. Of all the changes George W. Bush's administration had brought to American policy and governance, the opposition to the ICC was among the most radical. Under previous twentieth century administrations the United States had led the world toward international justice. I planned an exploratory trip to the US to probe this about-face.

—

It is February 10, 2004, and I am at my desk making last-minute arrangements when the ring of the telephone startles me. It is a friend who suggests that I turn on the television to watch a program being broadcast on C-SPAN, an American public service channel.

A gala award ceremony is taking place, sponsored by the American Enterprise Institute for Public Policy Research, perhaps the most influential think-tank on the contemporary neo-conservative right. Venerable (it was founded in 1943) and flush with corporate donations, the AEI has continued to attract some of the sharpest minds in Republican America, people whose work has frequently translated directly into White House policy. These have included Vice President Dick Cheney (President George W. Bush's influential Rasputin, who almost always occupies a seat just behind the throne, from which he smiles enigmatically); Paul Wolfowitz, formerly the deputy secretary of defence and later the president of the World Bank, a powerful insider who had worked for every Republican president since Nixon; and Bill Kristol, the editor and publisher of the right-wing *Weekly Standard* and the author of a book that laid out the ideology of the Bush administration: *The War over Iraq: Saddam's Tyranny and America's Mission.* Bill is the son of the late chameleon-like Irving Kristol, one of the first American intellectuals to effect a double political conversion: in the 1930s he cast off his Trotskyist cloak to reinvent himself as a liberal, and then, some thirty years later, he again transformed himself, this time into a neo-conservative.

At the televised gala, Charles Krauthammer, a widely read American journalist, is receiving the Irving Kristol prize. Now in his fifties, Krauthammer was once a Young Turk of the neo-conservative movement, and his star has risen even higher since September 11, 2001. His opinions appear weekly in more than a hundred newspapers, and his many awards include a Pulitzer Prize for commentary in 1987. I am intensely curious to hear what he will say to this audience of like-minded friends.

In 1997, Bill Kristol and many others at the gala had set the stage for the present era with the now well-known Project for the New American Century, which they described as "a non-profit educational organization dedicated to a few fundamental propositions: that American leadership is good both for America and for the world; and that such leadership requires military strength, diplomatic energy and commitment to moral principle." Shades of Plato and Thucydides, and not surprising, since nowhere had these two been studied more closely than in America. Over the decades various scholars and diplomats thought they could discern a parallel between their own Cold War competition with the Soviet Union and that of Athens versus Sparta. As early as 1947, Secretary of State George Marshall had argued that the Peloponnesian War was crucial to understanding the contemporary world. "I doubt seriously whether a man can think with full wisdom and with deep convictions regarding certain of the basic issues today who has not at least reviewed in his mind the period of the Peloponnesian War and the fall of Athens," he said.[1] In 1952, Louis J. Halle, then director of the State Department's policy planning staff, wrote that "the present, in which our country finds herself . . . called upon to assume the leadership of the free world, brings [Thucydides] virtually to our side. . . . He speaks to our ear."[2] Starting in the 1960s, Leo Strauss, the political science professor at the University of Chicago, and his intellectual disciple Allan Bloom also trained their sights on the Greeks, especially on Plato's (mid-life) authoritarianism as reflected in his enduring work, *The Republic*, which they saw as a model for top-down government ruled by trained elites. Their interpretations of the ancient texts encouraged the famil-iar "Athenian" view, via their reading of Thucydides: the might of a great empire is not merely self-serving (although there is nothing wrong with that) but is also in the best interests of the enemy. (As the Athenians explained to the Melians, "best interests" meant giving in to the empire in order to save them-selves from disaster. For contemporary neo-conservatives, "best interests" involved the installation of American-style democracy in unlikely places.) Strauss and Bloom inspired cult-like worship among generations of their students, many of whom passed through the portals of power in the administra-tions of Ronald Reagan, George H. W. Bush and George W. Bush. Paul Wolfowitz, a major architect of the drive to remake the Middle East through the March 2003 invasion of Iraq, was among the most influential of Strauss and Bloom's followers.

With the Cold War seeming to illustrate lessons from the classical past and academics drawing conclusions with foreign policy implications from that same ancient era, a common understanding about the contemporary uses of power emerged. As Alexander Kemos, a student in international relations at Harvard University, wrote in 1997, "[Contemporary] political scientists have treated the work of Thucydides as a coherent attempt to communicate silent universals that have served as the basis for American foreign policy and security doctrine in the post World War II era."[3]

The second historical marker underpinning this remark-able gala had occurred in January 1998, when the drafters of the Project for the New American Century sent a letter to President Bill Clinton urging him to revisit US policy on Iraq. Containment was "not succeeding," they wrote. Strategy should aim at "the removal of Saddam Hussein's regime from power." Not to remove Saddam, as the tyrant continued to develop weapons of mass destruction, would destabilize the Middle East, jeopardize world oil supplies and affect security in the world at large. American policy should be unilateral, if necessary, since subordinating national inter-ests to the United Nations Security Council would be "crip-pling." The authors firmly urged the president to "undertake military action, as diplomacy is clearly failing."[4]

On February 10, 2004, the day of the televised gala, just seventeen months have passed since the devastating al-Qaeda attacks on America. As the economist and writer Irwin Stelzer would later argue in the book *Neoconservatism*,⁵ it must have pleased President Bush to be able to turn to a group of advisers who already had a well-prepared response to the trauma of September 11, 2001. These, among others, were the guests at the gala; their success lay in having persuaded the president "to adopt a view of the world that [was] radically different from that favoured by the post–cold war foreign policy establishment, but which none the less [had] roots in earlier American history."⁶ They also were the men and women behind the president's National Security Strategy, introduced on September 17, 2002. Born of America's unparalleled power and fuelled by rage against the purveyors of terrorism, the presidential document spoke, as expected, of America's mission to spread "freedom," "justice" and "democracy"—but also of going it alone. Goodbye to Cold War "containment," the strategic brainchild of the American diplomat George Kennan, and to the "balance of power" so prized by Kennan and Henry Kissinger, President Richard Nixon's national security adviser and secretary of state. The new doctrine echoed the Project for the New American Century—and that century was now. It invoked a policy of pre-emption, of unapologetic hegemony in the name of security. The neo-conservatives at this gala now occupied the highest positions in Washington. A triumphant parade of like-minded men (and a few women) had crossed the threshold of power, where their newer, harder vision of America's place in the post–Cold War world was transformed into government policy.

The images from the televised award ceremony display several hundred members of this exclusive club, seated at round dinner tables. The men wear tuxedos, the women that enduring fashion statement known as "the little black dress."

But the gossip and laughter stop abruptly as a band strikes up to signal the entrance of Vice President Dick Cheney and his wife, Lynne. Everyone rises and applauds.

Dick Cheney has been associated with the AEI for thirty years—it is his intellectual home; but Lynne is also a formidable presence. She is a high-energy contributer to the culture wars that have racked the US for decades. She has authored or co-authored nine books, including *Telling the Truth*, which claims that too many teachers downgrade the United States and the heritage of the West in their classrooms; and several works for children, one a history of George Washington for "young patriots" as well as an alphabet book titled *America: A Patriotic Primer.*

The man in whose honour this glittering event is being held now enters the stage from the wings and positions himself at a table beside the draped folds of an oversized American flag. He is in a wheelchair; he has been paralyzed since the age of twenty-two, when he suffered a spinal cord injury in a diving accident. Vice President Cheney introduces him warmly, calling his work "that one clear note" in the cacophony of national commentary—and praising him as a man whose "great intelligence is guided by principle and an understanding of the world as it is." Charles Krauthammer listens carefully, his striking features mask-like and impassive. His face mirrors his fifty-four years; deep folds cascade in arcs from his nose to his chin, his dark eyes are almost expressionless and his thin lips are locked tight. Perhaps he has trained himself not to betray a hint of internal struggle, a thought that is reinforced when he begins to speak, for with every phrase he must momentarily joust with a stutter that threatens to overwhelm him. Writing has been his path to unburdened expression. He asks for no sympathy: the best advice to people who are injured, he once wrote, is to refashion their lives around what they are able to achieve in their newly configured bodies.

His hour-long speech is a brilliant overview of America's uneven foreign policy throughout the twentieth century, including the shifting background ideologies that have informed positions and choices. Like Goldilocks who tastes, then judges, the three bowls of porridge set before her, he begins by dismissing the old focus on isolationism, or "Fortress America," calling it an "ideology of fear" that is worse than useless in the post–Cold War unipolar world in which the United States has (unwittingly and unwillingly, he says) become the "accidental hegemon"—the most powerful nation since Rome. But not an empire, he explains with a small ironic smile, because Americans don't covet territory. Why, Americans don't *need* to go anywhere, nor do they need to speak foreign languages, he adds. "We like it here. We've got everything!" His friends laugh in appreciation.

The next bowl on Goldilocks' table serves up liberal internationalism, a policy that is at least principled, he concedes, because it strives to transform a dog-eat-dog Hobbesian universe where life is "nasty, brutish and short" into the law-based, international civil society of the seventeenth-century philosopher John Locke. This is a world ruled by multilateral institutions and treaties signed in good faith. Such thinking, he says, is "very nice, very noble . . . and very crazy." Its most absurd and dangerous characteristic is that it might be necessary to "transcend and even abolish the very idea of state power and national interest" in order to create a true international community.

"Realism" is what lies in the next bowl, and the realist, at least, knows a hopeless liberal project when he sees one. What the realist understands is this: "PEACE, noun: In international affairs, a period of cheating between two periods of fighting," quotes Krauthammer with deadpan irony. He is citing the tongue-in-cheek cynicism of *The Devil's Dictionary* by the nineteenth-century American writer Ambrose Bierce. His audience laughs in shared appreciation. Realists understand that the "international community" is a fiction, Krauthammer continues. "It is not a community, it is a cacophony of straining ambitions, disparate values and contending power."

Power—there's the right word, at last. Compelling and unsurpassed, *power* is the perfumed elixir that wafts from Goldilocks' third bowl. Power—to be deployed at will in the service of maintaining the status quo, the way a rich man will defend his stash of gold. American power is what keeps the international order orderly. America is the enforcer, the bulwark "between barbarism and civilization," he says. Pre-emptive attack is the only reasonable strategy in a world where the "existential enemy is undeterrable" and "yearns for heaven"; furthermore, if the choice of the liberal internationalists is to "tie down Gulliver" in order to achieve their multilateral aims, the true realist will refuse to be so governed. The meaning is clear: he who bestrides the world like a colossus cannot be held hostage to the will of those who would restrain him.

Exceptionally (and with apologies to fairy-tale aficiona-dos), there is a fourth bowl of porridge in this imaginary house, and not until he reaches the last does the speaker dis-cover the quality that is "just right." This he calls "democratic globalism," more popularly known as neo-conservatism, or neo-liberalism in its latest guise, the world-view that marries the American values of freedom and democracy to the hard fist of military persuasion. Democratic globalism incarnates a cloudless vision of America's exceptional place in the world. It is a pledge, a "sacred honour" that was entrusted to the nation at its origin and continues to live in the hearts of all American patriots; it is the "will to freedom," the struggle between "freedom and unfreedom and, yes, good and evil." It is the imperative to spread such ideals around the globe, by force if necessary, in order to make the world safe for America and its interests.

Today is Charles Krauthammer's opportunity to promote his personal version of this code, a refinement he calls "democratic realism." You don't go around the world knocking just any heads together hoping to turn people into democrats; you must choose your targets more carefully. Today, that means warring against "the new global threat to freedom, the new existential enemy, the Arab-Islamic totalitarianism that has threatened us . . . since the [Iranian] Khomeini revolution in 1979." And make no mistake, he continues, American military action does not need the approval of non-Americans or the United Nations to be morally legitimate. "It would be nice if we had more allies rather than fewer; it would also be nice to be able to fly."

The audience laughs again, nodding at the wisdom of the man who has just won their institute's most coveted award. He hasn't told them anything they didn't already know or agree with, but with this cleverly encapsulated presentation he has placed his thinking, and theirs, in a broader context than usual. What matters is power—then holding on to it against all challengers. For Charles Krauthammer and his colleagues, much of the 1990s was "a period of cheating between two periods of fighting." Then the new enemy dropped from the sky. Since that day he had assumed a plethora of grotesque shapes, starting with Lucifer himself, before taking up residence in Osama bin Laden, the Taliban, Saddam Hussein and the other (mostly) Islamic members of the axis-of-evil cabal whose home base was mainly the Middle East. America, Krauthammer's speech made clear, would not be deterred from its moral mission, which meant reshaping the region in its own image.

In retrospect, this speech, to this glittering audience, may have marked the high-water point of post 9/11 imperial certainties. If the convictions of Charles Krauthammer seemed dated, even hubristic, several years later, as the fruitless war in Iraq dragged on, his words—so charged with the aphrodisiac of unrivalled power—would remain perennially interesting. For what he described *ought* to have been an oxymoron: the unlikely marriage of utopian idealism, with tendrils reaching back to the Enlightenment, and contemporary government policies that were poised to alter the international landscape of the early twenty-first century. His very language invoked the familiar echoes of patriotism: the "sacred honour" that had bound Americans since the founding of their country; the ongoing struggle between good and evil in the world (with no doubt about who was clad in white and who in black); and that peculiarly disconcerting call to action—"the will to freedom"—which brings to mind "the will to power" of the nineteenth-century German philosopher Friedrich Nietzsche, the unwitting inspiration for Adolf Hitler, another "idealistic" ultra-nationalist.

Across American history, the conviction that God chose the United States as his agent of freedom and democracy in the world has never been far from the surface. The "shining city on the hill" metaphor was first articulated by John Winthrop as he led a group of Puritans on an ocean voyage to the Massachusetts Bay Colony in 1629. "We shall be a city set on a hill," he wrote with hope and deep religious conviction, quoting from the New Testament gospel of Matthew: "You are the light of the world. A city set on a hill cannot be hid."

The gospel of Matthew was appropriated to assign God to the new land, from the moment of its origins, but how many "lights of the world" can there be? The Jews had the oldest claim, but in his 1954 *Memoirs of War* Charles de Gaulle had insisted that his country also held membership in the exclusive club. Providence, he wrote, had chosen France for "an eminent and exceptional destiny." Marianne, the symbol of the French nation, was the nurturing mother of France, emblem of the nation's freedom and the incarnation of the warrior maid who led her troops into battle.

There were other members of the "we happy few" guild scattered about the globe. For example, South African Afrikaaners had invented a coherent ideology of racial, religious and political superiority that served them well during the era of apartheid (although it lost its cachet with the arrival of democratic black rule in 1994). But few could match the bred-in-the-bone exceptionalism rooted deep in America's self-image. You couldn't be a politician, let alone a president, without invoking the shining city on the hill, five words that summoned up a divinely inspired destiny. Abraham Lincoln, George Washington, John Kennedy, Ronald Reagan, Michael Dukakis, Bill Clinton, John Edwards, John Kerry, Howard Dean, and, of course, both George Bushes had all called forth the stirring rhetoric of patriotism by making Winthrop's words their own. In his speech to the nation on the fateful day of September 11, 2001, George W. Bush directly invoked Winthrop. "America was targeted for attack because we're the brightest beacon for freedom and opportunity in the world and no one will keep that light from shining," he told his grieving fellow countrymen.

Making the necessary nod to religious-political dogma at moments of national importance was a tradition. When he accepted his award from the American Enterprise Institute that day in 2004, Charles Krauthammer had captured, and made his own, a powerful mythology that resonated in the hearts of his audience.*

—

Krauthammer's openly expressed contempt, broadcast across the continent, for the "very crazy" liberal ideas and multilateral

---

* This enduring legacy made transferring even a degree of sovereignty to an independent body, such as the ICC, perennially difficult.

policies that had marked earlier eras may have been emblematic of the administration of George W. Bush; but beyond his withering scorn lay a long history during which Americans had made exceptionally important contributions to the rule of international law. They had done this in accordance with ideological commitments that sprang from the same sense of moral mission that inspired President Bush and his coterie of neoconservatives, including Krauthammer—although approached from a distinctly different angle. The American Creed promised liberty, justice, equality and democracy—and the light that beamed from the "shining city on the hill" would transmit these values, which were born of the Enlightenment, across continents. Whether they were translated to other places through peacebuilding or through war was, in the last analysis, less important than the bedrock imperative to propagate them.

President Woodrow Wilson, the peacemaker, had campaigned tirelessly at the end of the Great War of 1914–18 to create a multinational League of Nations. His famous Fourteen Points for an equitable settlement of the conflict sprang from his belief in reason as *the* essential tool for the creation of a just world order. On this basis he argued that a successful, pragmatic foreign policy needed to be premised on ethical grounds. By proposing a shift away from the conventional instability of secret alliances and strong armies, he looked toward "world government" grounded on the rule of international law.

Wilson's reputation has bobbed up and down with the decades and the changing seasons of politics; his belief, for instance, in the semi-magical powers of holding instant elections in war-torn countries as a means of building peace after periods of conflict (although still a powerful conviction in Western foreign policy circles) has been found wanting in a variety of ways. (As an example, it may be more important to ensure stability and build institutions first, since early elections can sometimes legitimize unresolved antagonisms between the same parties that fought the war, undermining stability.)[7] Similarly, his conviction that redrawing national boundaries in Europe after the Great War would permanently solve interstate problems exploded in the 1990s with the eruption of ethnic cleansing in the Balkan powder keg. All the same, Wilson will be remembered for having imagined the possibility of an international league of nations, even though the specifics of his dream eventually failed. Underlying everything he did, and stood for, was his idealized commitment to the American Creed.

George W. Bush held faith with the same creed, despite viewing it through a different lens. Although the radical nature of the Bush administration altered the focus of the message, as well as the means of delivering it, the intrinsic meaning of the creed, and the compulsion to promulgate it beyond the borders of America, remained constant.

From the cauldron of the Second World War, the United States, along with Britain, once again led the world in renewed efforts to establish international co-operation, justice and human rights. Previously, there were few rules in the international sphere. States could do more or less what they wanted; in fact, the League of Nations failed in part because it had no enforcement backup. There were no instruments or laws to protect or even identify basic human rights. Those who killed, or commanded others to kill, civilians were able to act with impunity, confident that they would not be challenged.

But Germany's strategically ill-founded invasion of the Soviet Union on June 22, 1941, turned the tide of the conflict in favour of the Allies, cautiously allowing them to look to the future. On August 14, Britain's Winston Churchill and the American president, Franklin D. Roosevelt, met aboard the US vessel *Augusta* in the remote port of Ship Harbour, Newfoundland. There, they laboured to draft guidelines for a more stable international order based on the rule of law and

functioning democratic institutions. They were more successful than Woodrow Wilson had been. In signing the Atlantic
Charter, the two leaders committed themselves to end land
grabs (with Hitler foremost in their minds), to legalize
restraints on the use of force (ditto) and, more radically, to
recognize individual human rights. Their agreement opened a
window into a fundamentally new era. As rumours of genocide leaked out of Europe in 1942, respect for the principles of
the Atlantic Charter rose ever higher. Just three years later, in
June 1945, fifty countries gathered in San Francisco to sign
the Charter of the United Nations. If the UN was created "to
save succeeding generations from the scourge of war," as its
founders stated in their preamble, the means would be international law. Enlightened reason—the peaceful settlement of
disputes—would (they hoped) stifle the drumbeat of war by
offering a real alternative to hostilities.

Since Franklin D. Roosevelt and his wife, Eleanor, were both
obsessed with the idea of a United Nations, it was unfortunate
that the American president died just twenty-six days before
the Allies declared victory in Europe and two months before his
dream of a world body was realized. But Eleanor Roosevelt per-
sisted. On December 10, 1948, the General Assembly of the
newly born United Nations adopted the Universal Declaration
of Human Rights—the first document of its kind. "Human rights
should be protected by the rule of law," stated the text in a short
revolutionary phrase. An emotional Eleanor Roosevelt predicted
that the doctrine of human rights would "creep like a curious
grapevine" into the consciousness of peoples around the world.
And so it has.

Just one day earlier, on December 9, 1948, the General
Assembly adopted the Convention on the Prevention and
Punishment of Genocide. This was followed on August 12,
1949, by the Fourth Geneva Convention, which (among other
things) protected civilians during combat and outlawed torture

and collective punishment.[8] The immediate postwar years were unparalleled in terms of reshaping international law—a process that began with the trials in Nuremberg and Tokyo (1946–48). Adolf Hitler had unwittingly propelled the world in a new direction.

—

When the Soviet Union crumbled and the Cold War came to an end, the United States once again endorsed the rule of international law by demanding accountability, by means of ad hoc criminal courts created by the UN, for the atrocities that had been committed against civilians in Bosnia and in Rwanda. The US also took the lead during the first years of the twenty-first century when it urged the United Nations to support other dedicated tribunals to prosecute individuals who had perpetrated crimes during the conflicts in Cambodia, Sierra Leone and East Timor. Most important, the US underwrote and guided more than a decade of preparatory work that would lead eventually to the creation of the permanent International Criminal Court.

But by the late 1990s, the United States had reversed itself. The ICC had become the sticking point of American defence policy. As the new millennium began, the idea of a permanent international criminal court had metamorphosed into the "bull's-eye" of the new Bush administration.[†]

—

For one dramatic moment before George W. Bush took power on January 20, 2001, there was new hope that the United

---

† In the words of Richard Dicker, the director of the international justice program at the NGO Human Rights Watch.

States might join the International Criminal Court. On December 31, 2000, as he prepared to leave office, President Bill Clinton asked David Scheffer, then the US ambassador for war crimes, to sign the Rome Statute as his proxy. The president had been lobbied tirelessly for his support and signature by (among others) Nelson Mandela—perhaps the world's most respected moral voice. Pushing for a rejection of the ICC were powerful Republicans in the US Congress, including Senator Jesse Helms. In his signing statement (signing statements allow US presidents some latitude in interpreting aspects of the law) Clinton stressed his country's "long history of commitment to the principle of accountability." He said he was signing the Rome Statute to allow the US to play a role in the selection of ICC judges and in the refinement of policy, rules and procedures. But, he added ominously, there were "significant flaws" in the treaty, and until these were rectified, he would not recommend that his successor send the statute to the United States Senate for approval.

Unsurprisingly, the purported flaws turned out to reflect the core of conservative objections to the court: the ICC's independence and its broad jurisdiction. Under the Rome Statute, the ICC is empowered to indict suspected perpetrators *from* any member state for acts committed *in* any member state, should the suspects' own countries be unable, or unwilling, to hold a trial.‡

But the drama of the Clinton signing paled in comparison with what came next. On May 6, 2002, George W. Bush formally "*un*signed" the Rome Statute. It was an unprecedented act in the history of international treaties, a highly irregular measure that may have long-lasting and unforeseen consequences,

---

‡ A state that wasn't party to the Rome Statute could also decide to transfer a case to the ICC, should it wish to do so.

said Robert E. Hirshon, the president of the prestigious American Bar Association, with its 400,000 members.

To the small number of people who had been following the unusual story of the creation of the International Criminal Court, the new president's dramatic withdrawal of assent came as no surprise, for behind George W. Bush sat John Bolton, a man so close to the "king's ear" that he was bruited to be Bush's alter ego. Bolton had asked for, and received, permission to append his own name to the "unsigning" document, which was delivered that same day to the UN secretary-general, Kofi Annan. In it Bolton wrote that the United States had "no legal obligations arising from its [earlier] signature. . . ."

"This is the happiest day of my government service," Bolton crowed to a cluster of puzzled reporters. The ICC was the incarnation of a world view he despised, a personal *bête noire* he would stop at nothing to destroy.

FOUR

The Man at the State Department

any Americans of both the Republican and Democratic persuasions were understandably wary about the possible implications of the International Criminal Court. What *did* the birth of this new institution mean for the post–Cold War status quo after the United States had emerged victorious over the Soviet Union at the "end of history," as the writer Francis Fukuyama so famously wrote in his article, then book, of the same name? Might the new world order in which the US had assumed the mantle of the world's sole remaining superpower be undermined by this upstart, supposedly independent, court far away in The Hague?

The question was a valid one—especially since there was little factual information available about the ICC (the US media seemed largely indifferent). The man who cared most about the subject was the ICC's implacable opponent, John Bolton; to understand America's rejection of the new court, it would be necessary to understand him.

The architect of America's uncompromising policy on the International Criminal Court had hopes of a State Department promotion after George W. Bush won a second term in November 2004, but in January 2005 Bolton was unceremoniously sidelined by the incoming secretary of state, Condoleezza Rice, in her first official act. Bolton's formal title, Undersecretary of State for Arms Control and International Security, placed him third in rank behind the secretary, and for weeks he had been lobbying to move up a notch, to deputy secretary, with the help of a few well-placed friends, especially Vice President Dick Cheney. But Rice chose the more moderate Robert Zoellick instead—a prescient move that signalled her intention to at least *try* to be her own woman at Foggy Bottom (the Lewis Carroll–sounding nickname for the State Department). Her predecessor, Colin Powell, had frequently been checkmated by Bolton, who did end runs around him with impunity; it was widely understood that he had been parachuted into his high position, with the help of Dick Cheney, expressly to keep Powell in check. Powell despised the American Enterprise Institute clique that surrounded the president. Privately, he called them "the crazies," and when they began to rattle their sabres threatening Baghdad and the other "axis-of-evil" capitals, he was known to call them "the fucking crazies."

Bolton's hardline stance on international treaties, including the ICC, made Colin Powell's other "crazies" look like peace-loving Quakers. Like Charles Krauthammer, Bolton didn't think the United States needed the approval of anyone before doing what it wanted to do. Nor did he believe that something as outmoded as tact might be necessary when his country leaned hard on others. On the contrary. Undersecretary

Bolton, whose job description included participating in some of humanity's most important and delicate negotiations, had married his single-minded defence of American interests to bullish outspokenness in the world's diplomatic chambers, where the highest decibel level is commonly the chime of silver spoons on china teacups. His supporters, including the crusty Senate warrior Jesse Helms, admired him as a "truth-teller" and a "patriot"; his opponents described him as a zealot, a confrontational true believer who acknowledged facts only when they served his purpose. But all agreed that underneath everything John Bolton said and did was an unqualified dedication to "America First"—and not first among equals.

His willingness to land punches in defence of his commitments went back decades. While still in his thirties (he was born in 1948), he became assistant attorney general in the Reagan administration; there, he vigorously supported the Contras guerrillas in their struggle to overthrow the Sandinista government of Nicaragua, before heading the campaign to withhold Justice Department documents during the congressional investigation into the government's illegal transfer of arms and money to the rebels. The Contras were a ruthless band of assassins whose atrocities against civilians inspired the human rights agency Americas Watch to conclude that murder, rape and pillage were their principal means of waging war. But a 1985 publicity campaign, sponsored by the Reagan White House in the hopes of encouraging ordinary Americans to "adopt" a Nicaraguan rebel for $12 a month, took a different tack altogether. It featured a peculiar Orwellian doublespeak created by Bolton. "There is no 'country' called Nicaragua," proclaimed the government's poster, "only a nation of people living under a totalitarian regime funded by Cuba and the Soviet Union."

Such disappearances (in the case of Nicaragua, the apparent departure of a verifiable place on the map that had been an independent republic since 1838) became a Bolton specialty. "There is no such thing as the United Nations," he announced in a talk to the conservative Federalist Society for Law and Public Policy Studies in 1994, adding, "The Secretariat building in New York has thirty-eight stories. If it lost ten stories, it wouldn't make a bit of difference." Nine years later, in response to a question by a *New York Times* reporter about the Bush administration's somewhat confusing policy on North Korea, he pulled a book called *The End of North Korea* from a shelf in his office. "That," he said, "is our policy."[1]

On November 17, 1997, Bolton published an op-ed piece in *The Wall Street Journal* expressing contempt for all international agreements. Such treaties were never legally binding, he wrote, but merely "political obligations." In other words, they were conveniently open to being ignored. International law didn't exist either, and "the goal of those who think [it] really means anything are those who want to constrict the United States." On yet another occasion, when he was being introduced as "an experienced international lawyer" to a class of law students at Washington's Georgetown University, he leaped to his feet to announce that anyone who described him as a supporter of international law was simply ignorant of his views.

His antics became Washington lore. Following the disputed election of George W. Bush in November 2000, he had joined a team hastily cobbled together by James Baker, the former secretary of state under Bush the Elder, to deal with the "hanging chads" scandal in Florida. "I'm with the Bush-Cheney team and I'm here to stop the count," he barked as he marched into a room where people were recounting the Miami-Dade votes. His peremptory rudeness created a small scandal, but the manoeuvre worked; he had earned his political stripes. When asked what job John Bolton should have in the new Republican administration, Dick Cheney didn't hesitate. "Anything he wants!" he replied with a smile.

His controversial nomination to the post of Undersecretary of State for Arms Control and International Security was narrowly confirmed in the spring of 2001 with all Republicans in favour and most Democrats opposed. Senator Joseph Biden, a Democrat, worried publicly about whether Bolton's history of "inflammatory rhetoric" would interfere with his ability to handle the job; but no one could better Jesse Helms's winning endorsement. Then in his seventy-first year, he rose to his feet on the Senate floor and boomed, "John Bolton is the kind of man with whom I would want to stand at Armageddon, if it should be my lot to be on hand for what is forecast to be the final battle between good and evil in this world." In the land where God reportedly speaks directly to significant numbers of people, including the president, praise didn't get better than that.

Once confirmed, Bolton wasted no time. From his high perch in the State Department, the man whose job involved negotiating international nonproliferation agreements and directing and coordinating arms control policy immediately brought the libertarian rhetoric of the pro-gun National Rifle Association to the international stage by informing the delegates at a UN conference (on illicit trade in small arms and light weapons) that the Bush administration would never agree to a treaty that tried to restrict Americans' constitutional right to bear arms. In November 2001, just weeks after the events of September 11 and the anthrax scare that followed in its wake, he snuffed out a bid to add a verification and inspection protocol to the 1972 Biological Weapons Convention. His rationale was, as usual, a defence of US sovereignty: such an agreement, he argued, might expose American military and commercial secrets.

"[The convention] is dead, dead, dead, and I don't want it coming back from the dead," he lectured the delegates who had assembled in Geneva. It didn't. However, months later Bolton was back on the stump, claiming that Cuba was not only developing biological weapons but providing the technology to other "rogue states." Congress demanded that he confirm his claim under oath. Bolton demurred.[2]

In 2002 he effectively killed the 1972 Anti-Ballistic Missile Treaty by withdrawing America's support, leaving the United States free to develop a new missile defence system that would confirm American hegemony on this last frontier and possibly restart an international arms race. He also revoked America's long-established commitment to use nuclear force only in response to an enemy armed with nuclear weapons. ("An unrealistic view of the international situation," he opined.) And when Hans Blix, head of the UN Monitoring, Verification and Inspection Commission, and Mohamed ElBaradei, director general of the International Atomic Energy Agency, each criticized the upcoming US invasion of Iraq as precipitate and lacking in sufficient evidence, he engaged the CIA to look for dirt that might justify the men's dismissal.[3]

His "America First" crusade reached its nadir in State Department relations with Iran and North Korea. It was clear by then that both countries either had or were developing nuclear arsenals. Carrots and sticks might have been a useful strategy, but such diplomatic subtleties bored him. ("I don't do carrots," he once said dismissively.) Instead, fortified with "axis-of-evil" rhetoric, he damned Iran as a rogue state "hostile to US interests." Rogue states that refused to adopt non-proliferation norms should be prepared to face the consequences, he threatened. "[This] is why we repeatedly caution that no option is off the table."

The Iranian foreign minister recoiled from Bolton's menacing remarks about "regime change." "Rude and undiplomatic!" his spokesman sputtered helplessly. ("Rude and undiplomatic" would also describe the language of Iran's next president, Mahmoud Ahmadinejad, who, in December 2005, publicly called the Holocaust a "myth" and declared that Israel should be moved to another place on the globe.) As for North

Korea, Bolton was barred from sensitive bilateral talks after he called that country a "hellish nightmare" in *advance* of a 2003 meeting. (North Korea returned the compliment by calling him "human scum.")

The sensitive security issues in John Bolton's portfolio were of critical importance to the world and deserved serious attention, but he will be remembered as the man who recklessly destabilized delicate international situations long before he became a United Nations ambassador in 2005. His "I don't give a damn" negotiating style damaged the United States in the eyes of the world a mere decade after the end of the Cold War, when the international community looked to the US for rational leadership. If the historical guidelines of diplomacy suggested starting with the tea cups before throwing down gauntlets and rattling sabres, someone forgot to tell the undersecretary of state—or if they did, he didn't care. He practised "diplomatic redneckery," as the American writer Ian Williams put it—breaking down the doors of international conference rooms with his guns already blazing.

Since the State Department is America's face to the world, it is hardly surprising that Condoleezza Rice shunned the man who had undermined her predecessor and contributed to the image of George W. Bush's administration as ideologically radical. And less surprising still that the beleaguered Colin Powell cleared his desk and slipped out the front door of Foggy Bottom at the first opportunity after the 2004 election.*

---

* John Bolton and Condoleezza Rice were reportedly still locking horns as late as April 2007. According to *The Nation*, Bolton, although no longer a part of the Bush administration, was trying to undermine his government's deal with North Korea, in which the latter had agreed to freeze its nuclear weapons program in exchange for foreign aid. For Bolton, any deal was a bad deal because it "legitimized" the North Korean regime. (David Corn, *The Nation*, April 23, 2007.)

—

Starting in May 2001, John Bolton unleashed a multi-pronged governmental strategy to maim, marginalize and (with luck) kill the International Criminal Court. His powerfully worded arguments were diplomatic bombshells. The ICC was "illegitimate," because it created a legal authority outside the US constitutional structure. The constitution was indisputably the standard reference for American law, but Bolton seemed to imply that the US Constitution also had to inform law *outside* the United States. Anything else would undermine American sovereignty.

Furthermore, according to Bolton, the prosecutor of the ICC would be "unaccountable." He or she (as yet unchosen) would be "politicized" and "unchecked." And members of the American military would become targets. Working in concert with the Republican senator Jesse Helms, Bolton became a general in the war against the ICC. He exhorted his troops to win the battle, and hurled verbal grenades at the enemy. He seized the ICC file with a ferocity that surprised even those who were familiar with his tactics.

The trigger for this diplomatic combat was a ceremony held at the United Nations headquarters in New York on April 11, 2002, a year before the judges were chosen, then sworn into office, at the formal inauguration of the ICC in The Hague. Ten new countries had ratified the Rome Statute, pushing the number past sixty—the magic threshold needed to legalize the court. That was the day Bolton readied his strategy: a month later, on May 6, 2002, he and President Bush dramatically "unsigned" the Rome Statute. When the ICC officially "came into force" on July 2 of that same year, Bolton led his soldiers into the fray with every weapon short of physical warfare—although the latter did briefly look possible on August 2, 2002, when President Bush signed into law the American Servicemembers' Protection Act (sometimes satirically called The Hague Invasion Act), which had been officially sponsored by Senator Helms and passed by the US Congress. This improbable legislation authorized US Marines to storm the beaches of Holland to rescue any American citizen who might languish in ICC custody as a suspected perpetrator of the core offences of genocide, crimes against humanity or war crimes. Was it to be taken seriously? Yes, very definitely. It had been the cause of a vote in the United States Congress. Was it fundamentally absurd? Undeniably. In spite of the gravity of the vote, there were many who could not resist giggling at the prospect of the US Marines swarming the beaches of one of the oldest, most peaceful, cities in all of Europe.

When the legislation was first introduced into Congress, puzzled observers might have been forgiven for scratching their heads. This was clearly a big deal—but why? They may have had a clearer understanding of the issue when Jesse Helms's reasoning finally emerged. The Rome Statute is "irreparably flawed," he explained to his fellow senators, because it would allow the ICC to "second-guess US foreign policy decisions."

The American Servicemembers' Protection Act also curtailed American participation in UN peacekeeping operations unless every US soldier and civilian was granted immunity from possible prosecution for war crimes and the other international offences. In anticipation, the US had used its veto in the Security Council the previous June (two months before the passage of the bill) to deny an extension of the UN Bosnia peacekeeping mission unless its soldiers were exempt from investigation by the court. There had been consternation in the General Assembly. During the heated negotiations, America's closest allies raised strong objections to the Bush administration's efforts to undermine the ICC (the US was pressuring the Security Council to exempt suspected perpetrators who were citizens of countries that were not party to the court). Canada's ambassador, Paul Heinbecker, sounded as angry as a diplomat is allowed to get: "The crimes [over which the ICC has jurisdiction] were meticulously defined in a manner acceptable to US negotiators and all states, with thresholds that exclude the isolated acts that a peacekeeper might conceivably commit," he told the Security Council. The Danish ambassador, Ellen Margethe (Denmark then held the presidency of the European Union), pointed out that under long-standing international law called "universal jurisdiction," *anyone* who commits a crime on someone else's territory can be put on trial in the country where the crime occurred. The authors of war crimes, such as torture, are considered to be "enemies of all humankind" (like the pirates of yore) and can theoretically be prosecuted anywhere. What the member states of the ICC had done was to delegate this already existing jurisdiction over crimes committed on their territory to the new international tribunal. Jean-David Levitte, France's permanent representative on the Security Council, pointed out that the Rome Statute contained stronger guarantees than the statute for the International Criminal Tribunal for the Former Yugoslavia. The latter had never caused problems for the United States. Why did it now? he wanted to know.

And so it went, as nation after nation defended the Rome Statute, the future of peacekeeping and the United Nations itself. In reply, John Negroponte, then the US ambassador to the UN, presented a short history of his country's important contributions to international human rights, international justice and the rule of law, starting with the United Nations Universal Declaration on Human Rights. He did not explain why any nation's peacekeepers should be immune from prosecution for acts that were defined as crimes within this same legal framework. It was a key moment in the history of the UN, the institution born in the aftermath of just such crimes; and (for those who thought about such things) it was a key moment in the history of the nation that had pressed so boldly for the UN's creation many years before.

The accumulated pressure from John Bolton, John Negroponte and others worked: on July 12, 2002, the Security Council adopted a resolution making UN peacekeepers immune from prosecution by the new ICC—but for one year only. The accord, they agreed, would be renewable. In 2003, the Security Council dutifully reconfirmed the resolution; but by April 2004 the atmosphere at the UN had changed drastically. Shocking pictures from the Abu Ghraib prison in Iraq showing grinning American soldiers posing over their naked, humiliated prisoners were circling the globe; torture was a war crime. This time, sensing that they would not secure the requisite support, the US declined to put the immunity resolution to a vote. "We have, I think, demonstrated that in the very unfortunate situation, [the] terrible situation, that developed at Abu Ghraib, that the United States does stand for justice, and will itself impose justice on any member of our services who might undertake things that constitute international crimes," said the State Department spokesman Richard Boucher defensively at a press conference on June 23, 2004. Instead, the US would review the ICC "risk" when deciding whether to take part in UN operations. (Following this diplomatic defeat, a handful of US peacekeepers were pulled from missions in Kosovo and Ethiopia-Eritrea, possibly for show.)

John Bolton's suggestion that America had come under surreptitious attack by an army of Lilliputians—the foreign diplomats and conniving lawyers who wanted to tie up Gulliver (to borrow Charles Krauthammer's imagery)—was soon being echoed so often by academics, analysts and the US media that it began to acquire the gloss of unassailable truth, although, with the exception of international law practitioners and scholars, few knew much about the text of the Rome Statute. For example, Jeremy Rabkin, a professor of government at Cornell University in Ithaca, New York, declared that it would be *unthinkable* to delegate authority to an external body not bound by the United States Constitution. "Policymakers at the Pentagon . . . could be liable for prosecution because they planned and ordered an air strike which the ICC's prosecutor regarded as a 'war crime,' even though the United States government took a different view," he wrote in his book, *The Case for Sovereignty: Why the World Should Welcome American Independence.*[4]

Rabkin argued the case for absolute sovereignty with the measured care one would expect from an expert in the field; but he is not a lawyer, and his suggestion that "foreigners" might have a different opinion than Americans about what constituted a war crime struck a discordant note. War crimes are not subjective impressions to be dreamed up over breakfast coffee. They are prohibited acts, conduct that has come to be recognized and defined as criminal under the law of nations. The most fundamental among them are the killing, torture or mistreatment of civilians or prisoners of war; intentional attacks on peacekeepers, humanitarian workers or civilian institutions; and the bombing of sites that are not military objectives. It had taken more than a century of wars and the peace negotiations that followed for agreement about such laws to emerge, and though the law itself was still evolving, there was no basic discord about the nature of such crimes.

Having thoroughly frightened many of the foreign policy elites, such as Jeremy Rabkin, who knew little about the tribunal, as well as elements of the mainstream media, who knew even less, John Bolton now accused the framers of the Rome Statute of "overreach" for claiming that the ICC had the right to indict suspected perpetrators from states that were not party to the Rome Statute (provided the crimes were committed on the territory of a signatory nation). The legal scholar and ICC expert William Schabas was unimpressed.

"The Bolton argument is simply bogus," he said bluntly. "As a lawyer [Bolton] would have known that genocide, crimes against humanity and war crimes—the crimes that come under the jurisdiction of the ICC—are international matters that fall *outside* the sovereignty of independent states, and they have done so since the time of the Nuremberg Tribunal more than half a century ago. The Rome Statute of the ICC does *not* bind non-party states, but the court *does* have jurisdiction over the nationals of states [that have not joined] if they commit crimes on the territory of member states."

What he meant was that under existing international law, all nations have the right to try the perpetrators of international crimes such as genocide, war crimes and crimes against humanity themselves, if they wish to do so. What the Rome Statute had done was to create an additional means for combating impunity, should states be unable or unwilling to hold their own trials.

If the detail of the law was complex, Bolton's tactics were not. The United States, including its constitution, its military and its high-ranking officials were *already* under attack, he warned. The Rome Statute and the International Criminal Court were not merely unwelcome, they were inherently dangerous.

One of the "high-ranking officials" he had in mind was Henry Kissinger. In his November 14, 2002, speech to the Federalist Society Bolton said that if officials had to worry constantly about the danger of being indicted, "over time that's going to have an effect on your decision-making. If you're Henry Kissinger and every time you to go this European country or that European country you have to worry if you're going to be served with a subpoena, it has an effect."

Although the acts of Nixon's high-profile secretary of state would not come under the jurisdiction of the ICC, which could deal only with events that had occurred after the Rome Statute came into force in July 2002, had the court been around in the 1970s and 1980s the redoubtable Mr. K. might possibly have been a candidate for investigation. He was President Nixon's national security adviser in 1973, when the Central Intelligence Agency helped engineer a coup that toppled Salvador Allende, the duly elected president of Chile, and replaced him with a military junta headed by Gen. Augusto Pinochet. According to CIA documents released in September 2000, Kissinger and Nixon had directed the organization "to prevent Allende from taking power"; furthermore, they were "not concerned [about the] risks involved."[5] Allende died during the coup, and during the seventeen years that Pinochet ruled Chile, more than three thousand people were murdered or "disappeared."

By the time the ICC appeared on the global horizon, the Western consensus about human rights and the accountability of people in high places was undergoing a profound shift. Kissinger-style machinations may have been winked at in the 1970s, or even welcomed as a strategic weapon in the struggle against Communism; but three decades later the author Christopher Hitchens was unabashedly calling Kissinger's manoeuvres in Latin America, Indochina, East Timor, Cyprus, Chile and Bangladesh "war crimes" in his best-selling polemic, *The Trial of Henry Kissinger*—language that would have been unthinkable in the seventies.[6] Before long Chile, France, Argentina and Spain (all of whom had citizens who had "disappeared") were inviting the former secretary to appear for questioning—requests he successfully ignored until May 28, 2001, when he was confronted at the door of his Paris hotel room by French officials delivering a subpoena from a judge investigating allegations that five French citizens who disappeared in Chile during the Pinochet regime had been kidnapped, tortured and killed.

Kissinger immediately decamped for Italy (the US embassy in Paris explained that he was unable to appear before the judge owing to a prior engagement), but not before French television cameras registered the alarm on his face—a sight that must have sent a shudder through the George W. Bush White House.

After the Paris escapade, the International Criminal Court was understandably on Kissinger's mind. In July 2001 he weighed in on the debate with an article in *Foreign Affairs*, in which he argued for a little *realpolitik*.[7] The very idea that heads of government and high officials should ever be held accountable for their political deeds was outrageous. "Judicial tyranny," he called it. That England had detained General Pinochet in 1998, after his indictment by Spain's crusading judge, Baltasar Garzón (taking advantage of the "universal jurisdiction" that adhered to every state), was "a dangerous precedent." Judge Garzón and his cronies were hypocrites: Spaniards had chosen to ignore their own unpleasant past after the death of Generalissimo Francisco Franco in 1975, and they were right to do so. Reconciliation after a war or political crisis meant putting the past away and looking to the future (a conviction Kissinger shared, not surprisingly, with Pinochet himself). Furthermore, the fiery passion of people who advocated for the ICC was "intimidating" and out of touch with reality.

Henry Kissinger had once been an international celebrity, a role he had revelled in. He had supped at the tables of kings and presidents and had perhaps grown careless about the need to place buffers between himself and certain of his government's less savoury initiatives. Nonetheless, Kissinger had misunderstood something fundamental: contrary to the theory and practice of *realpolitik* in which human rights and accountability are almost never a factor in international affairs, the memory of war crimes and human rights abuses does not fade away, as he claimed in his *Foreign Affairs* critique, nor are the "new" societies built on the bones of unacknowledged victims likely to yield long-term peace. Memories of past atrocities may lie dormant for decades, as they had in Spain since the death of Franco, but thirty years after democratic rule first assumed the reins of power, and four years after the publication of Kissinger's article, rumblings from the reawakened past were beginning to disturb that Mediterranean land. The first conference on suppressed historical memory took place in Barcelona in April 2005.

Although John Bolton's inflammatory rhetoric about the International Criminal Court fanned the fears of US conservatives who tended to distrust international institutions and worry about the erosion of national sovereignty, polls conducted by the respected Council on Foreign Relations as early as 2002 and 2003 suggested that the American public supported the principles behind the ICC. Like the populations of other Western democracies, Americans believe in fairness and justice; they expect to see people who have been charged with major crimes brought to account: their Constitution and the US Bill of Rights have bred this thinking deep into the bone. But the support was only theoretical, not specific. The public was not "engaged on the issue," said Richard Dicker of Human Rights Watch. "Americans don't really pay much attention to these sorts of [foreign policy] things, which is why the media don't bother investigating or explaining," he lamented. "This is sad because I believe that if we were successful in getting information out to people, they would see that there is no contradiction between their deeply held values and what the International Criminal Court stands for."

Dicker and other internationalists, who believed that a critical moment in the centuries-long struggle for global justice had arrived, seemed to be waging a losing battle. That they couldn't compete with John Bolton's bully pulpit in the State Department—where arguments could be constructed and disseminated in the national spotlight—was naturally a factor, but the ideological swing to the right that had swept a man like Bolton into high position was testimony to a far

larger obstacle, one that Charles Krauthammer had identified with irony and wit: the liberal consensus that had bound
America to a multilateral world order across most of the
twentieth century seemed to be in steep decline.

—

In May 2002, when the Bush administration "unsigned"
President Clinton's signature on the Rome Statute, John
Bolton announced a new benign-sounding policy: the Article
98 bilateral agreements based on an interpretation of a clause
in the Rome Statute with the same name.[8] Bolton's idea was a
simple one: the US proposed to sign reciprocal agreements
with individual countries in which both parties promised never
to send one another's nationals to the International Criminal
Court. In the hope that those who had already signed on to the
ICC might reverse their support, and that those who had not
yet joined would think twice before doing so, carrots and sticks
were dangled from the offer: Sign our document and you will
continue to receive foreign aid from the United States; refuse
to sign and your aid will be cut off. The starting shots were
fired in the summer of 2002. Jetstream clouded the skies as
Bolton and his associates winged past the ICC president,
Philippe Kirsch, and *his* associates, who also were circling the
globe signing up new supporters.

On August 1, 2002, poverty-stricken post-Communist
Romania (where the national average wage was at that time
approximately $80 a month) became the first to submit to the
Article 98 blandishments, a decision its government seemed to
regret when it found itself promptly condemned by the
European Union in Brussels. Struggling to defend himself,
Mircea Geoana, the foreign minister, admitted that Bucharest
had been unsettled by Washington's request. "I can't remember anything they put so much weight or interest into," he

confessed.[9] Next to yield were the Marshall Islands, the Dominican Republic and Palau, a tiny group of islands southeast of the Philippines in Oceania, a part of the world made memorable in *Nineteen Eighty-Four*, George Orwell's nightmare fantasy of totalitarianism. When Azerbaijan, Bahrain, Gambia, Tajikistan and Uzbekistan joined the roster, the list of international Article 98 signatories began to resemble the "coalition of the willing" that President Bush would cobble together several months later for the invasion of Iraq. All of them were small, needy states.

Albania, which had signed and ratified the Rome Statute, held the dubious distinction of being Europe's poorest, most backward state. It, too, succumbed. Since he happened to be on a swing through Europe, then Secretary of State Colin Powell dropped into Tirana on May 2, 2003, for the signing. "I've been wanting to visit Albania for some time. . . . This Article 98 agreement [shows] the closeness of the relationship that we enjoy, relationships that will grow even closer in the months and years ahead," he told the local dignitaries. Then, in the next breath, he made the announcement Tirana was waiting for. "A little bit later on, we will be signing the Adriatic Charter, which will align the United States with the three other nations that will be signing the Charter in a partnership that we hope will improve the possibilities for economic, and political and social development and move the three countries in the direction of eventual membership in NATO and the European Union."[10]

By December 2006, the United States had signed agreements with 102 countries. Fifty-four others had refused, among whom nineteen had subsequently lost US aid. One of the latter was war-torn Croatia, in spite of threats from the US ambassador, Lawrence Rossin, who raised questions about the country's chances of joining NATO should Zagreb decline to sign. But Croatian President Stjepan Mesić was an outspoken supporter of international criminal justice. He had been to the International Criminal Tribunal for the Former Yugoslavia in The Hague to testify against Slobodan Milošević, a highly controversial act in the aftermath of the Balkan wars. In a private meeting in Zagreb on November 26, 2003, he insisted to me that his country could not fully recover until factual evidence about what happened during the Yugoslav conflict emerged in that courtroom. He laughed aloud at the irony of being asked, by America, never to transfer an American to the International Criminal Court. The United States had been the prime mover in the founding of the International Criminal Tribunal for the Former Yugoslavia, which was currently trying suspected war criminals from his own region. As punishment, Croatia lost $5.8 million in US aid designated to train its military in advance of entering NATO.

Although it had been the site of a deadly US embassy bombing in 1998, Tanzania lost $450,000 that had been earmarked to bolster its security. Seven million dollars were withheld from South Africa, $500,000 from Benin and $250,000 from Mali—precious funds that had been allocated to "strengthening regional stability." Ecuador, a key ally in the US war on drugs, lost $15.7 million in promised funding, much of it set aside for military equipment to help detect narco-traffickers. In May 2003, US Assistant Secretary of State Stephen Rademaker told the foreign ministers of the Caribbean Community (CARICOM) that they would lose the benefits of the New Horizons program, which included rural dentistry and veterinary programs. Bosnia-Herzegovina foreign minister Mladen Ivanić was informed that it would be "very difficult to continue military and other assistance" if his government did not acquiesce.[11] President Beriz Belkić retorted that "Bosnia, with its long list of suspected war criminals, is the last country that should retreat from the ICC," but he signed anyway in May 2003.[12] Jordan was scheduled to receive

$209 million in military assistance and $250 million in economic support funds; although it had been one of the world's most ardent supporters of the ICC (through its UN representative, Prince Zeid Ra'ad Zeid Al-Hussein, who had spoken so eloquently at the inauguration of the tribunal), the government backed down and signed the immunity pact.

The saddest case was Lesotho, a tiny landlocked kingdom in the southeast corner of South Africa. Lesotho does not have to worry about joining NATO or the EU or anything more than basic survival. Thirty percent of its two million citizens have full-blown AIDS, including tens of thousands of young women who were infected by their husbands when they returned from working in the South African mines. Twenty percent of the country's children are orphans; many are HIV positive and not expected to live beyond the age of ten. AIDS has destroyed the economic and social infrastructure of the country. It is estimated that 70 percent of the population will die before they reach forty.

Yet Lesotho, which signed the Rome Statute in November 1998, refused to agree to the Article 98 immunity pact. It was severely punished; in retaliation, American aid designated to fight AIDS and HIV was withheld. In April 2005, former president Bill Clinton pledged $10 million to help Lesotho save its children, but this was privately raised money from his own foundation. In August 2006, Lesotho capitulated and signed.

Large, rich countries like Canada and the nations of Western Europe could refuse outright to sign the Article 98 agreements, and they did; but smaller, poorer nations were faced with painful choices. They desperately needed American aid, but they also faced pressure from the European Union and the other ICC signatories. In speeches to the American Enterprise Institute and elsewhere in November 2003, Bolton lashed out at the EU for placing impediments in his way. It was then that he called the ICC " . . . an organization that runs contrary to fundamental American precepts and basic Constitutional principles." The government of the United States was protecting its citizens from "the illegitimate assertion of authority over them," he said.

—

Bolton may have been abrasive and undiplomatic, but his arguments were influential and needed to be addressed. *Why* was the ICC "illegitimate" on US constitutional grounds? If it was, had the postwar international war crimes tribunals in Nuremberg and Tokyo (both directly sponsored by the United States) somehow reflected the American Constitution more faithfully? What about the International Criminal Tribunal for the Former Yugoslavia, which was sponsored and supported by the United States? Or the International Criminal Tribunal for Rwanda, which it also supported? Or the courts for Sierra Leone and East Timor? Were they also "illegitimate," and if so, why did the US see fit to sponsor them? These tribunals were creating new international criminal law with their verdicts. Were these legal precedents also "illegitimate"?

I put the questions to two well-informed professionals: Gary Solis, an expert on military tribunals, who teaches the law of war at the famous United States Military Academy at West Point, New York; and Jeremy Rabkin of Cornell University, who has written widely on the subject.

"Were [or are] any of the international war crimes tribunals, past or present, bound by the US Constitution?" I wrote Professor Solis in an email.

"Not at all!" he replied in an electronic instant. "Clearly, the post–Second World War military tribunals—Nuremberg and Tokyo—did *not* meet US constitutional standards, but there was no reason to be concerned with that. We were trying enemies who had violated the laws of war, not Americans. Constitutional standards are seldom a concern when non-US citizens are being tried extraterritorially. We are largely unconcerned [about] the ICTY [former Yugoslavia] and the ICTR [Rwanda] for the same reasons. . . .

"We, the US, essentially formed the post–Second World War International Military Tribunals. We had no objections because we would have been objecting to ourselves!"

I was taken aback at his directness; I could almost hear his laughter.

Since I had told him that I was researching the International Criminal Court, he went further still. "As for the ICC . . . the reason the US opposes the court is the irrational (in my opinion) fear that the president, vice president, secretary of defense, senators, et cetera will be snagged with an international arrest warrant while on vacation in Paris. There's no genuine concern for soldiers or their possible arrest. And the [Rome] Statute is worded such that the arrest of an individual soldier from any state is very unlikely, anyway.

"But I digress. We may say we object on constitutional grounds, but that's entirely bogus, in my opinion."[13]

There it was again, the word "bogus" as a description of the American position on the new court. The first person I'd heard use the word was the ICC expert William Schabas. And now Gary Solis, also an undisputed authority on the subject, had said the same thing.

I wanted to hear a thoughtful perspective from someone who, like Bolton, saw reason to fear that the ICC would erode US national sovereignty. In his well-argued book on sovereignty and the American Constitution, Jeremy Rabkin claimed that the United States could not permit international law to take precedence over the Constitution without undermining American democracy. By "deriding sovereignty," Europe has set off on the wrong historical track, he wrote. But in a less cautiously written newspaper piece angrily titled "The International Kangaroo

Court" he went much further. "Get ready for the ICC to go after Israelis and Americans," he warned in his article, cutting a lot closer to the core of the anxiety among Washington elites than he did in the studied prose of his scholarship.[14] He, too, worried about the "Kissinger effect."

Because his book struck a measured tone that was missing in the shouting diatribes of other political commentators, I wrote to him, in a follow-up to my conversation with Gary Solis. "One of the major US objections to the ICC is, as you discuss, constitutional . . . [but] I have difficulty understanding this because neither Nuremberg, Tokyo, the ICTY nor the ICTR were, or are, bound by US law, yet all were creations of the United States. Why is the ICC different, in your view?" I asked.

To my surprise, he agreed with Solis. "The reason those other tribunals could be established without a treaty [which might never have had majority approval in Congress] was that they weren't regarded as very serious commitments by the US—or regarding the US. At Nuremberg and Tokyo, the terms of jurisdiction . . . excluded American servicemen categorically. There was no chance whatever that any American could be tried by these tribunals. Same, of course, with the Rwanda tribunal. In principle the ICTY had jurisdiction over all forces fighting in the territory of Yugoslavia, [but] at the time [the court] was established there were no Americans there. . . . When [then secretary of state] Madeleine Albright negotiated this, she didn't imagine that there might later be American troops subject to that tribunal. . . .

"When the ICTY did go through the motions of examining US (or NATO) bombing practices in the Kosovo war, there was outrage in Washington. . . . It was regarded as absolutely outrageous that foreigners in The Hague should be allowed to second-guess American military tactics."[15]

As both Solis and Rabkin were independently acknowledging, the United States has long held a double standard with regard to aspects of international law, for two reasons. The first is the tradition of American exceptionalism, dressed up for new use. The second is power. Simply stated, the US is strong enough to do what it chooses, unless its military is already engaged elsewhere.

John Bolton's description of the ICC as "illegitimate" because it does not conform to the US Constitution was beginning to look like a red herring, but another of his claims—that the ICC would violate the usual protections of due process—was baffling. The presumption of innocence, the right to legal counsel, the right to present evidence and to confront prosecution witnesses, the right to be present at one's own trial and so on—these are the rights of an accused person in any of the world's working democracies. The Rome Statute is transparent, as even its enemies acknowledge. The full text is in the public domain; and it includes many cautionary references to the norms of due process. American negotiators helped to establish clear definitions of these rights during the decades of preparatory planning.

Monroe Leigh, a former legal adviser to both the State Department and the Defense Department, and a past president of the American Bar Association *and* the American Society for International Law, explicitly said that "due process rights guaranteed by the Rome Statute are, if anything, more detailed and comprehensive than those in the American Bill of Rights," and "I can think of no right guaranteed to military personnel by the US Constitution that is not also guaranteed in the Treaty of Rome."[16] There is one real discrepancy from the Constitution, as noted by John Bolton; but, contrary to his claims, it does not jeopardize fairness. Following European continental law, ICC trials will be heard not by a panel of jurors but by a panel of judges—as at Nuremberg, the ICTY and the ICTR. This has never before been an issue for the United States, which has long accepted that its citizens (including US service members) would not get jury trials when accused of crimes in countries where juries were not the practice.

In early 2001 Monroe Leigh had tried to stop the passage of Jesse Helms's American Servicemembers' Protection Act. Leigh wrote to Henry Hyde, the chairman of the House Committee on International Relations, warning him that the proposed bill was "replete with misconceptions." He also asserted that "the ICC would offer greater protection to Americans in military service than now exists at home or abroad." Ten former presidents of the American Society of International Law signed their names to his letter.[17]

From the depth of his experience and legal expertise, Leigh called the ICC "the most important international juridical institution that has been proposed since the San Francisco Conference of 1945" (which created the United Nations).[18] He mocked any anxiety about interference from the "politically motivated, unanswerable Prosecutor" by pointing out the exceptional safeguards against possible abuse in the statute itself. He noted, as had others, that under existing international law the "sovereign" [head of government] of a territory where a crime was committed *already* had the right to try the perpetrators; and that the suggestion that individual Americans could not legally be prosecuted for war crimes outside the United States because their government had not joined the ICC was false. He said that the strident demands for exceptionalism infusing every sham argument being brought against the new international court would only reinforce suspicions about "American hegemonic ambitions."

Leigh's plea to Henry Hyde was dated February 21, 2001. In August 2002, the American Servicemembers' Protection Act was passed. What happened in the interval?

During the seventeen months that separated these dates, airplanes reconfigured as bombs had pierced the towers of the World Trade Center; and in the aftermath, millions of Americans with the internationalist sensibilities of Monroe Leigh had been elbowed to the sidelines.

When questioned about the legitimacy of his strident opposition to the ICC and other multilateral institutions, John Bolton didn't hesitate. "Whether it is removing a rogue Iraqi regime and replacing it, preventing WMD proliferation or protecting Americans against an unaccountable Court, the United States will . . . follow its values when measuring the legitimacy of its actions," he said in a speech to the Federalist Society on November 13, 2003. So confident was he in his campaign that he sometimes didn't bother rationalizing his arguments. When asked about his certainty that the ICC would never be a deterrent to major criminals—in other words, that future tyrants in the mode of Slobodan Milošević or Adolf Hitler would be indifferent to the prospect of being brought to trial for fomenting wars or committing crimes in the service of their ambitions—he sounded more irritated than interested. The [ICC] court "does not, cannot and should not have enough authority in the real world to make that happen," he replied. "Why should anyone imagine that bewigged judges in The Hague will succeed where cold steel has failed?"[19]

—

Autumn 2004. I am about to meet John Bolton, the man *Salon* magazine once called "the most important administration official America has never heard of."[20] This comment preceded Bolton's controversial August 2005 to December 2006 term as United States ambassador to the United Nations—the organization he claimed to despise.[21]

The famous Washington, DC, monuments gleam in the warm autumn sun, and the occupant of one of them—the White House—has reason for satisfaction. Just forty-eight

hours have passed since Senator John Kerry conceded defeat
to George W. Bush. Stock in the souvenir shops at Reagan
National Airport has already been rearranged. Dozens of Bush
cut-out dolls line the shelves, along with Bush-Cheney inauguration T-shirts in every size from newborn to granny. Behind
them, lumped in undignified piles, Kerry-Edwards hats, shirts,
magnets and pens languish—all offered at a 50 percent dis-
count. The entrepreneurial class is profoundly unsentimental.

Two recent interviews with John Bolton run through my
mind as I make my way to the State Department where I will
meet the undersecretary. The first was with Jeffrey T. Kuhner,
the communications director for the Ripon Society, a
Republican think-tank in the city. Bolton's characteristic
bluntness during this conversation landed him in some trouble: He said that the International Criminal Tribunal for the
Former Yugoslavia was a threat to regional stability and might
create new animosities and new tensions. He had also complained that the ICTY had no democratic accountability or
checks against the misuse of power. Since the Bush administration publicly supported the ICTY, Bolton's intemperate suggestion that the government might be revisiting its policy were
wildly out of line. His irritated superiors left him twisting in
the wind. "[There] is no change," said Adam Ereli, then the
spokesman for the State Department, the day after the article
appeared.²² "The United States strongly supports the efforts of
the International Criminal Tribunal for the Former Yugoslavia
and its efforts to bring to justice those who have committed
serious violations of international humanitarian law."

Bolton was equally indiscreet with a journalist from the
other side of the political spectrum, the crusading Australian
television documentarist John Pilger. When Pilger asked him
a question about civilian casualties in Iraq, Bolton cut the
interview short and, in a comment reminiscent of another
era, demanded to know whether Pilger was "a member of the

Communist Party." Unfortunately for Bolton, the cameras were still rolling.[23]

—

Although it was designed and built in the architecturally florid era of the late nineteenth century, the US Department of State on C Street is a squat, no-nonsense low-rise made of serviceable grey stone with flat, steel-rimmed windows. Security is, naturally enough, formidable, at the physical location of America's department of foreign affairs. It starts with a confirmation of my appointment, a body pat and security scan outside the building, then continues at an indoor wicket where more questions are asked. Bolton's executive assistant arrives to escort me through a final scan, then through the locked glass partition that divides the inner from the outer section of the department before leading me up a flight of stairs.

Bolton's spacious outer office houses two female secretaries who are seated at large desks. The shaded lamps that illuminate their paperwork cast a light that is so low, so warm, so peculiarly enticing, that the entire room looks more like a lair than the reception area of a famously prickly individual. Only the wall decor hints at the man I am about to meet. First, a large framed plaque dated 1992, with words from Leviticus scrolled across the top: "JUSTICE, JUSTICE, SHALT THOU PURSUE." The honour came from the International Committee of B'nai B'rith, a respected organization of Jewish human rights and advocacy; but given his well-reported opinions on the supposed limitations of justice, at least the international kind, I am struck by the unintended irony of the Old Testament message, though to be fair, the B'nai B'rith tribute was presented for one specific aspect of Bolton's public service: "his conviction that UN resolution 3397 [in 1975] equating Zionism with racism would be repealed and his determination to bring it about."

It is a given that in the United States neo-conservative politics and militant support for Israel travel hand in hand. Bolton is not a Jew, but he used to be on the advisory board of the Jewish Institute for National Security Affairs (JINSA), a powerful lobby group dedicated to "US–Israel strategic cooperation [as] a vital component in the global security equation for the United States." He also has close ties with fundamentalist Christian constituencies that support the Jewish state for their own reasons (they believe that Christ will not return to earth in the prophesied Second Coming until all of the Old Testament "Land of Israel" belongs to the Jews alone). Part of his usefulness to his superiors in the White House is his ability to bridge these several Republican constituencies.

Second pride of place on the office wall goes to a framed blow-up of a *Wall Street Journal* profile published in May 2002, about the time Bolton personally overturned Bill Clinton's qualified acceptance of the ICC by "unsigning," with Bush, the Rome Statute. "Treaty Destroyer," shouts the headline over a picture of the smiling mustachioed undersecretary.

The executive assistant arrives to usher me into a spacious corner office with a "conversation area" containing a couch and two armchairs. Bolton stands in greeting. He is slim, of medium build, with bushy hair and a thick walrus moustache streaked with grey but showing signs of having once been blond. His manner is a mix of studied politeness and mild impatience.

"Have you read any of the stuff I've written on the court? Speeches I've given and things I wrote in *The National Interest?*" he asks. I assure him I have.

He wants me to understand that the opposition of the United States to the International Criminal Court is fundamental and unalterable. Foreign governments must not think that the concerns of the US can be addressed "with a technical fix here and there."

This is a given, but I know my welcome in this room has a time limit and I am intent on hearing his response to a central question: Why does the United States, which has been the world's strongest advocate for international criminal justice, call its opposition to the International Criminal Court "fundamental" and closed to negotiation? Is this not oddly implacable language from a State Department diplomat?

"The issue posed by the court has nothing to do with whether you're for or against war crimes, okay?" he replies, with an edge to his voice. "The United States has a record of prosecuting war crimes and human rights abuses committed by its own citizens that is, I think, unequalled in the world today. But we consider the ICC to be fundamentally illegitimate. We are aware of no other treaty in the world that anybody has ever accepted that binds a non-party to the treaty."

This double-sided argument is a known staple of the US position. But in the aftermath of the torture meted out at the Abu Ghraib prison, and the truly minimal response of the Bush government, I wonder whether many would agree that the record of the US in prosecuting human rights abuses is still "unequalled."[24] As for the treaty question, international law is clear, as we have seen. It is true that a *state* cannot be bound to a treaty, such as the Rome Statute, that it hasn't signed and ratified—but its individual citizens can be bound to this one if they are suspected of perpetrating genocide, war crimes or crimes against humanity.

"I'm sure you are familiar with [the US prosecutor] Telford Taylor's dictum from Nuremberg: 'The laws of war are not a one-way street,'" I say. "What is your understanding of that phrase?"

"I think Nuremberg was an example of victor's justice, and that doesn't trouble me at all."

"Why not?"

"Because we won the war over fascism. It was entirely appropriate for us to react the way we did."

True: the victor's justice delivered at the Nuremberg and Tokyo tribunals *was* only partial: the firebombings of Dresden, Hamburg and Tokyo, in which hundreds of thousands of civilians were incinerated, were not part of the courtroom story, nor were the nuclear bombings of Hiroshima and Nagasaki. Crimes of the Allies did not surface in those two postwar courtrooms. But what strikes me as I listen to this powerful man, is the profound chasm that appears to exist between his tough "might makes right" talk and the earlier humanist vision of Telford Taylor.

"You've written that the United States must be free to conduct 'controversial missions' without fear [of arrests]. What kind of controversial missions were you thinking about?"

"The recent war in Iraq is a good example of where complaints were filed with the prosecutor [of the ICC]; then there was the air campaign over Yugoslavia in connection with Kosovo, where complaints were filed with the ICTY prosecutor's office. Many things that are really not the subject of debate in the United States are often considered controversial abroad. That's what I was trying to say."

"You've said that you worry about someone like Henry Kissinger."

"The case is analogous. The fact is that people like [Kissinger], like Secretary Powell, or Secretary Rumsfeld would be at risk . . ."

I briefly recall an article in which he [Bolton] suggested that had there been an International Criminal Court in 1945 the United States might have been called to account for the nuclear bombings of Hiroshima and Nagasaki. And it's true: those unprecedented attacks on ordinary civilians *were* war crimes according to international law. But something more recent is missing from this conversation. It is a feature of the Rome Statute that was included, as it happens, at the insistence of American negotiators: the clause setting out the awkward-sounding principle of "complementarity," which states that the ICC will never trigger an investigation unless the national government of a suspected perpetrator fails to prosecute that person. The ICC is, in other words, a court of last resort. It will investigate a situation only if the home country is either unable or unwilling to conduct its own trial—something theoretically unlikely to happen in law-abiding democracies. I put the question to him. Since the United States has such an "unequalled" record of home prosecutions, as he describes it, why would it fear the International Criminal Court? Given that record, the ICC would never need to be involved in the case of an American citizen.

He smiles. "People *talk* about the doctrine of complementarity. That's what they call it—the *doctrine* of complementarity. Okay, so they say, Take it on faith that the doctrine will protect the United States. Well, I don't take anything this serious on faith. . . ."

There is one more thing. I have been told that the United States under its current laws could not prosecute its own citizens for the crimes of genocide, crimes against humanity and, in some cases, war crimes, even if it wanted to. Over recent decades, certain elements of international criminal law had been adapted into US domestic legislation to permit court trials for some offences,[25] but not these particular core crimes.[26]

"*Could* the United States try people at home for the core international crimes?" I ask him.

"Yeah, well, I think the Department of Justice determined that essentially everything that's covered by the Rome Statute is a federal crime. There may be some exceptions to that . . . but I'm not aware of any serious exceptions."

"Many lawyers say that is not so, that the US could *not* properly prosecute these crimes under its current laws."

"That is not the opinion of the Department of Justice."

He's too smart not to know he's mistaken, so he explains. "However, it is possible for countries . . . to undertake prosecutions of allegations of war crimes or gross abuses of human rights based on standards that they themselves have set. They can follow international standards *or* they can set other standards. We have our own standards that we follow. . . ."

It is startling to hear such a blanket dismissal of international law spoken aloud by an American undersecretary of state for arms control and international security. You don't like the rules of the game? No problem. Call a foul and make up your own.

"Have there been costs as well as benefits to your policy?" I ask.

"I think the benefits are that we have made it very clear we're not going to co-operate with the court, and that's now well understood. There are a lot of people who make a lot of complaints about American foreign policy, and I suppose you could call that one of the costs. . . . If countries disagree with us, that's certainly their sovereign privilege."

"In the long run it doesn't matter?"

"What has to matter to the president and the president's appointees is the protection of the American Constitution and our system, and I think that's what we're doing when we take on the court."

"You're said to be the architect and captain of this policy. Is that true?"

"I think the president is the architect and captain."

"But you are said to be the person who initiated things."

"He [the president] raised his opposition to the ICC in the 2000 campaign."

"*You* were talking about [the subject] long before that."

"I didn't talk to him about it."

He is starting to shift in his chair, but I am curious to learn what influenced his thinking as a young man. He studied law at Yale in the late 1960s, when ghettos were burning across America and the vast majority of students were either on the democratic left or off the democratic spectrum altogether.

He seems happy to entertain a personal question. "What

happened at Yale in the sixties was important for me because the radical left wingers had infiltrated the university and were subverting academic freedom. I gave a little talk at one point where I tried to convince the faculty members of the risks of what was happening, and I reminded them that they had all been opposed to Joseph McCarthy and his attacks on academic freedom in the 1950s. I said the difference then was that the barbarians were outside the gates. Today they're inside the gates. But I was a conservative long before then. I campaigned for Barry Goldwater when I was fifteen."

"Was your family conservative?"

"No, they were apolitical."

"So what was it that shaped you?"

"I read a lot of Karl Marx," he says with a smile.

—

Barry Goldwater was the first modern conservative on the American scene: a Republican from Arizona who opposed the Civil Rights Act of 1964, the transformational legislation that opened the vote to blacks and swept away the Jim Crow laws that enforced segregation in the South. He was called an extremist, a label he openly embraced during his nomination speech at the 1964 Republican Convention when he cried out, "Extremism in the defense of liberty is no vice!" Public outrage had swept the Democrat, Lyndon B. Johnson, into the White House that same year.

Bolton would have been a quirky outsider as a fifteen-year-old working for Goldwater in 1964, but the slow demise of the liberal consensus in the United States coupled with the steady rise of conservatism had borne him steadily toward power. He and his president both wore the rehabilitated mantle of Barry Goldwater with pride: Extremism in the name of liberty was, and is, no vice.

—

After the attacks of September 11, 2001, extremism in the defence of liberty coloured the policies that emanated from official Washington: from the desks of the president, the vice president and those of their deputies, including John R. Bolton. There was remarkably little public outrage of the sort that had once catapulted Lyndon B. Johnson into office. Although an institution such as the ICC seemed to incarnate America's deeply rooted principles of justice, accountability and the rule of law, these same civic values were badly undermined in the wake of 9/11, when it had seemed appropriate to many Americans to surrender liberties in return for a promise of greater safety.[27] In November 2001, just weeks after the assault, 60 percent of Americans polled thought it was acceptable to assassinate foreign leaders extrajudicially as part of the "war against terror," and 32 percent approved of torture: extreme abuse that had been repudiated as morally repugnant since the era of the Spanish Inquisition and legally forbidden since the United Nations Convention Against Torture entered into force on June 26, 1987.[28] On the other hand, 65 percent of these same respondents also feared that the very powers they had condoned would be used against the innocent[29]—as indeed they were.

The USA Patriot Act was signed into law on October 26, 2001, having swept through both Houses of Congress with minimal debate. The new law stripped away or sharply mitigated freedoms that had characterized America since its founding. The Bush government had empowered itself to arrest people on mere suspicion, to imprison them indefinitely and to prevent the re-entry into the country of permanent residents known to be critical of the clampdown. On November 13, 2001, the president had unilaterally invested himself with the authority to try terrorist suspects in secret military tribunals, thereby depriving them of the standard protections of civil and criminal law.

Military officers would serve as judges and jurors, he declared; and a two-thirds vote would suffice to convict in most cases. In May 2006, as the countdown to what became the mid-term Republican rout picked up speed, the Bush administration was forced to admit that it had illegally recorded the telephone calls of millions of its citizens.

Law and justice, the bedrock of democracy, seemed to be under siege, but there were surprisingly few public dissident voices. I wanted to hear these people. I decided to seek out several persons with impeccable legal expertise to hear the opposing view, should they wish to take such a position—and then another man whose pivotal role during the Vietnam War had shaped his country's history. The first was Michael Ratner, the president of the Center for Constitutional Rights in New York City, a man whom John R. MacArthur, the publisher of *Harper's Magazine*, had once called "America's most important civil libertarian." The second was Gary Solis, whom I had already briefly "met" by email; he was the authority on military tribunals who taught the law of war to officer cadets at West Point. He was also a retired marine lieutenant colonel and had commanded troops in Vietnam before working for eighteen years at the heart of the American military justice system, where he had prosecuted four hundred cases and been a judge in three hundred others. The third person was Cherif Bassiouni, a renowned Egyptian-American professor of international law at DePaul University in Chicago, who had been nominated for the Nobel Peace Prize in 1999 for his lifelong efforts in the cause of international criminal justice.

The fourth man was Robert S. McNamara, secretary of defence in the administrations of John F. Kennedy and Lyndon B. Johnson.

FIVE

The Activist, the UN Adviser, the West Point Prof

―――

The Activist

Michael Ratner, head of the Center for Constitutional Rights, works in Lower Manhattan, near Greenwich Village, not far from where the twin towers of the World Trade Center once scraped the sky. The neighbourhood is run down, or perhaps it is just bohemian, as people used to say, with lots of used bookstores and coffee shops. A mix of university students, grey-haired hippies, smartly dressed professionals and the indigent dodge one another on the sidewalks.

The Center for Constitutional Rights, a privately funded activist organization founded in the mid-1960s, was the creation of several lawyers (including the flamboyant William Kunstler) whose legal work with civil rights activists in Mississippi had led them to believe that ordinary citizens needed better protection. Ratner now presided in an era marked by a whole new erosion of civil rights, one that had the official imprimatur of the state given the radical nature of the Bush administration's policies after 9/11.

The CCR offices consist of a few tiny rooms linked by a narrow corridor on the seventh floor of a dilapidated building. There are a mere handful of employees, but every visible desk is piled high with papers and empty Styrofoam coffee cups. Everyone is wearing jeans. In spite of his David-versus-Goliath legal work, Ratner wears an expression radiating something positive, possibly even optimism. I wonder whether this is a reflection of inborn temperament, or whether he has perhaps made a conscious decision not to be cynical. It can't be easy to maintain equanimity when you are taking on the White House.

I know that Ratner was once a lecturer in international human rights litigation at the universities of Yale and Columbia. In the 1980s he represented persons who were tortured during the US war against Nicaragua, and in the 1990s he was the principal counsel in a lawsuit that successfully closed down a camp at Guantánamo Bay for HIV-positive Haitian refugees. But nothing in his personal history, he will tell me, led him to believe he might become a leading force in the defence of usurped laws in his own homeland.

At the time of my visit, the CCR was challenging what it characterized as violations of constitutional and international law on the part of the United States government, including Patriot Act restrictions on civil liberties and the use of the legally meaningless phrase "enemy combatants"—a lethal tag coined by government lawyers that deprived detainees, presumed to be al-Qaeda, of the protections that had been agreed to in the Geneva Conventions more than a half-century earlier. It was challenging the US government over its new policies of indefinite detention and imprisonment, without

charges, without legal representation, and almost always without evidence—all in the name of a permanent war against terrorism. Ratner and his colleagues were also fighting the
practice of sending terror suspects to third countries known to
embrace torture. In particular, they were suing John Ashcroft,
then the US attorney general, in the case of the Canadian citizen Maher Arar. Arar was deported from New York City to
Syria in September 2002 with the complicity of Canada's
national security apparatus, which, as would later emerge in a
public inquiry that shocked the country, couldn't do enough to
help the US administration.[1] (The Arar case had international
implications, as we shall see in a later chapter.) They had also
initiated a class action suit against the arbitrary detention of
non-citizens living legally within the United States, almost all
of them Muslim and Arab males.

"What precisely are you trying to accomplish?" I ask him
after he has cleared a place to sit amid the paper stacks.

"We're trying to protect the universal norms that every
country has to obey in order to be accepted in the world
community," he replies without hesitation. He leans forward
as if to underscore his words. "The United States ratified the
UN Convention against Torture,[2] and we have our own criminal statutes about torture. We ratified the International
Covenant on Civil and Political Rights that came into force in
1976, and that's a long time ago. We have bills that prohibit
sending foreign aid to countries engaged in gross violations of
human rights. In this country, the US Constitution is our secular bible—and it was founded on basic universalist principles
coming out of the Enlightenment, on the idea that reason is
better than non-reasoning, that law is better than Hobbesian
thinking. . . . That's what we're defending because these things
have come under attack in this country."

Perhaps because he has consistently maintained that no
event, including the most terrible, can be allowed to reshape

the laws of a democratic state, Michael Ratner is quick to insist that he has in no way forgotten what happened that eleventh day in September, nor will he ever. He needs to be explicit about this because every time he speaks publicly he is challenged as being unpatriotic to his country. At exactly 8:45 a.m. he was jogging past the World Trade Center, not far from his home in Greenwich Village. He heard an explosion, thought it was an accident, stopped to crane his neck, then stayed, riveted, for twenty minutes or so until he saw the second plane coming.

In the ensuing chaos, he ran blindly toward his home; his children, then aged eight and seven, were in schools very near the site, and his brother was in one of the towers that day. So were two cousins from Cleveland.

Miraculously, everyone in his family was safe, but he says it took two full weeks before he could think or feel again. Many of his downtown friends were living temporarily in his house, and "there were posters everywhere, dead people, it was really horrible. . . ." But after the numbness wore off, it wasn't long before a second reaction set in. "It soon became clear that we were about to go to war in Afghanistan on the understanding that we had to get rid of al-Qaeda and the Taliban, but the idea that you bomb people has always been a strain for me, and what I saw in New York made me think how truly awful war really is. You know, you look at the brutality and you say to yourself, What the hell is this world about?"

Slowly he returned to himself—to be confronted over and over again with the shock of the new order. First came a New York City police roundup of Muslim men, who were held without charges, beaten and shackled twenty-four hours a day. Then came the American-led war in Afghanistan, on October 7, 2001. Next in line was the USA Patriot Act, which gave the government the power to access citizens' private medical records, library use, financial records, medical histories,

Internet habits—in other words, every activity that left a trail. Then, on November 13, President Bush announced a military order setting the stage for trial by secret military commissions where, said the president, "it is not practicable to apply . . . the principles of law and the rules of evidence generally recognized in the trial of criminal cases in the United States district courts."[3]

President Bush's unilateral military order shocked a broad swathe of people across most of the political spectrum. Few were surprised when liberal journalists condemned the president's act, but when the conservative writer William Safire called the proposed commissions "a Soviet-style abomination,"[4] "Star Chamber tribunals" and a "dismaying departure from due process,"[5] it was clear that the prospect of secret trials appalled more than just those on the political left. "I wasn't used to living under a government where the president thinks he's at war and starts issuing military orders about terrorists," says Ratner. "All of a sudden he is saying he can point to any non-citizen he chooses. He can say, 'arrest them,' and they'll be held indefinitely; and secondly, that they can be tried before a military tribunal, which hasn't been used for sixty years. There's been a lot of water under the bridge since 1945 or 1950 in international agreements and our own domestic law. I go back to the Magna Carta of 1215 where it says you get a real trial!"

With considerable difficulty he put together a small team of lawyers to represent the jailed suspects—to act on behalf of their families, that is, since lawyers were not allowed to talk directly to their clients. But many of his colleagues refused to get involved. "They said, 'Why should I represent terrorists who blew up the World Trade Center?' So I said to them, 'How do you *know* they are terrorists?'"

The hate mail poured in. Most of those who wrote called him a traitor in a variety of redolent ways. One man (who may not have known that he was quoting the satirist Jonathan Swift) suggested that Ratner invite the Taliban to his home and let them eat his children. Another wrote the following, which I include as an example of the degree of apoplectic rage Ratner elicited: "My opinion is, You are a bald fat fuck, go over to Iraq and let them cut your big ass head off, you idiot scum sucking lawyer go play your bald weeny games somewhere in the mideast if you can fucking get there on your own. . . . I hope some SMART person shoves a nail up your fucking snake belly scum sucking low life lawyer butt fucking ass. If you have kids I feel sorry for them you low life piece of shit."

The ugly virulence of this letter and others like it under-score the courage that public dissidence demanded after September 11, 2001. Ratner spoke out because he found the White House's response to the terror strikes "utterly arbitrary." "It's no longer law that's governing," he tells me, "it's whatever the president or [Donald] Rumsfeld decides to do. Calling prisoners enemy combatants? There *is* no such category under the law. You could call them tables if you wanted to. You just make something up and pretend that it's law. We've reverted to a pre-modern system where the whim of the ruler becomes the law of the land, and what's interesting is just how quickly it happened."

Ratner was one of the first, if not *the* first, to articulate the breakdown of law: the shift away from Congress, with its dem-ocratically elected representatives, to the executive branch, with the president and his circle now assuming the right to invent, or remake, legislation as they saw fit. He was fighting to preserve what he considered endangered core values. Fundamental human rights such as the right *not* to be tortured, the right *not* to be detained indefinitely, the right *not* to be "dis-appeared" and the right to be tried in a proper court and not before some kind of secret tribunal.

It is impossible to exaggerate the importance of Ratner's Center for Constitutional Rights in challenging the legality of the Bush administration's response to 9/11. Starting in the winter of 2002, Ratner and his own "coalition of the willing"

visited prisons around the New York area, attempting to interview detainees. Most were being held on visa violations and
other immigration matters, and when that lawful justification
expired, people were detained in a legal limbo. In April 2002
the Center initiated a class-action lawsuit, seeking damages for
violations of the rights of detainees.[6] At the same time they
filed a petition with the Inter-American Commission on
Human Rights, arguing that the detention of the prisoners,
and the conditions under which they were being held, constituted a violation of international law.

That autumn, the CCR began to file briefs in American
courts challenging the legality of the Bush government's policies on "enemy combatants." Two among these cases were particularly striking: in October 2002, the CCR, together with
140 law professors and eighteen organizations, intervened in
the case of Yaser Esam Hamdi, an American citizen who was
being held in prison incommunicado. It was alleged that he
had fought in Afghanistan with the Taliban, but there was
apparently no evidence. No charges had been laid.

Their petition was rejected by a federal appeals court,
which ruled that in times of war the government had virtually
unfettered powers to incarcerate people who were suspected of
fighting with the enemy; but this early judgment merely
marked the beginning of the Hamdi story. There was an
appeal. And in early 2004, the United States Supreme Court
agreed to review the case. (Yaser Hamdi was then allowed to
see a lawyer, although not in private.) In June 2004 the
Supreme Court ruled that Hamdi had been denied due process
and should have an opportunity to defend himself against his
"enemy combatant" designation. But the Bush government
refused to allow a courtroom airing of the legality of the term
it had concocted; instead, Hamdi was summarily released
from custody, deported to Saudi Arabia (his parents' birth-
place) and deprived of his American citizenship.

The Supreme Court had been scheduled to hear another CCR case that same year, Rasul v. Bush. Shafiq Rasul and Asif Iqbal were British citizens who had been held in Guantánamo Bay for more than two years. It was alleged, again without evidence, that they had been with the Taliban in Afghanistan. Both men demanded the right to have their cases heard in American courts, under American law.

Several weeks before their scheduled date with the Supreme Court, both were set free in an act as arbitrary as their arrest. On their return to Britain, they wrote an open letter to President Bush and the Senate Armed Services Committee charging American military officials with deliberately misleading the public about the interrogation techniques being employed at the island prison. Statements made by US officials denying severe abuse in US-run prisons were "completely untrue," they alleged.

The techniques they had personally witnessed or experienced were

- forcing detainees to squat with their hands chained between their legs, and fastened to the floor for hours, while they were questioned;

- leaving detainees naked and chained to the floor while women were brought into the room—a particularly humiliating practice for prisoners from Islamic backgrounds;

- the use of strobe lights, loud music and freezing air to make difficult physical conditions worse;

- the use of dogs to intimidate the detainees;

- the use of physical force, including an assault on a man who had had a psychiatric breakdown; and another attack so vicious that the prisoner had to be hospitalized.

These techniques can accurately be called torture.

The letter did not elicit denial. On the contrary, on July 13, 2005, US military investigators informed the members of the Senate Armed Services Committee, who were probing possible abuses at Guantánamo Bay that had come to light through the release of FBI documents, that forcing a male detainee to wear lingerie and perform dog tricks was "not evidence of inhumane treatment." Yes, the inmate "was forced to dance with a male interrogator, was subject to strip searches, for control measures, not for security, and was forced to perform dog tricks," allowed the senior investigating officer.[7] All of this was "to lower his personal sense of worth."

It was the Nazis who had perfected the idea of "lowering [the prisoner's] personal sense of worth" when they forced elderly Jews to scrub the sidewalks of their cities with toothbrushes and tattooed numbers into their arms, to name just two of their memorable abominations. "Never again," the world subsequently intoned, referring not only to the spectacular cruelty of death by the poison gas Zyklon-B, the burning of bodies in crematoria, the murder of the infirm and genocidal medical practices, among other atrocities, but also to the distorted thinking that preceded those horrors: the cool certainty that there is nothing wrong with destroying the humanity of "the enemy," nothing wrong with "lowering his personal sense of worth."

It is possible that the legal suits brought by the Center for Constitutional Rights, including their later efforts to indict Defense Secretary Donald Rumsfeld and others for war crimes, will be seen by future historians as a turning point in the concerted struggle by a small coterie of American citizens to maintain law and civil rights after 9/11. Other organizations, such as the American Civil Liberties Union, under the unflinching leadership of Anthony Romero, also showed courage in the face of abuse. (The ACLU initiated a legal challenge against the

Bush government's program of domestic spying, which they won in August 2006, pending an appeal.) On April 24, 2007, Pentagon intelligence chief, James Clapp, halted the Defense Department's spying program.[8] In one respect, sheer coincidence worked to advantage: in April 2004, the pictures of detainees being tortured at Abu Ghraib were broadcast around the world: they included images of Iraqis with bags over their heads, being beaten, threatened by dogs and forced to perform degrading acts with leering US soldiers looking on. Within hours, a photograph of a hooded detainee standing on a box with wires attached to his outstretched arms had entered the realm of iconic photography.

On November 30, 2004, after the respected American journalist Seymour Hersh had detailed the "chain of command" behind what he described as a systemic policy of torture in certain US detention facilities,[9] the Center for Constitutional Rights filed its first complaint against Rumsfeld and other high-level officials. "From Donald Rumsfeld on down, the political and military leaders . . . must be investigated and held accountable," wrote the authors. In a formal statement Ratner asserted that "the existence of 'torture memos' drafted by administration officials and the authorization of techniques that violated humanitarian law by Secretary Rumsfeld . . . and others, make clear that responsibility for Abu Ghraib and other violations of law reaches all the way to the top."[10] Their strategy was to present their case outside the United States, since there wasn't a national court that would entertain such a charge.

Ratner and his colleague Peter Weiss hoped to open their lawsuit in Germany, under "universal jurisdiction." This was precisely the point that John Bolton and the other opponents of the International Criminal Court either misunderstood or willfully ignored: the right to try the perpetrators of such crimes already existed under international law, even if it had rarely been used.

The German federal prosecutor declined to take up the CCR petition, which was hardly surprising, given the reality of international alliances. A court case against the American secretary of defence would have been viewed as a diplomatic outrage. There was also the cautionary example of Belgium to consider. In 1993, the Belgians had opened their doors to possible prosecutions for war crimes. Charges against political leaders past and present streamed in, including complaints against the Israeli prime minister, Ariel Sharon, for his "command" role in the 1982 massacre of civilians in the Lebanese camps of Sabra and Shatila,[11] against the Cuban leader, Fidel Castro, for his alleged decades of abuse, against Hissène Habré, the former dictator of Chad, whose regime had disposed of at least forty thousand people before he was chased into exile in 1990, and complaints against Colin Powell, former US president George Bush Sr. and the current US vice president, Dick Cheney, for their alleged crimes against civilians during the 1991 Gulf War. The latter charges had crossed the line where justice intersects with politics: as one Belgian parliamentarian acknowledged, a complaint against George W. Bush for war crimes being committed in Iraq might arrive any day . . . and what would Belgium do then? It had a lot to lose if its new law remained on the books, including the continuing status of Brussels as the seat of international institutions, warned Colin Powell. The country's parliamentarians convened in haste. In the future, they decided, a federal prosecutor would decide whether to accept suits filed under the aegis of universal jurisdiction. Those that did not directly affect Belgium or its former colonies would probably not be approved.

—

What outrage to the soul had armoured Michael Ratner against the abuse he knew he would receive when he audaciously took on his own government? I ask this question as we sit opposite each other in his tiny office. He tells me that he was born into an ordinary family in Cincinnati, a liberal Jewish family with a strong commitment to social justice. His personal engagement came in the spring of 1968, when he was a law student at Columbia University. That was the year Martin Luther King, Jr., and Robert Kennedy were assassinated, the year of anti–Vietnam War riots, ghetto fires and an escalation in the struggle for, and against, black civil rights in the American South. In April, as the death rate in Vietnam increased, Ratner and a group of friends "occupied" several of the campus buildings, demanding that the university sever its ties to the US defence establishment via its sponsorship of the Institute for Defense Analysis. Ratner says he was radicalized not by the substance of the students' demands but by the behaviour of the authorities. After a week the university called in the New York City police, and in the ensuing melee he was badly beaten, along with many others. The physical wounds healed quickly. The continuing wound was interior and was transformed into an unshakable determination to defend civil liberties. He joined the Center for Constitutional Rights in 1972 and has never left.

The lifelong values of John R. Bolton, a man of approximately the same age, were also shaped by the unique environment of those turbulent years. His hatred of communism led him to despise the culture that embraced social democratic ideals, resisted the Vietnam War and celebrated the anarchy of so-called revolution. Bolton too had studied the law. The two men had never met, yet each reflected the legacy of that exceptional era. They hold starkly opposing views, though each considers himself a patriot and a believer in the American Creed: Bolton because he believes the awesome might of the United States at the start of the twenty-first century to be a value that must never be diminished; Ratner because he remains committed to the ideals that informed the Enlightenment origins of his nation as he understands them.

Conventional wisdom holds that the cultural, political and social divisions of the 1960s and 1970s have diminished with time, but they shaped these men; and now, in the early post-9/11 years, echoes from that stormy long-ago era are once again growing louder. The radical conservatism that was born with Barry Goldwater and his disciples has assumed the reins of power, taking over where Ronald Reagan left off. On the other side of the divide, millions of American liberals (or moderates, as they prefer to call themselves) have seen their ideological currency erode in the years following the election of George W. Bush.

The UN Adviser

In April 2005, Cherif Bassiouni was fired by the United Nations Human Rights Commission. He had been hired by the United Nations Secretary-General Kofi Annan just one year earlier, in April 2004, to "seek and receive information about, and report on, the human rights situation in Afghanistan in an effort to prevent human rights violations."

It hadn't been easy to find a visibly independent expert in this area, someone the Americans might find acceptable, and Bassiouni had seemed ideal. One of the world's foremost legal scholars, a professor of international law at DePaul University in Chicago and the author of more than forty books on legal topics, he was also president of the International Human Rights Law Institute, located in Chicago. And he had direct knowledge of the Muslim world. Born into a prominent Egyptian family, he had studied law in France, Switzerland and Egypt before immigrating to the United States, where he became a naturalized citizen. He was, in other words, the perfect internationalist—a man with a cosmopolitan point of view who spoke many languages with native fluency. He also had a long history with the UN. In the early 1990s he had served for two years as chairman of the Security Council commission to investigate war crimes in the former Yugoslavia. His much-lauded report had contributed to the creation of the ICTY in 1993.

Early in 2005 Bassiouni delivered a stinging report criticizing the US for the mistreatment of the approximately one thousand prisoners being held in Afghanistan. After a long, on-the-ground investigation, he accused US troops of conducting arbitrary arrests and inflicting torture that included "sexual abuse, beatings . . . and use of force resulting in death." He wrote, "When these forces directly engage in practices that violate . . . international human rights and international humanitarian law, they undermine the national project of establishing a legal basis for the use of force."[12]

This was not his first outspoken criticism of US actions. In a report delivered to the UN in October 2004 (six months after the torture of prisoners at Abu Ghraib had become public), he wrote that Coalition troops, which should have been "role models" in Afghanistan for international norms of human rights, were anything but. He pointed to alleged violations of international humanitarian law, such as breaking into people's homes without warrants, detaining them without the legal authority to do so, vicious beatings that resulted in death, forced nakedness, sleep denial, prolonged squatting, hooding and sensory deprivation. He said that an estimated three to four hundred detainees were being held at US detention facilities in Bagram, Kandahar and other transit facilities across Afghanistan, and that they were "without legal process," isolated and without recourse.

In his second report, delivered to the United Nations Economic and Social Council on March 11, 2005, he noted that the human rights situation in the country had improved only slightly. Continuing violations included repressive acts against women and children by the Afghan state, as well as arbitrary arrests and illegal detentions by the United States–led Coalition Forces.

In the suddenly changed environment of post–September 11, where war trumped rights, successive negative reports by the same author were viewed with alarm by the Bush administration. Bassiouni was *persona non grata*. At its annual meeting in Geneva during the week of April 18, 2005, the UN Human Rights Commission accepted most of his general conclusions, but neglected to take note of the US violations. Then the UN body decided it no longer needed an independent expert to keep an eye on what was happening in Afghanistan and refused to renew Bassiouni's mandate. Stunned by the cowardice of the world body, Bassiouni accused Kevin Moley, the permanent US representative to the United Nations in Geneva, of directing his staff to lobby the other delegations at the commission to force him out and cancel the position.[13] "The US was blatant about it," he said. "They strong-armed the delegates."[14] Whatever his private opinions, UN Secretary-General Kofi Annan appeared to be helpless.

It was absurd to suggest that Afghanistan no longer needed an independent human-rights monitor. Despite a relatively successful presidential election in 2004, the country's president, Hamid Karzai, presided over just one city, the capital, Kabul, while the warlords of opium ruled the rest. Bassiouni had documented many crimes in his reports, but there were other serious irregularities: in the widely touted parliamentary elections of September 2005, dozens of the candidates were accused war criminals. Law in Afghanistan was more facade than reality, more photo-op than governance; and as Bassiouni pointed out in his reports, the Western jailers' treatment of their prisoners matched the worst local abuses.

Just weeks after Bassiouni was fired, *The New York Times* published the leaked results of a US Army investigation into the deaths of two Afghan detainees who had been held in American custody. One was an educated man who had fought back fiercely; the other was an unschooled, submissive taxi driver who happened to be in the wrong place at the wrong time. Both men had been tortured mercilessly, kicked repeatedly, hung by their hands from ceiling hooks. They were dead within days of their arrests.[15]

—

I wasn't surprised to learn that Cherif Bassiouni hadn't pulled his punches. He was sixty-seven years old when I met him in Chicago in the winter of 2005—before his last trip to Afghanistan, and before the final report that resulted in his firing—and well past worrying about establishing his career. He had received countless honours, including the nomination for the Nobel Peace Prize in 1999 for his seminal work in creating an international criminal court. He was also physically large, direct and outspoken.

We had first met in the fall of 2004, in The Hague, at a conference he was chairing on the International Criminal Court. The meeting was poorly attended and might have been dull had it not been for his presence. He had dominated the speakers' table with his wit, candour, erudition and (it must be said) the self-aggrandizement that can characterize outsized personalities. He reminded his audience about genocides foretold: of Adolf Hitler who, when questioned about his plans for the Jews, had replied airily, "Who now remembers the Armenians?"; about the multiple advance warnings the world had received about the impending massacres in Rwanda; about the still-unaddressed crisis of 500,000 children, their parents and grandparents living and dying in the squalid refugee camps of Darfur. And about impunity, and the millions of civilians who had died during the six decades *after* humanity had first declared, "Never again!"

There was another speaker at that meeting. Pierre Prosper was then George W. Bush's "ambassador at large for war crimes." He had hands-on experience of the ad hoc international criminal courts as a prosecutor at the ICTR, the United Nations tribunal for Rwanda. Optimists had hoped he might try to nudge Washington away from its intractable position on the ICC, but he had not.

I awaited his presentation with interest; after all, as my neighbour whispered, hadn't he flown across the Atlantic to say *something?* Apparently not. He rushed in late, stood at the podium (all the others spoke from their seats on the stage) and delivered a boilerplate speech that began with "The US position is well known." He proceeded to elucidate it anyway. The Rome Statute was "fundamentally flawed"; the ICC prosecutor was "unchecked"; and the Article 98 bilateral agreements not to send American servicepersons to the ICC were an attempt to "bridge the gap" between Europe and the United States. This last claim produced an involuntary burst of laughter from the audience and an embarrassed smirk from the speaker; he was after all among former colleagues. Then he excused himself, without taking questions, to catch the next plane back to Washington.

Leaping into the void left by Prosper's precipitate departure, Cherif Bassiouni spoke diplomatically but with impressive candour. "The United States has made political choices, and that is its right . . . [but] hopefully, the ideological, knee-jerk reaction to international multilateral institutions will diminish," he said with a smile, managing to approve and condemn in a sentence.

As the meeting drew to a close Bassiouni spoke about the eternal "balancing act" between negotiated peace-making deals to end brutal conflicts and the inexorable demand for judicial accountability. At one end of the spectrum are those for whom bringing the perpetrators of massive crimes to justice is simply not an issue: What matters is settling the conflict, sometimes regardless of means or sustainability. At the other extreme are those who demand immediate courtroom trials for the perpetrators of atrocities. Bassiouni positioned himself at the centre of this ongoing debate. "Peace and justice are not necessarily exclusive," he said. "It can be a question of timing. Sometimes it may even be necessary to negotiate with war criminals, even secretly, as long as we do not prejudice the investigation of the crimes and the evidence that will be needed later. When the time comes, we can open the file. But if we pit *uncompromising* justice against the pursuit of peace, in terms of the timing, my guess is that we are not helping to achieve either."

It was a brave position to take. Many of the people in the hall were viscerally opposed to negotiating with suspected war criminals *even* to achieve peace. Slobodan Milošević had been emboldened by the (hypocritical) respect accorded to him during the Bosnian peace negotiations in Rambouillet in early 1999; cloaked in a false perception of personal immunity, he opened a new front against Albanian civilians in Kosovo, which led to the controversial NATO bombing campaign and eventually, for him, a prison cell in The Hague. I had met people in the Belgrade civic opposition who spoke bitterly, scathingly, about the Western leaders who were willing to negotiate with their lying, murderous butcher of a president.

———

It is early 2005. January-cold. A door at the end of a mundane-looking corridor at DePaul University College of Law opens into a suite of rooms where several people sit hunched over computer screens. Cherif Bassiouni's personal secretary, a researcher and a young assistant from Cambridge University in England, a PhD doctoral student under his supervision, all appear to be occupied with the great man's business.

Inside Bassiouni's large private office, every available space on the walls has been appropriated as testimony to his achievements. I count forty framed documents in a half-dozen languages naming international prizes and appreciations, including the French Legion of Honour. There are dozens of photographs of him with assorted luminaries, including Kofi Annan to whom he is proudly presenting a newly minted copy of the Rome Statute. A portrait of Abraham Lincoln peers into the room over a sketch of Don Quixote with his trusty steed, Rocinante. The drawing was given to him, he says, by a friend who thought he was as likely to tilt at windmills as the famous sixteenth-century cavalier. There are display shelves, too, with models of ancient Egyptian art, as well as more personal mementoes: a picture of himself as a young man on a motor-cycle, then age nineteen, in the Egyptian navy. And silly things: a Snoopy dog dedicated to "the world's finest teacher"; a cheap souvenir "donkey of diplomacy" from Paris that can be sepa-rated into two pieces, then reassembled any which way (head or rear end first, he explains); a small plaque that reads "First let's kill all the lawyers" (possibly Shakespeare's most quoted line) and another, more serious plaque, advising those who dream of peace to work for justice.

He is a man of strong appetites. When we lunched together at the conference in The Hague, I had observed that he helped himself to a larger-than-usual portion from the buffet table, after a careful examination of the offerings. Here, he keeps a plate of small Hershey bars on his beautifully polished wood desk, which he dips into frequently, taking care to lob one at Martin, his shy Cambridge assistant, whom he has asked to sit in on our conversation. The young man flushes deeply as he catches the small package sailing unexpectedly though the air.

I want to talk to him about the seeming breakdown of the rule of law in the American-led post-9/11 world; about the disturbing erosion of the civil rights that have been historically identified with democracies; and what these trends signify, if anything, for the future of the International Criminal Court. I am primed to begin—but there is a steady stream of visitors, each pictured on a video phone as he or she stands outside his office door. First his secretary, Kelly, who has been with him for years. Their talk reveals an edge of exasperation, like a long-married couple studiously intent on remaining polite. He signs letters with an expensive-looking pen; he discusses his book-in-progress on the legislative history of the International Criminal Court; he agrees to write prefaces for other people's works; he confirms his imminent travel plans to Afghanistan, and to his Institute of Higher Studies in Criminal Sciences in Siracusa, Italy. He talks on the phone in Arabic, English and Italian. His fundraiser pops through the door several times, trying to catch the attention of someone—*anyone*.

Forty minutes have already passed when one of his researchers enters the room. Bassiouni inquires about her health: she has been having medical tests, and the prognosis is serious. All business is interrupted as he doles out medical advice and makes calls to doctor friends on her behalf. He offers to be her advocate with hospitals and with her physicians. "Always get a second opinion!" he booms, before launching into two lengthy stories about his own several brushes with death.

In a moment of quiet, I seize my chance, diving in with a question I hope will attract his attention. "Can the International Criminal Court survive the opposition of the United States?" I ask him.

He looks at me with surprise. Perhaps he had forgotten I was here.

"They're marginalizing the ICC, no question. The opposition is not passive. They are not saying, 'We don't agree with what you guys are doing, so we're not joining,' although they try to present themselves that way. They are aggressively undermining the court by forcing other countries not to co-operate by saying that if they don't sign the bilateral agreements they will not receive foreign aid. So what they are doing is very damaging because, as a new institution, the ICC needs a great deal of material, as well as moral, support. But marginalization does not mean death. It means essentially that instead of taking five years to get on its feet, it will wind up taking fifteen."

As justice may wait until peace has been secured, depending on the circumstances, so the ICC may take a little longer than expected to establish itself. No big deal, he seems to be saying, although there are many who would be less sanguine. On the other hand, there are few people in the world who are closer to the court itself. In the early 1990s, he was the vice-chair of the United Nations' preparatory committee for the creation of an international criminal court; and at the 1998 Rome Conference he headed the all-important committee that drafted the language of the Rome Statute. Drafting clear legal language is the essential work of creating legislation, whether it concerns a parliamentary law, a judge's decision or an international treaty. The drafters must choose each word with the utmost care, for they are creating a reference that will bind others.

When he returned to the United States after the tumultuous meeting in Rome—after David Scheffer, President Clinton's delegate to the conference, had failed to find agreement between the US government and a majority of the other national delegations—Bassiouni made contact with Walter Slocombe, then the undersecretary of defence for policy in the Clinton administration. And since he clearly loves being an insider, he doesn't hesitate to report Slocombe's remarks about the collapse of the US position at the Rome meeting. "What I understood from him was that the uniformed military was opposed to the International Criminal Court for a reason almost nobody will articulate—and that is their strong distrust of the civilians in government and in the Pentagon," he says. "And I can assure you that everything that has happened since then in the Pentagon under [Donald] Rumsfeld confirms their fears. Torture? I can tell you there isn't a single judge-advocate within the US military who agreed with the position taken by the *civilian* lawyers of the Department of Defense, or by [Alberto] Gonzales at the White House [who gave President Bush the legal green light on "enemy combatants" and torture], or by the people at the Department of Justice. Not a single one. Rumsfeld marginalized the military by taking the responsibility from them and putting it into the hands of the civilians. There isn't a single military judge who agrees with [the prison at] Guantánamo and the 'enemy combatants' concept. That was a civilian decision imposed upon them."

"By whom?"

"First, by Donald Rumsfeld, the secretary of defence, who made the ultimate choice. And by Paul Wolfowitz [deputy secretary of defence], Douglas Feith [undersecretary of defence for policy] and a few others. The point is that even in the Clinton era, before these people were on the scene, the professional military was afraid of having an ICC that would see them, the military, as being responsible for war crimes, like torture. For example, if the ICC were investigating crimes against humanity committed in Iraq and arrested, let's just say, General Janis Karpinski [the commander of the Abu Ghraib prison when the abuses took place], the military would be left holding the bag because all the civilians—Rumsfeld, Wolfowitz, Feith and the others, like Alberto Gonzales—

would run for cover and say, 'We *never* told them to do that!'*
Or you could take the Kosovo intervention of 1999. The
military thinks, 'Okay, there's now a proposed doctrine of
humanitarian intervention, so the US has a right to intervene
militarily; but now they're telling us we have the right to bomb
Serbia—a car factory, a railroad, a bridge. But these are civilian
targets! Believe me, the military did not make the decision to
bomb there without direction from the top.

"What are you going to do if you're an ICC prosecutor?
First, you're going to go after the military! *Who* bombed this
bridge? *Who* killed these civilians? Okay, we're going to indict
Captain Smith. Who is his superior? Wing Commander So-
and-so. Who is *his* superior? Squadron leader So-and-so. Who
is *his* superior? The chief of the air force. It may get that far, but
no further, because the chief of the air force then says, 'This was
a political decision; I got my orders from the National Security
Council in Washington.' That's a no-no; that will be denied. So
the main concern of the military when the ICC negotiations
were taking place in Rome, and even more so now, is that in the
United States the military is controlled by civilians, and the
civilians, for all practical purposes, are unaccountable. It's a
matter of tradition. There has never been a case in United
States history where the responsibility has gone to the civilian
leadership. Did anyone go after [Robert] McNamara after the
Vietnam War? Or Henry Kissinger? The tradition is there to
protect the president. These cabinet officers are making decisions in the name of the president; to make them accountable

---

* On May 5, 2005, Janis Karpinski was demoted from brigadier general to
colonel on grounds of "dereliction of duty," but she was never tried. She
claimed to be a "scapegoat" for the actions of her superiors, especially
Donald Rumsfeld, and was, in fact, the highest-ranking officer disciplined
for the Abu Ghraib scandal.

would eventually lead to the president. But in the American system, the president is the golden cow that nobody ever reaches [on issues of war]."

Listening intently, I remember that more than half a century ago, during the American-led Tokyo Trials, Emperor Hirohito also was protected. Although every rapacious act committed by the soldiers of Imperial Japan during the Pacific war had required, at the very least, tacit approval from His Majesty, he never faced trial. Only the military entered the dock and paid the ultimate price. In a wink-wink deal brokered by the American general Douglas MacArthur, Hirohito was allowed to remain on his lofty throne in order to ensure cultural stability, which helps explain why the right-wing government of Japan, which has descended in a relatively straight line from that long-ago era, is still unwilling to offer an official apology for the atrocities that were committed against Chinese and Korean civilians and against American and British prisoners of war. The full truth about the emperor has never emerged.

"What about the rule of law since 9/11?" I ask. The question sounds faintly anachronistic even as I ask it. One day, long ago, I happened upon an acquaintance of my own age who had been practising law for several years. "How lucky you are to advocate for justice," I said admiringly. He guffawed so loudly that passersby on the street turned their heads in surprise. "Justice!" he shouted, "I haven't heard that word since law school!"

Cherif Bassiouni's idealism may have been tempered by pragmatism, but thankfully he has not lost his passion. "I will start by saying that recent events have demonstrated that the rule of law in the United States is only a thin veneer, although everyone thought for years, here and elsewhere, that two hundred years of legal development made it a place where the law was strongly established. And this is a shock, a surprise. . . ."

"To you personally?"

"Yes, to me. And I say this as a naturalized citizen who truly believed what the Constitution said and what the legal history of this country meant. When I took the oath of allegiance, I did it with full conviction. But to my great surprise, it has taken very little to wash away the rule of law. I think about the famous Boston Tea Party where, in the midst of general hysteria, a suspect was tried by a jury of twelve Bostonians—and acquitted. Now, in the days of John Ashcroft, we have the attorney general giving a press conference and telling the world that people who have been arbitrarily picked up are terrorists and using the entire pressure of the United States government to have them plead guilty. Without a shred of evidence—not a shred. When the inspector-general of the Department of Justice wanted to know the disposition of these 1,800 cases of 'pickups,' Ashcroft refused. When Congress wanted to know the numbers of people arrested, he refused. There is *no* legal basis for the attorney general to stonewall in that way, but he got away with it, which means the rule of law has no meaning any more. Think about it. The American Bar Association did not take strong measures against the Patriot Act. State bar associations did not take strong positions. Imagine! Imagine that in America a person might be convicted on secret evidence."

He is talking about the rule of law, which is the cornerstone of democracy. I wonder how many Americans would agree with what he has said. Would he be dismissed out of hand as a "liberal intellectual," as a "foreigner," even as "anti-American"?

He fortifies himself with a Hershey chocolate. "What this shows is that law isn't that important in our scale of values when we're confronted with fear. And so this has come to pass. We have become separated from the origins of our own legal system, from the notion of due process. What this shows is not only how insensitive our leaders are, but how precarious our legal system really is. We have lost our way."

"My own sense," I volunteer, "is that although the rule of law may have suffered a blow since 9/11, the fundamentals remain strong in America. I see signs of change, such as the court cases that challenged the arbitrariness of President Bush's new rules all the way up to the Supreme Court. That court delivered a judgment about the Guantánamo detainees that defied the will of the administration."

"It is true, the pendulum will readjust itself," he says. "But it's going to be much slower than you may think. The shock to me is that it could swing so far outside the bounds of the law and remain there for so long. You know, the day the president effectively said, 'I'm going to decide whether an American is outside the Constitution' [when American citizens were designated enemy combatants],[16] I would have expected less than three months for a federal court, or the Supreme Court, to say, 'Hey, wait a minute, we can't do that!' Not two and a half years. And there was so little indignation from people. . . . Think about the moral indignation of those who opposed the Vietnam War in the 1960s. They took to the streets. There has not been a single demonstration specifically targeted to torture."

He looks distressed, then busies himself with paperwork and several Hershey chocolates. I thank him for his time and slip out the door.

The West Point Prof

The hour-long drive from New York City along the banks of the Hudson River to the famous West Point Military Academy takes me through terrain so lovely, and so remote from urban life, that I momentarily forget the battle over the rule of law that has brought me here. West Point is the cradle of the American military: 20 percent of the officers in the United States Army receive their training here. The very fit cadets milling about in their green army fatigues and black boots, their hair shorn to within an inch of their scalps, are privileged by the beauty of this wooded hillside place—and rightly so, for many of them will soon risk their lives in Iraq or Afghanistan—or Iran, if the Bush administration's compass swings in that direction. A yellow ribbon symbolically embraces the girth of a large tree, marking the deaths of former students in the Hydra-headed "War on Terror."

After the shocking pictures from the Abu Ghraib prison circulated the globe in April 2004, Gary Solis went directly to the US media.[17] Where were the officers? he demanded to know—the lieutenants, the captains and the majors? Why did no one stop this? Since it is his job to teach the laws of war to the future military leaders of America, his reaction carried weight. In the hierarchical system of the military, as he told anybody who asked, responsibility always travels up the line.

Despite my having made an appointment, he seems surprised when I turn up at his office door in the law department just off the main street of the academy. But a person of such friendliness and natural charm is unlikely to remain reserved for long, if he has something to say.

And he does, this man of long military experience, as he leans back in his chair. "I'd have to say that I am disappointed—*offended* would be a better term—by the actions of my government. How can you take American citizens, put them in confinement, keep them incommunicado, without charges, without legal counsel, without habeas corpus,[18] without bail? To me it is just beyond belief that we would be doing this to US citizens. If they had a reason for arresting these people—and I'm speaking specifically here about Yaser Hamdi and José Padilla [the so-called dirty bomber][19]—they should have charged them with something. It's not a question of whether they were good or bad people; it's about the rule of law.

"And this is only one aspect. Torture? Disappearances? Rendition . . . ? Is this my country? I gave a speech in Mississippi recently and I said, 'I spent twenty-six years in uniform in the United States Marine Corps, my country right or wrong, and my country, right now, is wrong.'"

Solis holds three law degrees and knows more about war crimes than just about any one else in the United States. He is the author of *Son Thang: An American War Crime*, a chronicle of the courts-martial that followed one of the worst crimes of the Vietnam War, when, as he describes it, a five-man patrol that had dubbed themselves the "killer team" was sent to an area heavily infiltrated by Viet Cong guerrillas. It was the night of February 19, 1970. Adrenalin was running high in the young soldiers, in readiness, but there were no enemy fighters in the village. In a rage the Americans pulled seventeen sleeping women and children out of their huts and shot them at point-blank range.

The critics' response to the book was positive—powerful emotions still swirl around the memory of Vietnam in America. "But what about now?" I ask him. "Were the acts carried out at Abu Ghraib war crimes?"

"Absolutely. It was a clear breach of the Geneva Conventions. And I think one of the biggest crimes of Abu Ghraib is the fact that senior officers are walking. [Brigadier General Janis] Karpinski is going to get nothing, and that is criminal. Now *there's* someone who would be ripe for prosecution by the International Criminal Court if we, the US, didn't take action—and by the way, we're not. And what about Lieutenant General [Ricardo] Sanchez? Should he have known what was going on at Abu Ghraib? Of course you could go even higher, to the Joint Chiefs. How about [Donald Rumsfeld] the secretary of defence? At that point we move out of the Pentagon and into the [Bush] administration. These decisions [about whom to prosecute or not] are made at a very senior level."

The US government claimed that a few "rogue" soldiers were responsible and would be duly punished. It was the same argument that F. W. de Klerk, the former National Party leader and president of South Africa, employed in the mid-1990s when he said that the excesses of apartheid were due to "a few bad eggs" and not to government policy; and the same argument that the Serbian government trotted out in June 2005 when a video picturing Serb paramilitaries executing six Bosnian Muslims at Srebrenica surfaced at the Milošević trial. Also in 2005 (a year after the Center for Constitutional Rights' proposed case against Defense Secretary Donald Rumsfeld and other senior US military and civilian officials failed to find acceptance in Germany), the American Civil Liberties Union and the NGO Human Rights First had filed a federal court lawsuit against Rumsfeld in the United States. The defence secretary, they said, bore "command responsibility" for the torture and abuse of detainees in US military custody. He had "personally authorized unlawful interrogation techniques and [had abdicated] his legal duty to stop torture."

The term "command responsibility," which was coined at the Nuremberg Tribunal, refers to the authority to issue binding orders to those who will physically perpetrate a crime. At the moment of his untimely death, the former Serb president Slobodan Milošević was being tried in The Hague for "command responsibility" for the killing by Serb security forces of some 10,000 ethnic Albanians in Kosovo and the eviction of approximately 800,000 others. If the language of the law was dull, the politics surrounding "command responsibility" were anything but. Although the prospect of Donald Rumsfeld in a defendant's box still stretched credulity in 2005 when the ACLU filed its lawsuit against him, the idea of bringing charges against a politician of his stature would have been unimaginable just three years earlier, when a US federal court ruled, in late 2002, that the Bush administration could do virtually whatever it wanted "in time of war." In March 2006, Rumsfeld filed to dismiss the case, arguing that government officials were immune from any acts committed on their watch; but his claim made little sense in the post-Milošević era, particularly since the US had supported the rules and regulations of the ICTY. Although he is unlikely ever to see the inside of a courtroom, Rumsfeld's immunity defence was viewed with growing skepticism in some quarters—particularly after he resigned his office in November 2006, following the Democratic rout in the country's midterm elections.[20] International law seemed to be entering the United States by the back door.

Nonetheless, Gary Solis thinks the laws of war still don't work very well, although many of them have been on the books for more than a century. War crimes rarely come to light. In the US, Solis says, suspects may be court-martialled, but the sentences imposed by military courts are usually laughably short—for political reasons. Take the worst crime committed against civilians during the Vietnam War, the My Lai massacre of March 16, 1968, when five hundred civilians were slaughtered by soldiers under the command of Lieutenant William Calley. Solis thinks the military court-martial took its job seriously when it sentenced Calley to life imprisonment, but then politics took over. "The convening authority cut the sentence to twenty years. Then the secretary of the army, a civilian under political pressure, cut it to ten years, and President Nixon, who had his own problems with Watergate, cut it to 'time served.' So in the end Calley spent two weeks in a brig and two and a half years under house arrest. And he was the only guy convicted.

"You know, when you see violations of the laws of war, you always ask yourself, How did this happen? And the answer often comes down to [a failure in the command structure of the military] leadership."

All the same, long experience has shaded certain black-and-white judgments to grey, and he wants me to appreciate how extreme the pressures of the moment can be on the psyche of a soldier. "The massacres of Son Thang and My Lai were gross violations, and I'm not defending them. They were outright massacres of innocent civilians. But in cases when you're under fire, well, sometimes it is awfully hard to remember the laws of war. I know what it's like to be shot at and, as Churchill once said, there's no exhilaration like being shot at and missed. I would like to think I was a zealous prosecutor in my day, but I honestly can't square that with what I'm going to say now, because I know it's a violation: I would not prosecute someone who killed while actually under fire, or moments thereafter."

Judgment, he was arguing, demanded a case-by-case response, and in war there may be mitigating factors.

On the subject of Guantánamo, Solis has reached his own conclusions.

"We will never see a completed military commission [to try the detainees]. You heard it here first. We've used military commissions since 1849 and there have been literally thousands of them, so the military knows how to do it. But what was acceptable in 1945 is not necessarily acceptable today. Back then [our enemies] were seen as just a bunch of Nazis and a bunch of Japs. Nobody cared what happened to them. But the world has turned. Human rights, a term nobody had heard of in 1945, are high on the horizon now, and I don't think the world community is prepared to see trial, conviction and punishment based upon the lowered standard of rights and procedures that occur in military commissions."†

---

† On October 17, 2006, George W. Bush signed the Military Commissions Act in one of the most controversial acts of his presidency. For more on this see Chapter 13.

"What's your guess about what will happen to the hundreds of prisoners being held in Guantánamo Bay?" I ask.

"They're going to be sent back home to their country of origin, one by one. It's already starting. Eventually, we'll look around at an empty prison in Gitmo, and say, son of a gun, every one of those suckers walked. And what do you think is going to happen when they get home? How will their compatriots respond? Politically the United States will be paying for this for who knows how long."

He had already called John Bolton's constitutional argument against the International Criminal Court "bogus," and said the government's real worry was that the ICC might charge senior American officials with war crimes for having legitimized torture, or worse. Are the top brass in the Pentagon seriously worried that American "grunts" serving overseas might be indicted? I ask him. That, too, is a red herring, he replies. Anyone can commit a war crime, but the Rome Statute states that such offenses must be committed as part of a plan or policy, and on a large scale, before the ICC is allowed to initiate an investigation. "That's not an individual soldier shooting a prisoner, or even ten prisoners, but it *is* a commanding general who fails to control his or her troops. Like Janis Karpinski. The Pentagon may be a lot more worried about its senior generals having to face justice— you know, they might go on vacation to Portugal and get served on a beach with an international arrest warrant.

"The far greater obstacle to our joining the International Criminal Court is political—and I mean civilian politicians, the administration rather than the Pentagon. I oppose their thinking. I have spent most of my life dealing with war crimes in one way or another, and it seems clear to me that the ICC is the final step in the march toward personal responsibility [before the law]. The laws of war are like a reverse onion, putting on layers rather than peeling them off, and we've been moving in this direction since the 1907 Hague Regulations. The Nuremberg Tribunal was a great step forward, and now we have international tribunals for the former Yugoslavia and Rwanda. But they are merely a temporary step. The International Criminal Court is the final step.

"You know *we* were the principal proponents of the ICC until we didn't get our way on every issue! It's all about control." He laughs out loud.

Solis says he's realistic about what is likely to happen. "An institution like the ICC recognizes that it would be political suicide to charge an American politician—everyone knows that. But what the White House *can't* control is some guy walking in [to the ICC prosecutor's office] with an allegation [of gross abuses] and asking for an investigation . . . That's what happened with the ICTY. [There had been a complaint about the legality of the NATO bombing campaign in Kosovo.] Carla Del Ponte, the prosecutor for the ICTY, looked at it and initially declined to even *start* an investigation, let alone issue a warrant.‡ But instead of that being reassuring to the American body politic, it serves to illustrate the potential danger the Court presents."

"Wasn't that evidence of a double standard when she initially refused to investigate?"

"Well, yes, it was. Who was it who wrote that the strong do what they will and the weak seek justice?"

"Thucydides."

"Well, that's the way of the world. I'm not saying it is right, but it will always be thus."

"Are you suggesting that the United States should join the International Criminal Court on the understanding that the ICC will be willing and able to handle the politics?"

---

‡ Del Ponte did eventually open an investigation, which found there had been no wrongdoing.

"Yes, in my view, yes. After all, the ICC is a court of last resort. If we Americans take action ourselves with regard to crimes committed by our own people we have nothing to fear. That's the so-called principle of complementarity. On the other hand, if we commit massacres such as happened at My Lai, then we *do* have something to fear. Even though the ICC may appreciate the politics of charging Americans, if another My Lai–type incident were to occur and be handled in the same way, yes, we could have something to fear. Had the ICC been in existence in 1970, and had the US been subject to its jurisdiction . . . what would the court have made of our failure to prosecute nineteen [suspected murderers]? Or the failure to convict in five out of six other cases? Would we have been seen as having failed to undertake good-faith prosecutions? The ICC might *well* have assumed jurisdiction.

"Sure, it's true that America sends its men and women around the world. We are the spearhead that's exposed, and it's well and good for Iceland to condemn us—Iceland is at no risk. I understand that argument. But my perspective is influenced by my study of the laws of war and the eventual futility of try-ing to prosecute individuals on an ad hoc basis, as with the ICTY and the ICTR. You need a standing court of interna-tional reach with experienced people manning it—and that's the ICC. There have been so many perpetrators of major crimes who have gone scot-free. Just think of it! Maybe there will always be Idi Amins in the world, but it would be nice if we had a way of breaking through their impunity and forcing them to pay a price for their crimes."

He has indicated that he strongly supports the ICC *and* that he thinks it would be "political suicide" for a prosecutor to indict an American. But he also believes that if the US failed to conduct its own fair and transparent war crimes trials, the ICC might step in—and rightly so. The political issue he has raised is crucial, but the scenarios he has outlined might be contradictory. If a prosecutor chose, for political reasons, *not* to investigate a suspected perpetrator from one of the world's strongest countries, he could be accused of caving in to the politics of "might makes right." *This* might be "political suicide" for the International Criminal Court. The underlying charter of the ICC, the Rome Statute, opposes immunity, so if the court refused to acknowledge major abuses by a powerful state, its reputation would be placed in jeopardy. Conversely, if the strongest states came to believe that the tribunal was toothless and could safely be ignored, that would be equally dangerous. If the ICC looked helpless in the face of gross abuses, its member states might decide to withdraw their funding. None of this was likely to happen in the immediate future; the ICC was still in its infancy. But already, as we shall see in a later chapter, some of the court's watchdog supporters were not entirely pleased. Human Rights Watch—a prominent member of William Pace's Coalition for an International Criminal Court—had already expressed displeasure with the decision of Luis Moreno-Ocampo, the ICC prosecutor, to try just a single suspected perpetrator from the fracas in the Congo, as his first case.

The Rome Statute is a legal, not a political, document. Yet as Gary Solis made clear, politics are never easily ignored.

Solis admits that he sometimes finds himself groping to answer his students' questions. When eyebrows are being raised worldwide over the behaviour of some American soldiers in Iraq, he has to think fast. But he isn't King Solomon. "One thing I have some trouble with is when people ask, 'Why should we observe the laws of war when they cut off heads in Iraq?'"

I express surprise. "What's wrong with the simple ethic of two wrongs don't make a right? Because one person commits an abomination, does a second person then have the right to do the same?"

"Not at all," he replies, "but at the end of a conflict, war crimes can be unevenly prosecuted, as we know. The first thing I say to my students is, be sure you're on the winning side. I often get asked about the nuclear bombings of Hiroshima and Nagasaki. People say, 'How can you talk about the laws of war and not mention that?' In fact, I cannot justify [what happened there] except to say it was a different world then. But I do talk about the writer Paul Fussell's statement 'Thank God for the atom bomb.' He was slated to be in the front line and he thought the atom bomb was a right good idea."

"That's a personal argument," I remind him.

"Well, there were about a million of those personal arguments."

"There were some personal arguments in the streets of Hiroshima and Nagasaki."

"Absolutely."

What psychology leads a soldier to commit war crimes such as torture or the murder of civilians? Is it revenge for the death of his platoon buddies? Or a potent alchemy of adrenalin, testosterone and the conviction that the enemy is less human than oneself? The latter is a basic teaching concept of training, in spite of common denials, for how else can an ordinary non-violent person be re-educated to kill? Solis adds a fact that catches me off guard: I am astonished to learn that he is the first person ever to teach the Geneva Conventions to American officer cadets. There had never been such a course. He had had to invent it. In 1996.

"I came here and I said, 'Hey, who teaches the laws of war?' They said, 'We don't teach it.' I was amazed. How could it be that the West Point Military Academy doesn't teach the laws of war? Now it's true that unlike a civilian institution, we only have so many hours for academic subjects. There's the military department, the sports department—we actually had to kill a subject to get my course on the curriculum. But it's still optional. At the US Naval Academy they don't even have a laws of war course yet. The US Air Force Academy started their Laws of War course just last year [2004] as a result of an interaction between me and another retired marine colonel who teaches there."

"So officers go into the field without having studied war law?"

"Well, they study combat. They study what's gone wrong and what's gone right. They study My Lai, and hopefully they pick up some of it that way. Of course, ordinary marines and soldiers get trained in a rudimentary way when they join the services. They get lectures that nobody hears; they try to stay awake; the officer giving the lecture doesn't know very much about it, isn't interested in it, but it says in the training schedule that you will have an hour of laws of war training quarterly, so they have to do it. . . . There's been a change in awareness in the past ten years, and today the basic training requirements are somewhat stricter, but as I said, when there is a major breakdown, as in Abu Ghraib, you need to look to the [officer] leadership. And they may know very little about the law."

In his West Point classes he examines the moral and legal restrictions of the Geneva Conventions. Civilians in war zones are to be protected; surrendered or captured prisoners have defined legal rights and must be treated humanely. Officers-in-training must learn this—for their own protection.

"I present them with the facts, we talk, we look at war films like *Saving Private Ryan* and discuss the issues. But you have to remember that for these kids it's still abstract. Even torture is abstract. Some of them will say, 'Yeah, just kill them,' or 'Yeah, torture them.' So I ask what positive outcome might be expected from killing and torturing? Since the most important quality at West Point is honour, I say, 'Are you willing to risk your honour by torturing someone? To get information that is probably incorrect anyway? And even if it *were* correct, the information might be outdated? Is that worth your honour?' They listen, but every once in a while I get a kid who thinks the whole idea of circumscribing war is ridiculous. I don't argue. I just say with a smile, 'I suggest you pay attention anyway so one day you'll understand what you're being court-martialled for.'

"You know, they're so young. What they don't realize is that doing things like that corrodes the soul."

A silence drops between us. His experience in Vietnam drove him to study the law that was coded in the blood of earlier conflicts, the laws that were regularly ignored in that hellish place. "Vietnam remains the centre of my life; nothing that happened to me before or since has affected me so permanently," he says quietly.

"I was twenty-seven years old and not very sophisticated, but I knew something was wrong. My guys were killing people. I didn't know how to handle it. I didn't know if I was the only one, if I was a weak leader. I didn't know what the hell was going on. I couldn't talk to anybody. . . . My students here are just kids; they need to know what they're going up against. I want to protect them." His voice catches.

"When you teach your classes about the laws of war, is this what you are remembering?" I ask him gently.

"Yes," he replies, his voice a near whisper. "It sounds so corny, but there's not a day goes by . . . there's not a day goes by—"

He reaches across the desk and clicks off my tape recorder. "But you can't let that show," he says, directing his gaze away from mine. "You just look like a silly old man."

—

There is another man from another era who personifies the impunity of the powerful. He is Robert S. McNamara, the secretary of defence in the administrations of two presidents: John F. Kennedy and Lyndon B. Johnson. Decades ago, he was in charge of America's most disturbing war, the one that still haunts the daily lives of those, like Gary Solis, who were there.

I had watched him star in his own life story as presented by Errol Morris in his extraordinary documentary *The Fog of War*. Throughout that film, the man who had embodied the military face of America's Cold War pondered his personal history. The ghosts of almost sixty thousand dead Americans and millions of Vietnamese, most of them civilians, weighed invisibly on his shoulders as the camera lens captured his struggle to grapple with his past. Why did he subject himself to this painful examination? The film gives us no clue. He was almost ninety years old.

I place a phone call to his office in Washington, DC.

SIX

The Old Soldier

ince the early 1990s Robert S. McNamara has been
trying to shape the way historians will evaluate the
role he played in the Vietnam War. First, in 1993, he
agreed to be interviewed by Deborah Shapley,
whose well-regarded biography, *Promise and Power:
The Life and Times of Robert McNamara*, cleared a tentative path
through the dense forest of his past—a path he continued to
walk alone over the next several years with the publication of
three memoirs.

In his prologue to the first volume, *In Retrospect: The
Tragedy and Lessons of Vietnam*, which was published in 1995
when he was seventy-nine years old, he acknowledges that a
personal account of his Vietnam experience had been long in
coming. The reason, he writes, was his fear of appearing "self-
serving, defensive, or vindictive." And also, he adds ruefully,

"because it is hard to face one's mistakes." Yes, the Vietnam War was a mistake, he finally allows after the passage of three decades. "We were wrong, terribly wrong," he writes. "We owe it to future generations to explain why, and to absorb the bitter lessons of that era."

In Japan, after decades of hiding the truth about their wartime deeds, old soldiers were coming forward to tell a shocked and doubting public about the atrocities they had committed against Chinese and other civilians during the Pacific war. Since Japan's official stance over the decades was (and remains) denial, these perpetrators could have chosen to remain silent, taking their secrets to the grave. But guilt, and a desire to clear the slate of conscience as they approached the end of their lives, pushed them to confess.

A similar need for personal reckoning appears to have seized Robert McNamara.

In his books, and in the film *The Fog of War*, he draws eleven moral, cultural and strategic lessons from the failure of the war in Vietnam—all of them the result of serious misjudgments, in his view, that reflected America's ignorance of the history, culture and politics of the people in the region and the personalities and habits of their leaders. Among the misjudgments were the failure to recognize that the power of nationalism will frequently lead people to fight and die for their beliefs; the failure to appreciate the limitations of high-technology military equipment when confronting an unconventional enemy; and "the failure to recognize that [we] are not omniscient . . . and that where our own security is not directly at stake, our judgment of what is in another people's, or country's, best interest should be put to the test of open discussion in international forums. . . . We do not have the God-given right to shape every nation in our own image or as we choose," he writes.

In spite of these repeated *mea culpas*, many people were unwilling to forgive the old man, especially the bitter veterans of his war and the families of soldiers who died. During a panel discussion at Harvard University on April 25, 1995, shortly after the publication of *In Retrospect*, the academics were kind but the audience was not.

In question period a man jumped to his feet and said, "Mr. Secretary, my name is John Hurley. I'm a Vietnam veteran. And I have to tell you, sir, and there's no polite way to do this, your book and your presence is an obscenity. There [was] a time, sir, when your intentions in going into Vietnam were quite right, were quite moral, were quite valued and were respected by the entire country. But, at some time, sir, your opinion on this war changed. . . .

"At the end of 1965, 1,425 American troops were dead— 1,425. Exactly 58,191 died before it was over. My friend, my commander, Burt Bunting, died in Vietnam. McNally never saw Wyoming. Allen Perot never saw Needham, Massachusetts, again. Sunny Davis didn't come home. They were torn to shreds . . . You ripped the soul out of 58,191 families in this country, sir. And you remained silent. You said nothing. You let thirty years pass.

"My question is, sir, why did Burt Bunting die when you knew the war was a mistake? Why did McNally die? Why did Kirkendale die? Why did they die, sir? Why did you remain silent while another 57,000 US troops and 4 million Vietnamese died? Why?"

Supportive applause broke out before McNamara could reply. "You're going to have to read the book to get the answer," he said over the din, sounding flustered.

"Sir—"

"Wait a minute, *shut up!*" interrupted a rattled McNamara.

He tried to explain, but the audience refused to listen. The red-faced admissions of *In Retrospect* were not enough. In the aftermath of a failed war with high casualties, nothing would ever be enough.

—

During the Second World War McNamara served for three years in the Pacific, where he become a ranking military strategist under the direct command of General Curtis LeMay. This was not a happy assignment for a young man still in his impressionable twenties. General LeMay firebombed sixty-four Japanese cities where, to use his own culinary vocabulary, he "scorched, boiled and baked to death" some half million men, women and children. So chilling was he in real life that he was the model for the hilarious, terrifying, bloodthirsty Cold Warrior General Jack D. Ripper in Stanley Kubrik's 1964 film *Dr. Strangelove*.

McNamara is haunted still by the 100,000 men, women and children who were incinerated in a single firebombing attack on Tokyo the night of March 9–10, 1945—a murderous assault that he defended at the time as an "efficient" battle strategy. "Was there a rule of war that we could not bomb and kill 100,000 people in one night?" he asks himself in *The Fog of War*, sounding innocent and befuddled. "LeMay said if we lost the war, we'd all be prosecuted as war criminals. He and I were behaving as war criminals."

He was right—on both counts. When the Nuremberg Trials opened in Germany on November 20, 1945, followed by the Tokyo Trials on May 3, 1946, the victors, including General LeMay and Robert McNamara, were not standing in the prisoners' dock. That was a firm condition of the agreement that created the postwar international criminal tribunals. Instead, both men were promoted.

The laws of war were not on the minds of many people in March 1945, or if they were, men like LeMay and the young McNamara didn't care. What mattered was winning by whatever means necessary at whatever cost. Nor were the laws of war on the mind of Defense Secretary McNamara during the

Vietnam War, which began more than a decade after the 1949 Geneva Conventions were written into international law. "What is morally appropriate in a wartime environment?" he now asks himself. "While I was Secretary we used Agent Orange in Vietnam. Were those who issued the command to use Agent Orange guilty of crimes against humanity? What kind of a law says that *this* is acceptable, but *that* is not? . . . How much evil must we do in order to do good?"

Had he bothered to inform himself about the laws of war, Vietnam might have been a different battlefield. Now, in the twilight of his life, he believes, like Telford Taylor, that the laws of war are not a one-way street and that no one responsible for such crimes should be immune from prosecution. There is in him a worm of guilt that confounds and seeks redemption. The enemy can no longer be reduced to coloured pins on the bristol boards of civilian policy-makers and military strategists. Robert McNamara now thinks there should be no immunity for the perpetrators of acts that fall outside the thin moral line humanity has drawn for itself. In old age, he has become a proponent of the International Criminal Court.

—

Just a few blocks from John Bolton's office at the US State Department, and directly opposite a city park where the unemployed snooze on a soporific autumn day, stands the unremarkable building where Robert S. McNamara has an office. I take the elevator; a receptionist leads me down a narrow hall and knocks on a door. An elderly but strong-looking man answers. He beckons me in.

It is a large corner room with many windows. The old soldier indicates with a wave of his arm that we will sit together on the couch that lines one of the walls. His shoulders slouch with age, and he moves laboriously, but his regard is direct and intense.

I tell him I wish to understand the shift in his thinking about war crimes and impunity. I say I am aware that when the newly negotiated Rome Statute lay unsigned on the desk of President Bill Clinton, he, Robert McNamara, had contacted Benjamin Ferencz. I am interested to know why he did that. Ferencz had been agitating for the creation of a permanent international criminal court for half a century, ever since he experienced the cold chill of the Nazi genocide in the famous Nuremberg courtroom.

"I'd been interested in the International Criminal Court for some time as part of my concern about the limitations of existing sanctions, which are economic or military," he replies. "Economic sanctions are not very effective, and military action is a rough and crude response, but they are the only two we have against undesirable political or military conduct. So I came to believe a third sanction would be desirable, and I think of it as an international judicial system. They [the framers of the Rome Statute] agreed to standards of conduct to be adhered to by military and political leaders, and if those standards were violated, there would be a system to apprehend the violators and bring them before a court of justice. I came to see the International Criminal Court as that institution."

He himself would not be subject to indictment by the ICC—its jurisdiction was limited to events that occurred after it came into force on July 1, 2002; but deep in his bones he seems to believe that he ought to be. Naturally, neither he nor Curtis LeMay were charged with war crimes in their own country—something that would be compulsory today under the "complementarity clause" of the Rome Statute if a signatory nation wanted to avoid triggering an investigation of one of its citizens by the ICC. But sixty years ago the rights of civilians on the enemy side were not on anyone's military map, although McNamara's personal suffering stands as proof that such breaches can take up permanent residence in conscience. By the time of the Vietnam conflict, non-combatants had been protected under international law for almost a century, but war crimes were no one's priority then either. When individuals *were* charged, as in the case of Lieutentant William Calley, the punishment was laughably slight.

"Do *you* believe the people who ordered the firebombing in Japan and Germany, and the nuclear bombings of Hiroshima and Nagasaki, should have been in the dock after the war?" I ask.

He declines to engage. "I don't want to argue the point, but at least the issues [of law] should have been considered, and I certainly know they weren't considered at the command level where I was. I just know that this was not an element of our decision-making process."

Perhaps we are both thinking the same thing: that he is responsibile for the millions who died on his personal watch, those unquiet shades who rob his final years of sleep; but short of that accounting he has a message to impart about the learning an old man is privy to, about the wisdom that sometimes descends when the clatter of active life falls away. What he now believes about war and politics is far removed from the urgencies of battle, rapid decision making and the stresses of war. His focus now is on a peculiarly human quality—one that commonly suggests interpersonal, not global, relations. Had he replied candidly to the still-grieving veteran who confronted him at Harvard, he might have mentioned this concept aloud, although it is possible that some people might have laughed. That necessary (and usually ignored) quality, he says, is empathy: the ability to put oneself in the shoes of another, including an opponent.

Empathy has a long pedigree; it is what the ancient Greek dramatists sought to trigger in their audiences, as did Sophocles in his play *Antigone*. Because it prompts an acknowledgment that the hated enemy remains a human being, empathy is a tool for understanding events from an opposing point of view. McNamara now thinks that knowledge so gleaned can and should be a strategic element of military planning.

His proof is embedded in a startling personal story. In 1995 he travelled to Vietnam to talk to the man who was the North Vietnamese foreign minister during the war. "I was shocked because it became clear to me that we didn't understand them and they didn't understand us," he says. "For us, the war was about keeping the security of the West from weakening by pre-venting the Communist Chinese and the Communist Soviets from controlling South Vietnam. We thought they wanted to use it as a base from which to extend their operations across East Asia and South Asia. But *they* thought of it as a *civil* war. They actually saw us as a colonial power—substituting for France.[1]

"[The foreign minister] told me, 'You were totally wrong. We were fighting for our independence and you were fighting to enslave us.' He said, 'Mr. McNamara, if you had ever read a history book you would have known that we are not the pawns of the Chinese or the Russians. We have been fighting the Chinese for a thousand years. No amount of pressure from the United States would have stopped us from fighting for our national independence.'"

"Did hearing this undercut the rationale for the war in your mind?" I ask him.

"Well, it supported my view that we each could have obtained our objectives without the terrible loss of life."

"Without going to war?"

"I think so, yes. On their side as well as ours."

It was a sobering image: two once powerful, now elderly men belatedly clarifying fatal misunderstandings that had cost the lives of millions. Ironically, they—both of them—still lived.

"Do armies and their political bosses still misread the story?"

"Sure. I don't want to argue whether we're right or wrong in what we're doing in Iraq, for example, but we're poles apart in the way we see the Iraqis and the way they see us. I won't comment any further except to say there is very little of the kind of understanding I call empathy on either side."

As a young man he studied the Greek philosophers, Plato and Aristotle, with a professor at the University of California who had greatly influenced him. The moral foundations of that thinking interest him, he says; and now he had returned to that long-forgotten part of himself. Years ago, his late, beloved wife, Marg, had brought to his attention a stanza from "East Coker—1940," the second of the "Four Quartets," by the twentieth-century Anglo-American poet T. S. Eliot. This work has become increasingly important to him; he mentioned it in *The Fog of War* and quoted the last line, which includes the words "In my end is my beginning . . . ," and added his own recollection of another line from the poem: "We shall never cease from exploring, but at the end we shall return to our first starting place."

I had looked up that section of the Eliot poem. The exact phrasing was this:

> *Old men ought to be explorers*
> *Here or there does not matter*
> *We must be still and still moving*
> *Into another intensity*
> *For a further union, a deeper communion*
> *Through the dark cold and the empty desolation,*
> *The wave cry, the wind cry, the vast waters*
> *Of the petrel and the porpoise.*
> *In my end is my beginning.*

And the words of the second quotation, from "Little Gidding," the fourth "Quartet," were these:

We shall not cease from exploration
And the end of all our exploring
Will be to arrive where we started
And know the place for the first time.

I have brought the book with me, and I hand it to him, saying, "What is it, if I may ask, that you have returned to?"

"One thing I know is that every human being, no matter how smart he is, makes mistakes, and one should try to separate one's wise decisions from unwise decisions and consider how the latter were made and what can be learned."

"Are you at peace with yourself now, with your life?"

There is a long pause. "Well," he says, "I don't feel at peace with the world, I'll tell you that. Look at what's going on in Sudan. It's a godawful mess, and we haven't properly grappled with it. That's a perfect example of where the Security Council could refer a case to the International Criminal Court.[2] The leaders of the future Sudan should know that their predecessors were referred to the court and convicted."

"You have lived a long, momentous life, Mr. McNamara. What would you like people to say about you after you are gone?"

He is silent. I try again. "How would you like to be remembered?"

He hesitates, then speaks of two things. "I would like to be remembered as having fought against the use of nuclear weapons and to some degree prevented their use the last fifty years." Again, he falls silent. I think once more about the toxic mushroom clouds that rose over the ruins of Hiroshima and Nagasaki in August 1945. Whatever acts of barbarism McNamara was responsible for as a commander, they did not include dropping nuclear bombs. Those came later, when his time on active duty had ended. I am also aware that he helped the Kennedy administration sidestep nuclear disaster during

the Cuban Missile Crisis of 1962, and I know that he has publicly described the Bush administration's nuclear weapons policy
as immoral, illegal, militarily unnecessary and dangerous. Then
he adds, "I would also like to be remembered, though perhaps
with less success, as having fought against poverty in the developing nations and also reduced poverty to some degree." This
was indeed his priority during his presidency of the World Bank
(1968–1981), when he instituted a large increase in development
loans for Third World countries around the globe.

He looks tired, this eighty-eight-year-old man. We end
the interview and take leave of each other. As I wait in the hall
for the elevator, he passes by in the next corridor. He does not
see me. He is bent over, deep in thought; he shuffles a little as
he walks.

While I watch him, another part of the "East Coker" poem
runs through my mind:

Home is where one starts from. As we grow older
the world becomes stranger, the pattern more complicated
Of dead and living . . .

—

He seemed genuinely remorseful, but the still-grieving survivors of the Vietnam debacle remain unreconciled. Yes, a
major memorial has been erected on the Washington Mall,
the monumental locus of the nation's history; and yes, thousands of Vietnam "war pilgrims" travel to the capital every
year to visit the stark free-standing columns that soberly
memorialize the names of the dead. But other pieces of the
reconciliation puzzle are still missing. Forty years after the
conflict ended, there is still no consensus over that failed war,
let alone an apology for wasted lives, and since public opinion
mirrors the continuing political and ideological split in the

American population, this resolution is unlikely to happen. Furthermore, the civilian and military leaders who led America into a war built on misunderstood foundations and threaded through with war crimes have remained immune from meaningful censure.

History repeats itself, and the ironies are many. The man who stood at the centre of the Vietnam War command structure today finds solace in the knowledge that a permanent international criminal court exists in the world, knowing that it might have indicted him for war crimes, or worse, had it been operative all those years ago.

But reconciliation, forgiveness and resolution elude him. As he knows better than his enemies, he has never been called to account.

SEVEN

The Things Robert McNamara Didn't Know

T hat the defence secretary of the world's most powerful nation had opted *not* to know the laws of war during his tenure at the top mirrored Thucydides' observation that the strong will refuse to be bound by rules, if possible. The decision *not* to teach international war law to the upcoming generations of US military officers derived from the same thinking. Between 1864 and 1949, the Geneva Conventions were fought over, then finally agreed to, by the global powers—and they were, and remain, a work-in-progress. To profess ignorance of their existence was, itself, a political act.

Within this context, Gary Solis's personal resolve to teach the Geneva Conventions to American officer cadets was a sign of change—in spite of the Bush administration's attempts to circumvent the protections that the conventions provided. Among other safeguards, the conventions set out rules for the protection of the sick and the wounded, the rights of captured prisoners, and, most recently, the welfare of civilians who find themselves caught up in the whirlwind of armed conflict, or actually targeted by the belligerents, as has happened with frequency since the end of the Cold War.

What Gary Solis called the "onion" of war law—an entity that adds layers to its inner core—was (and is) created in the aftermath of armed conflict, when nations that have recently fought one another to the death rush to conference. Their assembly, which is called to set the terms for peace and, very occasionally, the punishment of the vanquished, is the second phase of a *pas de deux* that has been rehearsed a thousand times across the centuries. The first steps are frenzy: young men clash and kill amid a cyclone of gunshots and bombshells. The second steps more closely resemble a quadrille: when the noise has subsided and the blood has been ploughed into the ground, the diplomats bow to one another and smile over canapés. They discuss peace and possible punishment, but at times they go further still, conferring over the severity of the crimes committed on the battlefield—though not, of course, by themselves.

Vae victis—"woe to the conquered." The phrase, first recorded by the Roman historian Livy, conveys a conceit that has endured from the ancient world to the Middle Ages and beyond, into our own times. Anyone who has looked upon the Arch of Titus in the ancient Roman Forum—a monument built in 81 CE to commemorate the defeat of Judea eleven years earlier—will understand the intoxication of total victory. After more than two thousand years, the elation of the emperor's triumphal entry into Rome remains visible on the stone relief. His soldiers carry the spoils of war, including the branched candelabrum and the silver trumpets from the destroyed temple of the Jews in Jerusalem.

Booty? A standard ritual of war. In eleventh-century Spain, knight mercenaries signed up to fight with the Christian Holy Reconquest Against the (Arab) Infidel or, conversely, with the Arabs' forces against the infidel Christians, depending on who they thought would win the battle and (perhaps more important) the quantity and quality of the potential loot. But *vae victis* has also been a favoured rejoinder of the vanquished themselves as they strive to deflect accountability. En route to France in 1983 from Bolivia, where he had been captured, the Nazi war criminal Klaus Barbie voiced the conviction that he had done nothing wrong and that the only crime (if crime there was) lay in Hitler's having lost the war. *Vae victis*, he muttered under his breath, brushing off the details of his personal history.

Two decades later, Nebojša Minić, a Serb who fled to Argentina after having executed a family of Albanians in cold blood during the Kosovo war of 1999, was interviewed on his deathbed in the city of Mendoza, where he was dying of AIDS and Hodgkin's disease.[1] He acknowledged having killed many people (he didn't remember how many), but he did not feel guilty. He was a patriot and a soldier, he said. There were no laws in war, so there were no crimes. He was a God-fearing man. He knew that God loved him.

On the northern Canadian lake where my family owns a summer retreat, we once had a neighbour who had fought in the German Wehrmacht and still thought the only thing Hitler did wrong was to lose the war. He was well into his eighties when he told us this. I was reminded then of a basic truth: that the loyalties impressed on young minds can endure a lifetime, and that the abandonment of the moral thinking of one's early years requires not just determined re-evaluation but courage. War propaganda can so dehumanize a designated enemy that those thus inspired can kill their former friends and neighbours. These messages of war are particularly useful during military training. Not long ago I happened to see an American television documentary called *Enemy Images*, which traced the progressive strangulation of wartime television news. The Vietnam War was the last time independent photo-journalists were permitted to record a conflict freely from both sides of the battle lines. The work of these independents had contributed to the eventual souring of public opinion, in spite of the boosterism and fake heroics produced by the usual authorized sources. Televised pictures of suffering among the Vietcong helped many Americans to reassemble the frag-mented "enemy" into a recognizable human shape; and since we seem to be hard-wired to respond to the visible pain of others (hence the need to recondition military recruits), such reporting subverted the official story. Even the most rudimen-tary understanding of "the enemy" as people like ourselves can be a transforming experience.[2]

In spite of successive conflicts, and unrepentants such as Klaus Barbie, Nebojša Minić and my lakeside neighbour, the warrior nations have historically tried to temper the violence of the battlefield with various codes of military honour and the governance known as international law. This has not been easy. The road leading to the Geneva Conventions traces a long, arduous effort to override the philosopher Thomas Hobbes's harsh assessment about the nature of human life ("nasty, brutish, and short")—even if the same nations that make the rules don't always follow them. One early effort originated with the fifteenth-century French king Charles VII, a belea-guered unfortunate with a deranged father (Charles VI, known unaffectionately as "Charles the Mad") and a mother who expressed her devotion by describing her royal son as "the so-called dauphin." Charles has been excoriated over the cen-turies for having made no effort to save the life of Joan of Arc, whose mystical visions led him to the throne in 1429; but in spite of his overwrought beginnings, he later proved to be a unifier of his country, as well as a shrewd politician and a man of moderation. He reorganized the administrative services of government, created a standing army to serve the royal house and—presciently—promulgated a law of war on remarkably modern-sounding principles. In 1439 he ruled that military officers would be responsible for "the abuses, ills, and offences" that were committed by their underlings. If the officer did not take action against his soldier in a timely manner, *he* would be punished as though he were the perpetrator, added the king.

Little attention was paid to Charles's attempts at reform over the next centuries until Napoleon Bonaparte's rampage across Europe propelled the frightened Great Powers of the early nineteenth century to the conference table. Britain, Austria, Prussia and Russia (France came on board soon after) met at the famed Congress of Vienna; negotiations began in early September 1814, and continued, with interruptions, until June 1815. Their plan was to restore peace, determine the laws of war and create a new "balance of power" map of Europe after what they thought had been the defeat of Bonaparte at the Battle of Leipzig in October 1813.

Among the delegates were some of the world's most famous men. They were Prince Klemens von Metternich of Austria, who was emerging as the most powerful statesman in Central Europe; Czar Alexander I of Russia, a man of shifting commitments whom Metternich called "a madman to be humoured"; Prince Karl August von Hardenberg of Prussia, whose formidable career was almost ruined when his wife had an affair with the Prince of Wales; the greatly admired British diplomat Viscount Castlereagh; and Charles Maurice de Talleyrand-Périgord, one of the most influential diplomats in European history, who arrived from France. They had been making excellent progress in redefining the post-Napoleonic borders of Europe—until February 1815, when the news of

Napoleon's escape from his exile on the island of Elba reached them by letter.

The work of the congress screeched to a halt as the diplomats waited anxiously to see what the self-crowned emperor would do next. For one hundred days they held their collective breath. So little business was accomplished that Emperor Francis I of Austria, the host of the event, felt obliged to hold frequent balls and banquets to entertain his bored guests, leading one wit to remark, "Le Congrès ne marche pas; il danse" ("the congress doesn't 'work' [or 'walk']; it dances"), an observation that was mirthfully reprised a century later in the name assigned to a new waltz: The Congress of Vienna. When they returned to work the following June, shortly before Napoleon was definitively defeated at the Battle of Waterloo, the diplomats set the stage for a more concerted approach to keeping the peace in Europe—one that would, they fervently hoped, prevent more puffed-up "Napoleons" from assuming centre stage. Most important for our story, they ruled that it was a crime for Napoleon (or anyone else) to go to war in breach of a treaty.

The significant word is, of course, "hoped," since Napoleon paid no attention to their deliberations. But a half-century later, the brutality of the American Civil War did inspire something revolutionary and new—the Lieber Code of April 24, 1863: the first formal classification of disparate rulings on "the laws and customs of war." So seminal were Francis Lieber's remarkable "Instructions for the Government of Armies of the United States in the Field" (he was a professor of international law at New York City's Columbia College) that President Abraham Lincoln quickly promulgated them as law, for reasons that are not hard to fathom. That year, the memorable catastrophes of Gettysburg, Chickamauga and Chancellorsville would destroy the lives of 115,835 American soldiers on both sides of the Mason-Dixon line.

Lieber's "Instructions" were applied for the first time two years after they were written into American law. Captain Henry Wirz, the commander of Camp Sumter—a Confederate prison near Andersonville, Georgia, where more than a third of the thirty-three thousand starved Union Army inmates died during 1864—was tried and executed for "conspiracy to . . . destroy the lives of soldiers in the military service of the United States . . . in violation of the laws and customs of war." Although there was sufficient eyewitness testimony to convict the captain of cold-blooded murder many times over, the trial was condemned by many Southerners as victors' justice—and it's fair to say that triumphalism did play a part. Wirz was deliberately executed in the same Washington yard where the conspirators who had planned the assassination of Lincoln were dispatched to the next world, and even as he hung by his neck, gloating Union soldiers chanted, "Wirz, remember Andersonville." Although he insisted to the end that he was convicted for obeying orders and was innocent of any crime, Wirz's death confirmed the law of the Lieber Code and set a legal precedent.

(In May 1908, a highly politicized memorial to Wirz was erected at the site of the Andersonville prison. Part of the inscription reads "In memory of Captain Henry Wirz . . . Sentenced to death and executed at Washington, DC, Nov. 10, 1865 . . . To rescue his name from the stigma attached to it by embittered prejudice, this shaft is erected by the Georgia Division, United Daughters of the Confederacy.")

—

In June 1868 (perhaps inspired by the Lieber Code), Czar Alexander II of Russia organized the world's first international military commission to discuss the rules of armed conflict. Alexander II had reformed his country's education system as well as the government bureaucracy, the judiciary and the military. He had liberated the benighted Russian serfs in 1861. Now he sought, in his words, "[to alleviate] as much as possible the calamities of war." In the czar's view the situation had become urgent: in 1863 the Russian military had invented a bullet that exploded on contact with a hard substance (the object was to blow up ammunition wagons), and in 1867 it had been "improved" to explode within a soft substance, such as the body of a human being. These so-called dumdum bullets terrified the Great Power leaders, including the Russian czar himself, who feared that his *own* troops might find themselves on the receiving end. He wanted the bullets outlawed.

The commission, which was held in the magnificent imperial city of St. Petersburg, was attended by delegates from eighteen of the world's most powerful countries, including Austria-Hungary, Belgium, Denmark, France, Great Britian, Bavaria, Greece, Persia, (Ottoman) Turkey and what was then called the North German Federation; the United States declined to attend. By the time the session ended, the participants had signed the world's first collective agreement prohibiting the use of certain weapons during war. All agreed that the legitimate aim of war was to win by weakening the military capacity of the enemy. This could be accomplished, they said, without the kind of ammunition that produced unnecessary suffering in the wounded. The use of explosive dumdum bullets was "contrary to the laws of humanity," wrote the participants in prescient language that would come into its own almost a century later at the Nuremberg Tribunal. (Mirroring Gary Solis's "reverse onion" metaphor about the building of war law, the Declaration of St. Petersburg was echoed in the expanded legislation that was agreed to at the Hague Peace Conferences of 1899 and 1907.)

Concern about the suffering and pain of soldiers was a major step toward regulating the conduct of war: an early statement of the modern principle of "proportionality," according to which combatants must not cause damage that is disproportionate to the military advantage they are trying to achieve. (Today, proportionality prohibits inflicting harm on civilians, as well as infrastructure, including buildings with cultural or religious significance. An attack must also be in accordance with the planned military aim.) Although more than a hundred years passed between the Declaration of St. Petersburg and the Geneva Convention of 1977, which contained the first formal definition of this concept, something new emerged on the international scene in December 1868: the collective desire to prohibit raw brutality.

Reforming winds were blowing across Europe, and in 1874 a second international conference was convened in Brussels. This time the delegates from fifteen European states went considerably further. In the Brussels Declaration of 1874 they agreed to protect civilians by prohibiting military attacks on undefended towns; henceforth, armies would be required to distinguish between military and civilian targets. Although these protections were already included in the American Lieber Code, the Brussels Declaration was a breakthrough on the international front. Attacks on ordinary citizens had characterized war since ancient times, when aggressors, such as the Athenians, massacred civilian populations, or, like the Romans, laid siege to walled cities, starving the population within.

Unfortunately, international agreements signed by diplomats had to be ratified by their governments, and the Great Powers of the day (Germany, Russia, Great Britain, Austria-Hungary and France) pointedly refused. The Brussels Declaration was "too humanitarian," they complained. Power politics seemed to have overwhelmed international law-making in the old familiar ways, but if two steps forward and one step back was an advance, slow progress was in the making.

It was Hugo Grotius, the seventeenth-century Dutch legal thinker, who had first advanced the unprecedented notion that civilians should be shielded during conflict. In his seminal (and controversial) work, *On the Law of War and Peace* (1625), he proposed that war could be—*ought* to be—circumscribed by ethical considerations, such as whether the hostilities could be justified (only when they were conducted in self-defence, he argued); proportionality (the damage inflicted by a military action vis-à-vis the desired strategic goal); whether there was a reasonable chance of success on the battlefield; whether advance fair warning had been provided to the enemy; and whether the decision to wage war was truly a last resort after diplomacy and other means had failed. (As might have been expected, Grotius's ideas did not please the rapacious booty-and-territory-seekers of his day, which may help explain why the man now known as "the father of international humanitarian law" was thrown into jail after the book's publication.) A century later, the Genevan philosopher Jean-Jacques Rousseau returned to the question of protecting civilians during warfare, arguing, like Grotius, that morality could not be separated from politics, and that a state that ceased to act ethically lost its authority over its citizens. In Book One of his influential work *The Social Contract*, which was published in 1762, he wrote, "The object of . . . war being the destruction of the hostile State, the other side has a right to kill its defenders, while they are bearing arms; but as soon as they lay them down and surrender, they cease to be enemies, or instruments of the enemy." Once soldiers move off the battlefield, he continued, they "become once more merely men, whose life no one has any right to take." Civilians, in other words, were never legitimate objects of attack. The purpose of war was not to destroy an entire nation but to overcome its armies. (Rousseau fared no better than Grotius. Because *The Social Contract* privileged the inherent freedom of the individual over the authority of the state, it was banned in both Geneva and France, forcing the philosopher to flee to avoid arrest.)

Although Grotius and Rousseau helped create the intellectual groundwork for the birth of international humanitarian law, it was the nineteenth century before these elements of their thinking were formally codified, in the Lieber code. Lieber wrote, "As civilization has advanced during the last centuries, so has likewise steadily advanced, especially in war on land, the distinction between the private individual belonging to a hostile country and the hostile country itself, with its men in arms. The principle has been more and more acknowledged that the unarmed citizen is to be spared in person, property, and honor as much as the exigencies of war will admit."[3]

After Lieber, the principle (if not the practice) of protecting civilians achieved such wide acceptance that on August 11, 1870, just one week after his army battered its way into French Alsace at the start of the Franco-Prussian war, the bellicose Kaiser Wilhelm I thought it suitable to announce, "I wage war against French soldiers and not against the French people!" This pronouncement may have come as a surprise to the citizens of Paris, who were subsequently encircled and starved by the kaiser's army. Wilhelm's words, weasely though they were, found their roots in an emerging set of international rules.

—

The Lieber Code also inspired the First Geneva Convention of 1864, which protected the sick and wounded by allowing privileged access to medical organizations and personnel—especially the newly created International Committee of the Red Cross. The ICRC was founded in 1863 by Henri Dunant, a young businessman from Geneva. In 1859, needing water rights for one of his international projects, he brazenly decided to ask Emperor Napoleon III for permission, stubbornly (or perhaps naively) ignoring the fact that the emperor might have had other things on his mind, such as providing help to the Italians who were trying to drive the Austrians out of Italy. Dunant made his way overland to Napoleon's head-quarters near the northern Italian town of Solferino, arriving just in time to witness one of the bloodiest battles of the nine-teenth century. He was traumatized by what he saw that day of June 24, 1859. In his riveting book, *A Memory of Solferino* (1862), he wrote of "chaotic disorder, despair unspeakable, and misery of every kind"; of injured soldiers dying unat-tended beneath the pitiless blaze of the sun, or run over by charging cavalry. His work was a sustained plea for a relief society to care for the wounded.

The public responded with emotion (the famous French *littérateurs*, the Goncourt brothers, wrote, "One finishes this book cursing war!"). Ten countries signed the First Geneva Convention, which formally incorporated the new International Red Cross. Called "the Convention for the Amelioration of the Wounded in Time of War," the Geneva treaty established "immunity from capture and destruction of all establishments for the treatment of wounded and sick soldiers and their person-nel, impartial treatment of all combatants, protection of civilians rendering aid to the wounded, and recognition of the Red Cross symbol as a means of identifying those covered by the agreement." Within three years all the European powers of the day had ratified the convention. (The United States rati-fied it in 1882.)

In 1872, Gustave Moynier—a founder of the International Committee of the Red Cross—became the first to call explic-itly for an international criminal court. There was ample rea-son. The Great Powers of the day might have been willing to agree to the growing body of war law, but that did not mean they intended to follow their own rules. During the Franco-Prussian War of 1870, both sides had committed atrocities.

Moynier suggested that anyone violating the terms of the Geneva Convention should be tried in a court of law, but his idea was coldly rebuffed: the very thought of granting an international tribunal that much power was anathema. But in spite of the reluctance of many governments, international humanitarian and criminal law developed increasingly solid foundations as the nineteenth century dissolved into the twentieth. At the turn of the century, millions of people felt unbounded hope for the future.

In 1899, then in 1907, before the madness of trench war-fare strangled the dreams of the era, delegates from around the world met once again to end the European arms race, seek peace and (in the absence of peace; they were realists) to tie together a coherent bundle of wartime law from the disparate conventions, protocols and agreements that had been agreed to over the previous half-century. In 1899 they convened, once again at the invitation of a young Russian czar (Nicholas II), in The Hague, in a seventeenth-century Dutch royal palace known as the Huis ten Bosch or "House in the Woods."

As usual, although they spoke earnestly about lasting peace, the Great Powers brought their self-interested agendas to the table. (For example, Czar Nicholas favoured disarma-ment because he worried that the pace of arms production in Germany and England was outstripping his country's ability to produce guns, shells, and bullets.) But the robust idealism of the age had succeeded in driving the players to the negotiating table, and now, for the first time, ordinary people played a sig-nificant role. Newly created peace groups summoned their members to write petitions and to speak on public platforms; Quakers and other religious assemblies lobbied for peace, as did municipal councils and ad hoc gatherings of private indi-viduals, one of which named itself "The People of Bedford" (England). More than 750 resolutions in favour of the peace conference were sent from England to the British Foreign Office; a petition from Belgium carried 100,000 signatures; one from the Netherlands was signed by 200,000 persons. The chief American delegate, Andrew Dickson White, wrote in his diary that he was besieged by people with "plans, schemes, nostrums, notions and whimsies of all sorts," and that their idealism was "more earnest and widespread than anything I had dreamed."[4]

The Hague Conference of 1899 heard the first public call for "universal peace." Andrew Carnegie, the New York philanthropist and the wealthiest man on earth, was personally preoccupied with "the quest for world peace," as he put it. His idea was a simple one: civilized societies are governed by domestic law and have procedures for resolving conflicts. What was needed was a system of international institutions.[5]

On May 18, 1899, 108 jurists, politicians and military men from twenty-six countries gathered in the Huis ten Bosch, satisfiedly calling themselves "The Chosen Ones" in a phrase they hoped might attach God to their project. Foreshadowing the revival of internationalist civil society organizations in our own *fin de siècle* era, large contingents of writers, scientists and peace activists travelled to the Dutch city to hold their own meetings outside the periphery of the conference. Their leader was the Austrian countess, Bertha von Suttner, an extraordinary woman who was internationally acclaimed at a time when women were thought to be children inhabiting adult bodies.

Her exceptional life is worth a small detour. She was born in Prague in 1843, into an aristocratic military family whose resources dwindled so quickly that she was obliged to move to Vienna as a governess in the noble von Suttner family. She became romantically entangled with their youngest son, Arthur, and when the von Suttners expressed outrage (in spite of Bertha's aristocratic beginnings), the young people eloped. They were disowned, and for the next nine years they lived in the Caucasus, where they survived by giving language and music lessons, then from the proceeds of Bertha's writings. During this period she produced the poetic *Es Löwos*, a paean to the happiness of their life together; several works of fiction; and an influential non-fiction book titled *Inventarium einer Seele* (Inventory of a soul), which detailed her thinking about social progress. Advancement, she wrote, would be brought about through world peace.

The next phase of her life began in the late 1880s (the elder von Suttners had relented and welcomed Bertha and Arthur home to Vienna) after she and her husband learned about the International Arbitration and Peace Association in London, a group that espoused negotiations in lieu of armed force. What followed was a second book of non-fiction: *Das Maschinenzeitalter* (The machine age), which caused a similar stir. Bertha wrote prophetically about the likely outcome of the new nationalisms that were sweeping Europe. She was one of the first to do so.

By 1899, the year of the Hague Conference (she was the only woman invited to attend), von Suttner was known internationally as one of the world's most passionate advocates for peace; and in 1905 she won the Nobel Peace Prize—the first woman so honoured. "History constantly demonstrates the great influence of women," remarked Jørgen Gunnarsson Løvland, the chairman of the Nobel Committee, as she was awarded her prize on April 18, 1906.* "You, Madame Baroness, have taken the lead among women of today. You have attacked war itself and cried to the nations: 'Down with arms!' This call will be your eternal honor."[6]

The delegates to the Hague Conference made no substantive progress on stopping the arms race, in spite of the heady excitement surrounding their meeting; but they did reach agreement on a Convention for the Pacific Settlement of Disputes, which led to the creation of the landmark Permanent Court of Arbitration—the world's first international tribunal for the settlement of inter-state quarrels. After much debate,

---

* "History" had done nothing of the kind, but his heart was in the right place.

they also reaffirmed the 1874 Brussels prohibition on dumdum bullets and banned the use of poison gas in warfare and balloon-launched munitions.

Perhaps the bowing and smiling of the diplomats made the inevitable disagreements more palatable, for none of the world's most powerful nations wanted further limitations on arms or curbs on military expenditure. Ominously, the military delegate from Germany proclaimed that the "patriotic" German people would not tolerate a reduction in such spending, while the chief military delegate from the United States argued (with happy cynicism) that new weapons were always denounced as horrific until they had been proven useful, at which point everyone included them in their arsenals. (In his autobiography, Andrew Dickson White writes, "Since the world began, never has so large a body come together in a spirit of more hopeless skepticism as to any good result.")[7]

Only the United States and Britain voted against the proposed ban on dumdum bullets (which Britain was producing in India and had already used in its colonial wars in Africa). Speaking with the racism that infected the age, the British delegate, Sir John Ardagh, reminded his colleagues that ordinary bullets were not effective against colonized peoples. "In civilized war, a soldier penetrated by a small projectile is wounded, withdraws to the ambulance, and does not advance any further," he informed his audience. "It is very different with a savage. Even though pierced two or three times, he does not cease to march forward, does not call upon the hospital attendants, but continues on, and before anyone has time to explain to him that he is flagrantly violating the decision of the Hague Conference, he cuts off your head."[8]

In spite of major setbacks and failures, the 1899 Hague Conference was deemed to be so successful that even the delegates agreed to be impressed. The British peace campaigner William Stead wrote in his diary, "A month of amicable discussion of the gravest problems has worked the happiest change in the spirit of the Conference. The fact is that the intrinsic absurdity and unreason of the existing international anarchy are such that honest men cannot seriously consider them without the conviction growing that a little good faith and sincere effort are alone wanting for a great step toward a happier future."[9]

Such was the pleasant sense of general well-being and progress that a second Hague conference was planned for 1907 to add to the evolving body of humanitarian law. Disarmament, too, was back on the agenda; and Andrew Carnegie—ever committed, ever optimistic—wrote to the American president, Theodore Roosevelt, asking for support.

Roosevelt was interested but cautious. "I hope to see real progress made at the next Hague Conference," he replied to Carnegie on August 15, 1906. "If it is possible in some way to bring about a stop, complete or partial, to the race in adding to armaments, I shall be glad; but I do not yet see my way clear as regards the details of such a plan. We must always remember that it would be a fatal thing for the great free peoples to reduce themselves to impotence and leave the despotisms and barbarians armed. It would be safe to do so if there were some system of international police; but there is now no such system."[10]

The second conference, which opened in The Hague on June 15, 1907, expanded some of the earlier successes by elaborating, among other things, "The Rights and Duties of Neutral Powers and Persons in Case of War on Land," as well as crucial humanitarian legislation concerning "The Status of Enemy Merchant Ships at the Outbreak of Hostilities." With ill-omened foresight, the delegates also created rules circumscribing "The Laying of Automatic Submarine Contact Mines." But though progress was made, talk about disarmament ended once again in failure. Never mind, said some people, success will come. Elihu Root, the American secretary of state, spoke with sanguine confidence as he tried to placate the critics. "The question about each international Conference is not merely what it has accomplished, but also what it has begun and what it has moved forward,"[11] he said soothingly. Progress was the watchword of the day—the satisfying belief that the world would move onward and upward evermore. There were now regulations to minimize civilian casualties in occupied territories and to respect "[f]amily honors and rights, individual lives and private property, as well as religious convictions and liberties."[12] What no one knew was that the "civilized world" was about to explode.

The bubble of nineteenth-century optimism burst in the streets of Sarajevo on June 28, 1914, when a bullet felled Archduke Franz Ferdinand, the heir to the throne of the Austro-Hungarian Empire. The man behind the gunsight was nineteen-year-old Gavrilo Princip, a Serb nationalist who hoped to bring about his country's independence. Little did he know that fateful, sunlit morning that his act would redirect the course of the century.

The outbreak of world war just two months later figuratively lifted the good men from their negotiating tables, where they had tried to humanize war through law, and spun them into an abyss from which neither they, nor the rest of the world, would emerge intact. Respect for the new rules (especially the agreement not to use poison gas) quickly fell by the wayside.

It is sobering to read Theodore Roosevelt's dark comments of January 1915, a few months after the start of the war:

> It was well worth going into these Hague conferences, but only on condition of clearly understanding how strictly limited was the good that they accomplished. The hysterical people who treated them as furnishing a patent peace

panacea did nothing but harm, and partially offset the real but limited good the conferences actually accomplished. Indeed, the conferences undoubtedly did a certain amount of damage because of the preposterous expectations they excited among well-meaning but ill-informed and unthinking persons. These persons really believed that it was possible to achieve the millennium by means that would not have been very effective in preserving peace among the active boys of a large Sunday-school—let alone grown-up men in the world as it actually is. A pathetic commentary on their attitude is furnished by the fact that the fifteen years that have elapsed since the first Hague conference have seen an immense increase of war, culminating in the present war . . . with bloodshed on a scale far vaster than ever before in the history of mankind.

And again in February 1916:

The Hague conventions were treaties entered into by us with, among other nations, Belgium and Germany. Under our Constitution such a treaty becomes part of "the supreme law of the land," binding upon ourselves and upon the other nations that make it. For this reason we should never lightly enter into a treaty, and should both observe it, and demand its observance by others when made. The Hague conventions were part of the Supreme Law of our Land, under the Constitution. Therefore Germany violated the *supreme law of our land* when she brutally wronged Belgium; and we permitted it without a word of protest.[13]

The strongest nations—those able to cloak themselves in the "might makes right" doctrines described by Thucydides, Machiavelli and others across the centuries—continued to ignore the same global agreements they had been signing with great fanfare; in fact, there may be no better way to appreciate the turn-of-the-century roller coaster of hope and despair than to list the major conflicts that followed on the heels of the Hague conferences: the Boxer Rebellion (1899–1901); the Anglo-Boer war (1899–1902); the Russo-Japanese war (1905–1906); and the 1905–1907 colonial war in German East Africa. Independently, these slaughters trailed universal pessimism in their wake. Collectively, they fatally weakened the shared nineteenth-century belief in moral progress.

But in spite of wars, including the Great War, the bedrock rules that were agreed upon, proclaimed, declared and celebrated with balls and champagne toasts across five decades remained theoretically intact. The nineteenth-century diplomats and peace acitvists who laboured to protect civilians and to circumscribe the conduct of battle had reached a hitherto unimaginable consensus about the humanity of those who did the fighting, and the responsibilities of those who led them. They saw their efforts as emanating from the great Enlightenment tradition—the triumph of civilized reason over crude brutality.

—

As the First World War drew to an end, there were renewed calls for criminal prosecutions—trials that would, it was hoped, include the waging of war itself. In January 1919, the hopeful delegates to the Versailles Peace Conference in Paris created the Commission on the Responsibility of the Authors of the Laws and Customs of War, which in turn proposed that designated nationals of the Central Powers be tried by an international tribunal for violations of the laws of war and "crimes against the laws of humanity," meaning atrocities committed against civilians. Kaiser Wilhelm II was first in line to be prosecuted by the proposed Allied military tribunals "for a supreme offense against international morality and the sanctity of treaties." Other indictees would include Germans, as well as the Turkish officials who were thought to have been responsible for their government's attempted genocide of the Armenians beween 1915 and 1917 in which more than a million men, women, and children were killed.

Need one note that the charge of offending "international morality and the sanctity of treaties" was purely unilateral? Few have a finer sense of the intinsic tensions between justice and the conflicting demands of *realpolitik* than Cherif Bassiouni, or a better appreciation of the patent hypocrisies. For two months, he wrote,[14] the commission met behind closed doors to prepare a list of indictable individuals; and when they had finished, they submitted the names of 895 alleged war criminals—a list that included several Turkish officials. The charges were based on the "Martens Clause" from the preamble of the 1907 Hague Convention, which stated, "Until a more complete code of the laws of war has been issued . . . the inhabitants and the belligerents remain under the protection and the rule of the principles of the law of nations, as they result from the usages established among civilized peoples, from the laws of humanity, and the dictates of the public conscience."

In August 1920, the Allied Powers and the government of the Ottoman Empire duly signed the Treaty of Sèvres, which provided for the surrender of the accused Turkish officers. But the agreement was never ratified, and no action was ever taken. Then in 1923, the Sèvres accord was supplanted by the Treaty of Lausanne. It contained *no* provisions for prosecutions, but it did include an (unpublished) section granting the accused Turks amnesty for all offences committed between August 1, 1914, and November 20, 1922.

What had precipitated this about-face? Something huge. The Russian Revolution of 1917, which overthrew the czar and brought Lenin to power, was sending nervous shudders down the spines of the British and the French. Turkey was strategically located on the border of Russia. It was needed in the new alignment of Western powers.

Nor was Kaiser Wilhelm II ever prosecuted for his crimes; in fact, he proved to be an embarrassment both at home and abroad. The German people had reacted to their defeat with despair; and in the last month of the war some of the military had dreamed up a prestige-saving fantasy: they wanted their kaiser to sacrifice his life to save his country's honour, a dramatic gesture they hoped would give rise to a latter-day myth rivalling the defeat of the heroic Spartans at Thermopylae in 480 BCE.

Wilhelm was distinctly unimpressed with this scenario in which he was supposed to play a tragic role, and instead of falling gallantly at the head of his troops he waited for a moonless night, then escaped to the neutral Netherlands.[15] The Allies duly sought his surrender, but the sitting Dutch monarch happened to be Wilhelm's cousin, and his reply was a firm no.

This development might have come as a relief, suggests Cherif Bassiouni. "[The Allies] were not ready to create the precedent of prosecuting a head of state for a new international crime."[†] Given the entanglements of pre-war international alignments, both open and secret, Bassiouni was right. In 1919 the British politician Austen Chamberlain (the half brother of Neville) pointed out that should the kaiser be prosecuted, "his defence might be our trial."[16]

The wording of Wilhelm's indictment reflected the Allies' reluctance. The tribunal, they agreed, would be guided not by law, nor by a statement of the crimes imputed to the German

†Another eighty years would pass before Slobodan Milošević would be indicted by an international tribunal.

leader, but "by the highest motives of international policy . . ." By politics, in other words.

Kaiser Wilhelm lived to a ripe old age, but a touch of irony surrounds his passing. He died on June 5, 1941, not long after the Netherlands fell to the Nazis—the new rulers of Germany.

———

It was the Leipzig trials of 1921 that sharply exposed the chasm between politics and justice. Fearing to disrupt the fragile postwar Weimar Republic, the Allies agreed to allow Germany to prosecute its own wartime offenders. The Germans proposed a list of forty-five names (reduced from the original 895 put forward by the commission), but under domestic law the country's supreme court had the right to decide who would be brought to trial. Of the forty-five suggested persons, the prosecutor chose only twelve; and among these, some "could not be found" (although one man was living openly in Leipzig). Others were acquitted outright. The few who were eventually convicted received sentences ranging from six months to four years—and not all of them served their terms.

In spite of this juridical pretence, local crowds surrounded the Leipzig courthouse to cheer the accused, who were portrayed as national heroes unfairly singled out by the victors' justice of foreigners. But it hardly mattered. By 1921 the Allies had lost their appetite for postwar justice and barely cared about the outcome.

———

In the mournful aftermath of the incomparable devastation of 1914–1918, the major powers were willing, even eager, to sign international treaties promising mutual restraint. The First Geneva Convention of 1929 detailed specific protections for the sick and the wounded, and for captured prisoners, who were to be treated "humanely." That same year, the United States and fourteen other countries proclaimed the Kellogg-Briand Pact, which renounced war as an instrument of national policy. (Germany, Japan and Italy were notable among the signatories.) On the legal front, a committee of jurists appointed by the postwar League of Nations once again advocated a "high court of international justice," recommending that the tribunal's jursidiction include offences "recognized by the civilized nations, but also by the demands of public conscience [and] the dictates of the legal conscience of civilized nations."[17]

Although the Third Committee of the Assembly of the League would decide that a concept as radical as international criminal justice (which might apply to them) was highly "premature," the International Law Association and the International Association of Penal Law pressed ahead; and in 1937, the League agreed to adopt a treaty titled "The Convention for the Creation of an International Criminal Court." The document opened for state signatures in an atmosphere of great anticipation, but when the implications began to sink in, few countries proved willing to join. The proposal died on the drawing board—but global justice had come closer than ever before to the birthing place.

For the moment. On the political front, Japan, Italy and Germany formed a new axis in 1936. The civil war between Nationalists and Republicans in Spain continued to rage. In 1937 the Japanese army attacked the Chinese city of Nanking, viciously killing an estimated 260,000 civilians. In 1938 Germany annexed Austria, then Czechoslovakia. All the while, the League of Nations, which represented the system of international law, stood by helplessly as the armaments race speeded up in expectation of imminent war. By the end of 1938 the Kellogg-Briand Pact and its ideals of internationalism had effectively disappeared from sight.

Between 1939 and 1945 enhanced killing technologies such as submarines fitted with torpedoes, airplanes carrying bombs, poison gas and long-range weaponry made it possible to wage war from afar. Ordinary people became prime wartime targets in order to lower enemy morale. The hard-won distinction between combatants and civilians was undermined. Approximately fifty million people were killed, of whom more than half were civilian men, women and children.[18]

When the carnage came to an end, the familiar dance of the diplomats resumed. The Fourth Geneva Convention was born in 1949, in the aftermath of the Holocaust against the Jews of Europe, the firebombings of civilians in Dresden, Tokyo and Hamburg and the destruction in Hiroshima and Nagasaki. In the shadow of these humanitarian tragedies, the community of nations reaffirmed the earlier conventions and sought to strengthen already existing protections for civilians and prisoners of war. In July 2006, the four Geneva Conventions achieved universal acceptance (the tiny country of Nauru had long been the last holdout).

Humanitarian law and political interests had been permanent sparring partners in the seesaw struggle for law and justice, starting with the Lieber Code of 1863. The *pas de deux* between the generals and the diplomats was as predictable as a marital squabble followed by sex. What never changed was the sequence. In the invisible spaces between the men who danced to this ancient tune, the battle between power and the rule of law raged on.

EIGHT

Birth Pangs at Nuremberg

n November 11, 2005, just days before the sixtieth anniversary of the creation of the International Military Tribunal at Nuremberg, the American Bar Association held a small conference at Georgetown University in Washington, DC. The subject to be discussed was the legacy of the most important and memorable trials in twentieth-century history.

The idea for this meeting had come from the American lawyer Henry King, eighty-six years old and one of the three surviving Nuremberg prosecutors. It was he who told me, when we met at the inauguration of the International Criminal Court, that conversations with his parents at the family dinner table had instilled in him a lifelong commitment to the cause of peace and the search for law and justice.

Seated beside King at a raised table in one of the university's lecture halls was Ben Ferencz. He had been chief prosecutor of the case against the Einsatzgruppen death squads that murdered more than a million civilians: intellectuals, Roma and functionaries of the Communist Party, but overwhelmingly Jews: men, women, children and infants in arms. I had met him on an earlier occasion, in January 1999, at a conference titled "Hate, Genocide and Human Rights Fifty Years Later: What Have We learned? What Must We Do?" at McGill University in Montreal. He told me then that something had hardened and gathered strength in him when he prosecuted his cases in Nuremberg, as a young man still in his twenties. The almost incomprehensible number of the dead (he was in charge of tallying the figures in reports sent from the field to Berlin); the lack of remorse among the defendants; and, most disturbing to him, their high levels of education (many were members of the elite Waffen SS, with graduate university degrees), had shocked him. Compounding this personal trauma, he had battled his way across Europe after the D-Day invasion on June 6, 1944, and been among the first wave of US troops to enter the concentration camps of Buchenwald and Mauthausen. The horrifying encounter with the blank-faced, emaciated inmates had etched deep crevices into his memory. From that time on, his life had assumed a new direction. More than anyone else, he incarnated the dream of a permanent international criminal court to try persons accused of crimes against humanity.

As the 2005 anniversary of the Nuremberg Tribunal approached, few among the assembled failed to notice the irony in holding a conference on the rule of law in George W. Bush's Washington. Karen Mathis, the president-elect of the American Bar Association, addressed the meeting. Everyone in the room had come to discuss "the just rule of law," she said. Then she quoted the US Supreme Court Justice Anthony M. Kennedy:

"Government must abide by, and be bound by, law. . . . Within each person is a core of dignity and humanity."

"Nuremberg is proof that legal processes can be used to repair great wrongs," she told her audience. "The tribunal reminded us that the world had not gone mad permanently, that when governments abuse their people and others, we return to the rule of law."

—

The nationalist fervour aroused in Germany by the Leipzig trials of 1921 reached its zenith just twelve years later, when Adolf Hitler came to power in free elections. The international community had failed in its fleeting, half-hearted attempts to hold international trials after the First World War. Moreover, the princes, generals and diplomats who convened at those post-conflict conferences to thrash out the global laws of war had had the conduct of *states* in mind, not individual actors, when they strained to reach consensus in the face of opposed national interests. The rules they had devised for nations were good ones, even if they were frequently ignored.

But November 20, 1945—the day the Nuremberg Tribunal first opened its doors to try the top leaders of the Nazi enterprise—witnessed a breakthrough. The new court was empowered by its founders to prosecute the acts not of states but of individual perpetrators, for the crimes they had committed or had ordered others to commit. For the very first time, individuals would be held responsible for their acts under international law.

Among the Allies there was unrestrained optimism—the existence of the tribunal was a sign that human reason had resumed prominence over madness. Robert H. Jackson, the American chief prosecutor of the court, expressed this Enlightenment view in his famous opening address to the court: "The wrongs that we seek to condemn and punish have been so calculated, so malignant, and so devastating that civilization cannot tolerate their being ignored, because it cannot survive their being repeated. That four great nations flushed with victory and stung with injury stay the hand of vengeance and voluntarily submit their captive enemies to the judgment of the law is one of the most significant tributes that Power has ever paid to reason," he added in a compelling inversion of ancient "might makes right" logic.

No one, including the twenty-two notorious defendants, had a clear idea of what to expect. In one enduring image, the prisoners are seated in two long rows in a box along one side of the courtroom. The men who had recently terrorized the world by masterminding Hitler's genocidal war, then found themselves charged with crimes against peace, war crimes, crimes against humanity and conspiracy to commit all of these, look shockingly ordinary. Among them, the theatrical Hermann Göring, formerly the chief of the German Luftwaffe and Hitler's designated successor, stands out from the rest. He slouches at the end of the first row, looking incongruously like someone's bemused portly uncle. Hans Frank, the governor general of the occupied Polish territories and the principal architect of the destruction in that country, is in the front row: in his forties, thin faced, balding. I once met his son, Niklas, in Hamburg, where he worked as a journalist. Although then in his late fifties, he was still struggling to sort out the passionate hatred (laced with love) that he felt for his father. What obsessed him was what Hans Frank might have become: he had once been president of the Academy of German Law.

Hans Frank's vacillating testimony becomes interesting against this background. It was he who initiated the plan to use slave labour, and he who oversaw the creation of the first ghettos for the Jews. He had been quoted as saying, "Poland shall be treated like a colony; the Poles will become the slaves of the

Greater German World Empire." Yet this man who once said, "We must annihilate the vermin Jews wherever we find them" expressed remorse. "A thousand years will pass and still this guilt of Germany will not have been erased," he told the court. Niklas rejoiced when he learned this, but he soon felt crushed again, for his father retracted his words in his final statement to the tribunal. "Every possible guilt incurred by our nation has been completely wiped out . . . by the tremendous mass crimes of the most frightful sort which . . . have been and still are being committed against Germans. . . . Who shall ever judge these crimes against the German people?"[1]

Hans Frank could have been among the German patriots who shouted their outrage outside the doors of the Leipzig tribunal. It was there that law was subverted by patriotism.

Of the original twenty-two defendants, twelve were sentenced to death by hanging (including Frank), seven were sentenced to various terms in prison and three were freed.

—

Like the earlier failed attempts at international criminal justice, Nuremberg almost did not happen. The decision to put the Nazi leaders on trial came about quite late, according to the British historian Richard Overy.[2] The Allies initially planned to prosecute just the conventional illegalities of warfare as defined in the nineteenth and early twentieth centuries. But there was a problem: the shocking felonies of the Nazis appeared to be unparalleled in scope. Furthermore, as Winston Churchill put it, in language that will sound familiar to post-9/11 ears, their crimes seemed "to have no special geographical location."

When rumours of the atrocities first filtered into Western capitals in 1942, the plan on the part of both the Americans and the British was summary executions of the Nazi leaders.

"Hitler is the mainspring of evil," Churchill told his war cabinet on July 6, 1942. "He should be executed by electric chair [which is] no doubt available [from President Roosevelt] on Lease Lend."* Trials seemed to be out of the question. As late as April 12, 1945 (the day FDR died), the British prime minister continued to reject the idea of a courtroom solution: "All sorts of complications ensue as soon as you admit a fair trial," he advised his war cabinet in the best tradition of *realpolitik*. "Execute the principals as outlaws . . ."³

The "outlaw" designation, which had been abolished in English law in 1938, was applied to perpetrators deemed to be outside the law—much like the George W. Bush administration's "enemy combatants." "The guilt of such individuals is so black that they fall outside and go beyond the scope of any judicial process," wrote Churchill's foreign secretary, Anthony Eden, in support of his prime minister.⁴

But the French and the Soviets were beginning to favour courtroom prosecutions, Stalin almost certainly because the war had interrupted his show trials of real and imagined enemies, during which everyone conveniently confessed after being tortured, and he hoped to repeat the process.

In July 1944, as the evidence of Nazi atrocities against Allied prisoners of war mounted, the United States appointed Lieutenant Colonel Murray C. Bernays to investigate and make recommendations. Bernays, a practising lawyer, not a politician, forcefully promoted justice over summary vengeance. International law should reflect the "conscience of humanity," he argued, reprising the now familiar phrase. The punishment of Nazi war criminals should be seen as a cornerstone of postwar peace and justice, not as revenge.

---

*The correct name was the Lend-Lease Act. It was passed by the US Congress on March 11, 1941.

Bernays won over the US secretary of war, Henry Stimson, who reminded President Roosevelt that Western justice viewed due process as a right, regardless of the crimes committed. When the president remained unconvinced, "an unlikely alliance of Communist lawyers and American liberals were mobilized to . . . insist on a judicial tribunal," wrote Overy. Eventually, all parties agreed that firing squads might not look good in the history books.

Just weeks after Roosevelt's death, his successor, Harry Truman, authorized preparations for criminal trials, although his timing was, to say the least, ironic. Just as he was endorsing courtroom justice for the Nazi war criminals, the new president gave the order to drop atomic bombs on two heavily populated Japanese cities, in full knowledge of the devastation they would wreak.[5]

When the major powers met in San Francisco on June 26, 1945, to discuss the wording of the charter of the new United Nations (mustering the same hope that had accompanied the creation of the League of Nations more than two decades earlier), Truman appointed Robert H. Jackson, a former United States attorney general and associate justice of the Supreme Court, to preside over and shape the war crimes court. It was agreed that the trials would be held in the Palace of Justice in the southern German city of Nuremberg—for symbolic, as well as other, reasons: if Nuremberg had been the scene of Hitler's most famous propaganda rallies, it would also be the place where his movement was condemned. On August 8, 1945, after conferencing over the summer months, the four participating nations met in London to sign the charter of the new court. (Britain had since conceded the point about trials, optics and history.)

Robert Jackson was fifty-three years old when he stood in room 600 of the Nuremberg Palace of Justice to deliver his opening address: he was a forceful-looking man in a dark suit with a white handkerchief folded in his breast pocket, a man who neither minced his words nor tried to camouflage his sense of righteousness: "We must never forget that the record on which we judge these defendants today is the record on which history will judge us tomorrow," he told the hushed court. "To pass these defendants a poisoned chalice is to put it to our own lips as well."

—

The Nuremberg Trials are still controversial after sixty years. The tribunal's charter codified a category of law—"crimes against humanity"[6]—that had never previously been made explicit, although the phrase had been articulated many times, starting with the preamble to the 1907 Hague Convention, which was the legal bedrock for the decision to investigate war crimes at the end of the First World War. The experts who drafted the charter believed that their definition of crimes against humanity was "the expression of international law existing at the time of [the tribunal's] creation . . ."[7] But to many critics, the new law was suspect. It was, they argued, a serious breach of *nullum crimen, nulla poena, sine lege*, the generally accepted proposition that no one can be punished for an act that was not defined as criminal when it was committed. The court defended itself vigorously. "The law of war is to be found not only in treaties, but in the customs and practices of states which gradually obtained universal recognition, and from the general principles of justice . . . ," wrote the judges. "This law is not static, but by continual adaptation follows the needs of a changing world."

There was also widespread condemnation of "victors' justice," in which the winning side in a war presumes to judge the vanquished while excusing its own crimes.

Since these criticisms cannot easily be refuted, we may ask why the Nuremberg Tribunal is nonetheless seen as a landmark achievement, even by Germans who are today among the world's strongest supporters of Nuremberg's "daughter," the International Criminal Court. Even if they resented the court, postwar Germans saw for themselves that the trials were conducted according to the highest standards of due process; nor did they fail to notice that several of the defendants were acquitted, although the Nazi judiciary had conspicuously sentenced people to death in the name of a future Reich. There was also the emerging reality of the Cold War. When politics began to change gears in the late 1940s, the tribunal was pressed to think carefully before convicting educated defendants who might become useful in the shifting world order. The West was going to need Nazi Germany's best minds. But Robert Jackson refused to allow politics into his courtroom.

Jackson's vision of justice also informed the Nuremberg Principles that emerged from these landmark trials: the legal and philosophical standards that have helped to shape international criminal justice in the postwar West. Chief among them is the idea of personal liability for committing, or commanding others to commit, criminal acts. Another deals with the tricky subject of "superior orders." No one was foolish enough to suggest that obeying orders was not fundamental to military life, but the Nuremberg judgments presumed an underlying code of universally understood common law and morality that transcends the command to commit atrocities.

———

It is possible that our collective aversion to "crimes against humanity" is bred in the bone, since its first expression—in literature, not politics—also assumed awareness on the part of an audience. When Sophocles' Antigone confronted the mighty Creon, she called on a resonant knowledge that was understood in the deepest recesses of mind and conscience. "I did not think your edicts strong enough to overrule the unwritten, unshakeable laws of gods, you being only a man," she told the king. "They are not of yesterday or today, but undying, though where they came from, none of us can tell. . . ."

Fashionable or not in an era of science and painstakingly drafted law, Antigone's "unwritten" understanding directly informed the decision to penalize "crimes against humanity," although the offences were not formally codified in the law books of international criminal justice at the time they were perpetrated. The same "unwritten law" was seen to supersede the rule that orders from military superiors must always be obeyed.

What the judges meant was that the first loyalty of human beings must be to the preservation of humanity. This is surely what Robert Jackson had in mind when he said that the survival of "civilization" would depend upon the fairness with which the Nazi defendants were treated. His "poisoned chalice" metaphor, with its Shakespearean, even Sophoclean, echoes of retribution, emanated from the core of his humanitarian vision.

NINE

Against Impunity

The two-step between politics as usual and the demands of international justice resumed during the decades of the Cold War. For almost fifty years after the Nuremberg Tribunal spelled out its "lessons" of criminal accountability and personal responsibility under the law, tyrants ruled and their subjects suffered. Thousands were "disappeared" in Argentina, Chile, El Salvador and Guatemala, to name just a few such places. Josef Stalin (who sent more than 50 million to their death), Chairman Mao (who was responsible for the murder of 40 million) and Pol Pot (who carried out a genocidal massacre of 1.7 million Cambodians) all died of natural causes, leaving their respective nations to combat the corrosive legacy of unaddressed crimes. (Pol Pot's most urgent post-genocide problem seems to have been repeated surgery for pesky hemorrhoids.)

In 1989, eight thousand ethnic Kurds in Iraq were massacred by Saddam Hussein with a chemical derivative of
Zyklon-B, the gas used by the Nazis in their concentration
camps, but Saddam did not become a pariah until his leadership was seen to block, rather than facilitate, the interests of a
superpower, at which point his human rights record was
unearthed and found wanting. In 1994, under the controversial regime of the UN secretary-general Boutros Boutros-
Ghali, the United Nations ignored the open call to genocide
on the airwaves of Rwanda and the pleas of its own commander
in the field, General Roméo Dallaire; and at the beginning of
that same decade, no one came to the aid of the Muslim
minority in Bosnia as thousands were massacred by their former friends and neighbours. Not until 1999, when Serb atrocities resumed in Kosovo *after* Slobodan Milošević had been
honoured as a respected participant at the peace talks in
Rambouillet, did NATO make a first attempt to rescue a persecuted minority within a sovereign state.

The United Nations failed to prevent, or intervene in, the
Bosnian and Rwandan genocides. At this writing, a genocide
rages in Sudan. And still the United Nations does nothing. In
his powerful book, *Complicity with the Devil: The United
Nations in the Age of Modern Genocide*, the British journalist
Adam LeBor blames the anachronistic structure of the UN
Security Council. Its permanent members are the five great
powers of the immediate post–Second World War period.
Any one of the council members can veto any resolution
passed by the General Assembly, which is far less influential.
The council also has an often obscured connection with the
UN Secretariat—the "home" of the secretary-general. LeBor
is especially critical of Kofi Annan, whom he accuses of caving
in to the United States, the strongest member of the council.
(This became evident when Annan did not come to the aid of
Cherif Bassiouni, whom he had hired one year earlier to

report on human rights in Afghanistan, when Bassiouni was summarily fired.)

On the other hand, the United Nations did create two after-the-fact international criminal courts to try perpetrators of war crimes from Rwanda and the former Yugoslavia. That these milestone tribunals—the first of their kind since Nuremberg—actually came into being was little short of a miracle. The UN had been losing credibility; shocking images of starved prisoners were appearing on television screens in private homes around the globe. Among these, one became instantly iconic: a row of emaciated men with sunken eyes staring out from behind barbed wire at the Bosnian Serb concentration camp of Omarska. The picture reawakened the appalling memory of starved skeletal prisoners in the Nazi camps. It was this image that forced the United Nations to take action: the world body had to be seen as doing *something*.

On October 6, 1992, the UN Security Council adopted Resolution 780, which became the 780 Commission, with a mandate to "make recommendations for further appropriate steps." (The UN Commission of Experts was chaired, as it happens, by Cherif Bassiouni.) In February 1993, the commission reported on the situation in Bosnia. It inaugurated the legal use of the phrase "ethnic cleansing"[1] and concluded that such acts fell under the definition of crimes against humanity, war crimes and genocide as defined at Nuremberg.

History, memory and the Nuremberg principles were much in the air on February 22, 1993, the day the resolution to establish the International Criminal Tribunal for the Former Yugoslavia (ICTY) was debated in the Security Council; and it was Madeleine Albright, then the US ambassador to the UN, who best articulated the emotion of that day: "The Nuremberg principles have been reaffirmed. We have preserved the long-neglected compact made by the community of civilized nations forty-eight years ago in San Francisco to

create the United Nations and enforce the Nuremberg principles. The lesson that we are all accountable to international
law may finally have taken hold in our collective memory."

The ICTY was born on May 25, 1993. Underpinning it
was the section in the UN Charter known as Chapter VII,
which empowers the UN to order military force, create agencies relating to the maintenance of international peace and
security and override national sovereignty if necessary. The
ICTY was to be a temporary institution with a single mandate: to prosecute the perpetrators of the core crimes of
genocide, crimes against humanity and war crimes in the
territory of the former Yugoslavia, starting in 1991.

The court's beginnings were dubious, to say the least. The
UN had appointed Richard Goldstone as chief prosecutor in
July 1994. He was an ideal candidate: a respected judge and
lawyer from South Africa and a member of that country's
Constitutional Court. Three years earlier he had headed a
national commission of inquiry into South Africa's Third
Force (described by his commission as "a sinister and secret
organization orchestrating political violence on a wide front"),
which courageously implicated the ruling National Party in a
systemic pattern of murderous activities. Goldstone personified the changed face of South Africa—and he had the support
of Nelson Mandela.

But he could not have anticipated the start-up problems he
would face. "We had to create the court from scratch," he told
me when we met in Toronto in early 2006. "There were no
rules. There had never been an international criminal tribunal
of this kind. . . . Nuremberg, don't forget, was a military court.
And I certainly didn't expect money problems!"

Goldstone arrived in The Hague to find a bare-bones
office without secure financing and without investigative or
intelligence materials. (He insistently lobbied governments for
help, with some success.) But he appeared to hesitate before

taking the next step: the indictment of a perpetrator from the Yugoslav conflict. It was rumoured that he was reluctant to anger the diplomats who were trying to negotiate a peaceful end to war in Bosnia and on whose goodwill he depended.

The newly appointed ICTY judges twiddled their thumbs impatiently, as did the member states of the United Nations. Eventually, the world organization threatened to withhold its budgetary financing, such as it was: payment, they said, would depend on forthcoming events. So in late 1994 and early 1995, Goldstone charged two "small fish": Dragan Nikolić, the Serb commander of the notorious Sušica camp in eastern Bosnia, and Duško Tadić, a torturer who had operated in the dreaded Omarska camp.

At the time of these indictments, Radovan Karadžić, the political leader of the Bosnian Serbs, Ratko Mladić, the commander-in-chief of the Bosnian Serb army, and Slobodan Milošević, the president of Serbia, were still viewed as potential peacemakers by the West. Karadžić liked to brag about his influence. That he had personally directed the destruction of Sarajevo, the Bosnian capital, was indisputable: the BBC had filmed an extraordinary documentary on the crest of a mountain overlooking the city in which Radovan (as he was known to his familiars) played a starring role. In the film he talks excitedly on the telephone to his wife, Ljiljana, as a famous Russian writer named Edouard Limonov adjusts the telescopic sites on his machine gun and aims at a woman running in the street below. The camera captures Karadžić giving Limonov a history lesson: "The Turks defeated us in 1389 and some of the Serbs here converted to Islam . . . but *we* own this country. The world must understand that we are not besieging Sarajevo but reclaiming Serb territory."

The ICTY judges waited and waited, but the "big fish" like Karadžić were out of reach as long as they kept up a pretense of participation in the peace process. Then, at 4:15 p.m.

on July 11, 1995, Ratko Mladić committed an unthinkable crime: his forces entered the supposed international safe haven of Srebrenica, where tens of thousands of people had taken shelter. More than seventy-five hundred men and boys were executed over the next five days.

On July 24, Goldstone indicted both Karadžić and Mladić for crimes against humanity and genocide for acts they had committed *prior* to Srebrenica (he would re-indict them for the Srebrenica massacre four months later). But in the eyes of some people he had been slow off the mark.

Should these two men have been indicted sooner? I asked Goldstone when we met. No, he replied. He could not have brought indictments before completing the investigations; that would have been unprofessional. In any case, NATO was clearly *not* prepared to arrest them. He has no regrets about his term as chief prosecutor, he told me. "Starting with the [small-fry] Tadić case was a good decision. It gave the judges a chance to cut their teeth and, importantly, it created new international criminal law on rape as an instrument of war." His most important achievement, he believes, was getting the office of the prosecutor up and running. When he arrived at the ICTY there was a staff of forty, almost all of whom were American or Australian. When he left, there were more than two hundred people from forty countries.

He did not mention this, but his other major achievement—and it is ongoing—has been public relations in the cause of international criminal justice. Goldstone lectures around the world, educating his audiences about the advances of the past decade and a half and their significance for the future. Sometimes he tangles with nationalists, as he had the evening before I spoke with him, at a public lecture in a Toronto synagogue. Although the majority of the audience received him warmly, he was confronted by several speakers whose point of view was anti-internationalist, anti-UN and, above all, opposed to the International Criminal Court (Israel had signed the Rome Statute but never ratified it). A Jew himself, he offered them no quarter.

At this writing, neither Radovan Karadžić nor Ratko Mladić has been apprehended, although rumours suggesting their imminent capture circle the globe on the Internet every other week. They have remained elusive in spite of the presence of NATO, then European Union troops; in spite of the fact that each man has a bounty of $25 million on his head; in spite of frequent warnings to Serbia from the United States, the European Union and Carla Del Ponte, the current chief prosecutor of the ICTY. Mladić is believed to be hiding somewhere in Serbia, Bosnia, Montenegro or Russia. Who can say where he is? Certainly not the Serb government in Belgrade, which prefers not to offend the unrepentant ultra-nationalists among its supporters—believing (perhaps correctly) that the present leadership would be driven from power should either man be delivered to The Hague.

It is a fact that Mladić and Karadžić remain heroes to many. When I travelled by bus from Sarajevo to Belgrade in the late 1990s, Karadžić's stronghold, Pale, was festooned with outsized pictures of the Great Man. Coloured streamers flew in his honour from municipal buildings and private homes. At a coffee stop in a run-down, barn-like building, men with weather-creased faces were huddled at long tables, chain-smoking cigarettes and drinking coffee and plum brandy under giant posters of the smiling leader-in-hiding. It was the same in Belgrade in 2003, when I once again visited that city: street kiosks sold cheap trinkets plastered with pictures of the two heroes; and the same in 2006, when "T-shirts, calendars, posters, lapel pins and wooden icons emblazoned with [their] faces" were still available everywhere, according to Ljiljana Smajlović, the editor of *Politika*, a major newspaper in the city.[2]

She added that Slobodan Milošević's son was allowed to collect his father's army pension until November 2005, and that in January 2006—almost five years after the former president was sent to The Hague—the Serb government still had not frozen his assets. "A culture of impunity," she fumed.

Something basic to this culture of impunity had touched me personally during my 2003 visit to Belgrade. My previous book, which investigated the way nations shape their history after times of crisis, had been translated into the Bosnian-Serb-Croatian language, and the Zagreb publisher had invited me to the publication launch.[3] The reception in Croatia had included a meeting with President Stjepan Mesić, who was strongly interested in the ICTY. (We now know he testified for the prosecution as a protected witness at the trial of Colonel Tihomir Blaškić, who was charged with war crimes against Muslims in central Bosnia.) I had also been invited to launch the book in Belgrade by Borka Pavićević, once a famous Yugoslav dramaturge and now director of the ironically named Center for Cultural Decontamination.

I can only describe what happened at the Belgrade book launch as reflecting the changes that had taken place since the arrest and transfer of Milošević to The Hague. There had been a shift in the thinking of the intelligentsia. Those whom I had met back in 1997 had been hopeful and anti-Milošević, but now a different powerful conviction seemed to have taken hold: that Serbs were the victims of the war and of the West. Two speakers sat to the left of me at a panel table. One, a historian, was the head of the Serbian archives; the other was Miloš Vasić, a star reporter for the liberal magazine *Vreme* during the war, a man who had dared to write the truth about the atrocities then taking place. When I interviewed Vasić in 1997, he was distraught; he spoke about Serb-instigated lies and mass murders in Bosnia and about what he was trying to accomplish through his work. He volunteered that he felt guilty "as a human being" about what had been done by the Milošević regime in his name and in the name of all Serbs. His statements to me were all the stronger because he acknowledged the shared human potential for group violence; because he refused to excuse his own people on grounds of tribal commonality; and because he would not generalize about the specific tragedy of what had taken place in Bosnia.

We exchanged greetings before the launch event began. "I remember you," he said with an ironic grin. "I felt desperate then. Now I don't give a shit." A warning bell sounded in my ears, but I didn't know what it signified.

After formal introductions, the archivist on the panel began to talk about Serb history. Thirty minutes passed, then forty. Then it was Vasić's turn. He told the audience that I was "anti-Serb," and that I believed in "collective guilt." I was surprised at how brazenly he misrepresented me.

Finally, it was my turn. As I began to speak, Vasić and the archivist, both of whom were still sitting beside me on the stage, began to talk and laugh loudly in an attempt to drown me out. It seemed that Vasić (who had already read the translated edition) was embarrassed to read in his own language what he had said in 1997, now that he had adopted the line that the West was anti-Serb. It also occurred to me that this scene might not have been an unfamiliar one here: this was the way Communism had operated in Yugoslavia, as elsewhere. By seizing control of a situation, you can undermine your opponent before he or she has a chance to express a view; and when she does speak, you make sure she isn't heard over the din.

The hopes of people like Miloš Vasić, who ten years earlier had risked his life to write the truth, had not been realized, even after the removal of Slobodan Milošević. The ICTY had not performed entirely as expected; the corruption at home had not ceased. After the panel, my interpreter put the bleakness best. She was forty years old, she told me, and penurious, with barely enough money to feed and house herself and with no prospects for bettering her life. She also said, with obvious sorrow, that the wars of the 1990s had stolen the years when she might have married and had children.

After the book launch, the audience departed to another room to drink slivowitz, leaving me with the sad translator, the Canadian ambassador to Serbia, Borka (the fine woman who had invited me), Nikola Barović, her husband (one of the country's most committed human rights lawyers) and my own loyal spouse, who had accompanied me on the voyage.

On a train to Zagreb the next morning, police officers boarded and dragged a protesting male passenger off the car. A silence fell over the other travellers, who averted their eyes from the scene, minding their own business as the long decades of totalitarian rule had taught them to do. Close by, on the eastern side of the Serb-Croat border, another distressing sight came into view: tent colonies where hundreds, perhaps thousands, of Serb refugees lived. Their ancestors had made their home in the Krajina region of Croatia since the sixteenth century, but these people had been expelled into Serbia in August 1995 during the infamous Operation Storm. Eight years later they were still there, in the gathering cold of late November, waiting and hoping to return to their homes—someday.

Such was the nature of "peace" in Serbia almost a decade after the end of the Bosnian conflict. War criminals in hiding, a destitute population and a bitter intelligentsia that had hoped for better days.

—

The International Criminal Tribunal for the Former Yugoslavia had major image problems in Serbia. Slobodan Milošević was grandstanding in the courtroom, claiming that the tribunal was biased against Serbs; and the tribunal's long-term reputation was bound to be affected by its continuing failure to bring the two fugitives, Karadžić and Mladić, to justice. Every one of the three successive prosecutors-in-chief knew this. Goldstone had been followed by the Canadian jurist Louise Arbour, who despaired of their ever being arrested. When I met her in The Hague, she had talked about the "psychological fusion" of the Bosnian Serb community with Karadžić, their leader. She wondered how this community would react to his possible trial for war crimes—acts in which they had been passively acquiescent, or had actively supported. The subject was a reminder of German ambivalence at the time of the Nuremberg trials, and later. Guilt, especially associative guilt, is a complex human issue, a grey area that far transcends the black-and-white functionality of a courtroom.

On May 24, 1999, a few months after my conversation with her, Louise Arbour indicted Slobodan Milošević in absentia on sixty-six counts of crimes against humanity, genocide and violation of the laws of war. He was arrested in April 2001, and transferred to The Hague the following June. Serbian nationalists were enraged. It was not until June 2005, four years later, that the Serb government finally acknowledged the truth about war crimes, having only then been forced to do so. That month, the ICTY prosecution had entered into evidence a videotape showing the fearsome Serb paramilitary group called "the Scorpions" executing six Muslim men from Srebrenica during the massacres that took place there in July 1995. In the film the victims are taken from a truck with their hands bound. They are kicked brutally and ordered to lie face down on the ground. Four of them are shot from behind. The two remaining prisoners are forced to carry the bodies into a nearby barn, after which they too are murdered.

Within hours, the tape was being broadcast across the airwaves of the former Yugoslavia and around the world on the Internet. In Bosnia, the families of Safet Fejzić, Azmir Alispahić, Sidik Salkić, Smail Ibrahimović and Saib Salkić, who had been waiting for a decade for news, at last learned what had happened to their missing son, husband, brother or father. (The sixth victim remained unidentified.) In Serbia, the video elicited outrage. The timing couldn't have been worse for the government; an opinion poll published by the Belgrade-based Strategic Marketing Research just two months earlier had revealed that more than 50 percent of respondents either did not know about war crimes in Bosnia, or did not believe they had taken place. Now the government was forced to admit that such crimes had indeed been committed.

By the end of 2005, the Scorpions were on trial—the government had finally taken action. It was an important test of the Serb judiciary, which had been notoriously corrupt for decades under Communist rule—and one that it seemed to be failing. According to the Belgrade Humanitarian Law Centre, the chief prosecutor amended the indictment to charge the accused with a less serious criminal act *before* the incriminating video was entered into evidence, thus opening the door to an acquittal, or a lesser conviction.[4] On April 12, 2007, the Serb court sentenced four of the five Scorpions to jail terms ranging from five to twenty years (a fifth man was freed), but the judge refused to link the killers directly to the Srebrenica genocide. This angered the survivors. They thought the judge's decision was a political act.

The trial of former Serb president Slobodan Milošević, which opened on February 12, 2002, was the second key to the ICTY's future reputation. It was one of the most remarkable courtroom events in modern history—certainly the most important judicial event since the Nuremberg trials where the senior perpetrators of the Nazi enterprise had been convicted for similar crimes. Chief among the great hopes was the expectation that the evidence that emerged would produce a factual record of what had taken place in the region, and that the eventual assimilation of this knowledge would lead to reconciliation among the parties.

The defendant's deeds were known in general terms. After the death of Marshal Tito from cancer in 1980, the "new" framework for power had turned out to be the same as the old one: ethnic nationalism. Inciting hatred in mixed societies is never hard to accomplish, especially for a determined elite that controls the microphones and other communications media. Milošević had fomented such division in the name of a Greater Serbia, "cleansed" of inhabitants of other ethnic origins or religions, with the support of many of Serbia's most renowned intellectuals. But now that it had the former strong man in the dock, the ICTY was itself on trial. Every move by the prosecution was certain to be watched nervously by the friends of the court and hawkishly by its enemies. The tribunal would be under pressure to be excruciatingly careful and transparently fair. In his pretrial appearances, Milošević had painted himself as the victim of a NATO-backed conspiracy that was determined to destroy him and his country. He described himself as a man who had engaged in war for the sake of peace. He was a negotiating partner of the West in its efforts to settle the conflict in Bosnia, but now he had been singled out for a show trial. The prosecution needed to counter these attacks with evidence.

Like many tyrants, he turned out to be smaller than life once the props of power were removed. Acting as his own lawyer, and unfamiliar with the novel rules that combined elements of both Anglo-American and Continental courtroom procedures, he at first refused to recognize the jurisdiction of the court; and when that failed, he relied on the political propaganda he knew best, as though saying something loudly and aggressively made it so. I happened to be in the ICTY courtroom on March 12, 2003 (behind bulletproof glass), when he cross-examined an important witness: Dr. Helena Ranta, the head of the Finnish forensic team that had investigated the killings at Račak, Kosovo, on January 15, 1999, where at least forty-one people were found shot to death after an assault by Serbian paramilitary forces. The debate inside and outside the courtroom was between those, like Milošević, who maintained that Račak was a faked scene staged by the Kosovo Liberation Army and NATO in order to justify NATO's intervention against Serbia, and those who insisted that the attack was an indiscriminate assault on a civilian population.[5] In lieu of asking the witness questions, Milošević accused her of taking part in a Western conspiracy against Serbia. Judge Richard May constantly reprimanded him as though he were talking to a child. At times the two men snapped openly at each other.

It was more than a little strange to see Slobodan Milošević "defanged" in this environment; on the other hand, he was maintaining his influence elsewhere: the soapbox effect was working back home in Serbia. Indeed, that very day, as we sat in an international courtroom far removed from Belgrade, Zoran Djindjić, the democratically elected, pro-Western prime minister of Serbia, was murdered by Milošević's ultra-nationalist supporters.

Milošević was frequently sick; he didn't like the court-appointed lawyers who were supposed to be helping him with his defence; his cross-examinations were often off the mark legally; occasionally the proceedings seemed to veer out of control. So improbable was his behaviour that in 2004, the ICTY, perhaps sensing its faltering public relations, felt the need to publish a list of five of its vaunted successes.[6]

Appearing after each of the five achievements cited below is the ICTY officers' assessment of their work (followed by my comments).

1. "Spearheading the shift from impunity to accountability." By holding individuals, including those in the most senior

positions, accountable for war crimes and other serious violations of international law, the ICTY personalized guilt and
shielded entire communities from being labelled collectively
responsible for the suffering of others. *(Yes, the court grounded
the Nuremberg concept of personal responsibility under international
criminal law. But the psychological problem of collective, or group,
responsibility for acts passively agreed to went beyond the courtroom
and was far more complex than the ICTY suggested.)*

2. "Establishing the facts." By means of its evidence gathering,
the tribunal was creating a factual record of the conflict in the
former Yugoslavia. *(Correct: Just as the Nuremberg Tribunal had
recorded the facts about the attempted genocide of the Jews, thus
making it impossible for a reputable movement of Holocaust denial to
take hold, so the record being pieced together by the ICTY would create an authentic historical record of events.)*

3. "Bringing justice to thousands of victims and giving them a
voice." More than three thousand witnesses testified in court,
providing them with a real sense that they and their communities were involved in the work of the tribunal. Making those in
authority responsible for their crimes brought a sense of justice
to the victims across the region. *(This was the weakest claim, as
we shall see.)*

4. "Achieving 'major accomplishments in international law.'"
The ICTY was expanding upon elements of the Geneva
Conventions of 1949. It had confirmed the general prohibition of torture in international law and made significant
advances in international humanitarian law regarding the
punishment of sexual violence in wartime, among other
advances. *(This was a triumph of both the Yugoslav and the
Rwandan tribunals, fleshing out older legal concepts and creating
new law to serve the twenty-first century.)*

5. "Strengthening the Rule of Law." The ICTY served as an incentive to reform the judiciaries in the former Yugoslavia and a catalyst for the creation of specialized war crimes courts in the region. The ICTY was actively involved in training legal professionals in the territory to enable them to deal with war crimes cases using international legal standards. *(These functions were critical, since courts in the former Yugoslavia and during the subsequent Milošević era were merely tools of the state. Given growing international impatience with the length of its trials, the ICTY had agreed to prosecute only top-rung perpetrators. Acccess to highly trained personnel meant that local tribunals, especially in Bosnia, could co-operate with the ICTY in the trials of lesser perpetrators.)*

By 2004, there were also major criticisms of the court, many of them emanating from Serbia and the Bosnian Serb "entity."

• A disproportionately large number of the indictees are Serbs. *This was numerically true, and to the Serbs it was proof that the ICTY was biased against them, a position Milošević reinforced in his testimony during his trial. However, since the former Yugoslav People's Army was under Serb control, they had the weapons and the military command structure to commit major crimes on a wide scale, and the evidence showed that they had made use of the opportunity. Muslim Bosniaks, on the other hand, were under an international arms embargo. The fact that the Serbs outnumbered the Croats as indictees could be explained on the same grounds of Serb military strength; however, if the Croat president, Franjo Tudjman, and the Bosniak leader, Alija Izetbegović, had survived, they too might have been indicted for war crimes.*

• The tribunal's power to issue secret indictments creates uncertainty among people who fear they might be possible indictees, placing an unreasonable strain on their ability to proceed with their everyday lives. *This concern was understandable.*

But if such people knew in advance that they were about to be arrested, would not some of them have planned strategic disappearances, à la Karadžić and Mladić?

• The tribunal makes no distinction among the Bosnian, Croatian and Serbian languages, issuing documents in what it terms "B/C/S" ("Bosnian/Croatian/Serbian") with no regard to differences in the three. *This was nationalist nonsense. Before Yugoslavia splintered, all three were considered to be the same language, although Serb uses the Cyrillic alphabet.*

• The tribunal did not prosecute NATO or its military as a result of controversial attacks during the 1999 bombing campaign over Kosovo and Serbia. *This criticism had merit. Civilians were killed, and the American NGO Human Rights Watch, among others, called for an independent commission to investigate possible violations. NATO spokesman Jamie Shea responded, none too subtly. "NATO countries are those that have provided the finances to set up the Tribunal," he said, leaving no doubt about his meaning. In June 2000, ICTY prosecutor Carla Del Ponte formally declined to investigate. Her decision was a stunning example of the power of politics over international law.*

There were other general criticisms:

• Major indictees had not been apprehended, which reflected badly on the tribunal. *Yes, Karadžić and Mladić remained at large, and the tribunal had no powers of arrest. Louise Arbour talked about this problem, comparing her situation with the prosecution at Nuremberg. "It's the technical things I think about," she said. "[The Nuremberg jurists] had every defendant in custody, and the ones they didn't have they tried in absentia. They had no appeals; they had every document; they had translators by the zillions. I'm not saying I would approve, or even want, all these things, but it made their job a heck of a lot easier. . . ." In other words, the work of the ICTY depended on international co-operation that was not always forthcoming.*

• The tribunal's costs are too high. *The two-year budget for the tribunal for 2004 and 2005 was just under US$272 million, a cost borne by all UN members. The allocation for 2006–2007 was US$275 million. Was this too much to establish a legally authenticated historical record of the crimes committed during the recent Balkan wars and to advance the principle of accountability for major human rights violations? By the end of September 2007, the cost of the futile war in Iraq, in which tens of thousands of Iraqi civilians and more than three thousand Americans had been killed, was expected to reach more than $500 billion.*

• The trials are too long, some extending for several years. *Although open trials, especially those requiring simultaneous translation, can certainly be long and tedious, the ICTY was making a great effort to be fair. There was, though, a lesson here for the International Criminal Court which had yet to launch its first prosecution. It would have to expedite its major cases, while upholding the dignity of the court. Not permitting the accused to strut and preen on televised transmissions to his supporters at home would be a good start.*

—

The untimely demise of Slobodan Milošević on March 11, 2006, was a blow to the ICTY, but not a fatal one. In Croatia and in Bosnia, regret was tinged with anger. Within hours of the death announcement, the Croatian president Stjepan Mesić said, "It's a shame he didn't live until the end of the trial so he could be given the sentence he deserved." The question of Milošević's involvement in attacks by Serbs on Croats living in the Krajina region would now never be resolved. In

Belgrade, even those who had opposed Milošević expressed concern. The human rights activist Nataša Kandić worried that his death would cause "historic damage" to Serbia, and she may have been right: the ultranationalist Serbian Radical Party immediately promised that it would "no longer tolerate the harassment of the Serbian patriots and their families." (Ominously, they were referring not to the ICTY but to their political enemies, Serbia's pro-Western president, Boris Tadić, and his foreign minister, Vuk Drasković.)

But Slobodan Milošević did not escape justice, for the goals of the International Criminal Tribunal for the Former Yugoslavia transcended his case, important though it was. In the long term, the achievements of the ICTY, though perhaps not as stellar as optimists may have hoped at the outset, will outweigh the loss of its most important defendant, for the many reasons mentioned above. Future historians of the court will note the demise of Slobodan Milošević as unfortunate—but a footnote.

—

What did need questioning was whether or not the ICTY was contributing to the reconciliation of former enemies in the Balkans, especially in Bosnia. As a judicial body, the tribunal could rightly be considered a success, in spite of setbacks and difficult beginnings, but without reconciliation between the victims and their former persecutors, there was no guarantee that hostilities would not resume when the Office of the High Representative eventually closed down. (The OHR was created under the 1995 Dayton Accords "to ensure that Bosnia and Herzegovina is a peaceful, viable state on course to European integration.")[7] The scope of suffering in the country was overwhelming. Approximately 100,000 were dead; at least 20,000 women had been raped; and two million people had been displaced from their homes. Yet only a small number of perpetrators had been indicted and tried in the distant court in The Hague, and there had been minimal outreach into the communities of the victims.

The international community largely failed these people. NATO "couldn't find" Mladić and Karadžić, the leaders of the genocide. The United States supported the ICTY tribunal— but without helping to locate the master criminals. The United Nations had neglected to protect the thousands of Muslim families that sought refuge in Srebrenica.

How relevant was the ICTY to the lives of the Bosnian survivors? Did they feel that justice had been served?

TEN

Return to Bosnia

I first visited Sarajevo in the fall of 1997, just two years after the Dayton accords purportedly brought peace to the region. The word itself was a misnomer, for "peace" in this case meant little more than the cessation of killing, crucial though that was. Nothing even hinted at the recovery of pre-war communal life; on the contrary, by dividing the Bosnian territory into ethnic enclaves, the Dayton accords seemed to have legitimized the outcome of the morbid ethnic cleansing that had characterized the conflict.

In 1997, the once beautiful city of multiethnic Sarajevo, a former jewel in the Austro-Hungarian crown, was a destroyed husk of its former self. Bullet holes pockmarked the walls of elegant buildings, some of which had been reduced to jagged remnants of their earlier splendour; plastic stretched across the cavernous mouths of blown-out windows; my taxi driver's face was hideously burned. Because the airport was closed, I had arrived by way of a nightmarish car trip from Belgrade along mined mountain roads. The driver and his friends were Sarajevans who had been attending the first inter-ethnic conference on war refugees in the former Yugoslavia, and the car's Sarajevo licence plate identified us as Muslims, or friends of Muslims; in other words, as "Turks," in the racist nomenclature of the region. For better camouflage, we had travelled in the dark of night; to avoid trouble, we had detoured around a huge swath of the Bosnian Serb Republic, driving along the Croatian side of the border until we reached an area south of Sarajevo from which it was safe, or at least safer, to circle back to the city.

There was no passport check in Bosnia then—no "country" to issue such a document; but on my return to Belgrade by local bus I had had an absurd (in retrospect) encounter with nationalism and its limits. My fellow passengers, Bosnian Serb peasants with ruddy weathered faces, were openly curious. They smiled at me, whispered to one another and sometimes pointed as they buzzed conjecture in one another's ears. I smiled back, and by the time we reached the border with Serbia several hours later we were all "friends" of sorts, as happens to travellers. When a border police officer unceremoniously marched me off the bus, they looked as concerned as I felt.

The walls of the one-room shack that passed for a border control station were covered with pictures of Radovan Karadžić (this was his territory). The three men on duty looked deeply bored as they sat, feet up on chairs, chain-smoking cigarettes. My appearance stirred them to sudden attention. Where is your Republika Srpska visa? one of them demanded to know. I didn't have one: Republika Srpska was not a country—their evident wishes to the contrary.

The officer-in-chief examined my Canadian passport closely, then after a whispered conference with his colleagues demanded payment of 100 deutschmarks. I agreed with alacrity. After turning the document in every possible direction, as though expecting to discover unknown and possibly useful information, he looked at me and sighed audibly. "Ah, Canada," he said, with a sad, wistful smile. How extraordinary, I remember thinking. The bones of thousands of civilians still moulder in the ground; millions have been displaced; the country is in ruins, its centuries-old cultural heritage destroyed. And for what? If an "immigration officer" of this pretend nation still sighed for a place across the world, where he probably assumed that people did not massacre their neighbours, what had been the point of the deadly nationalist violence?

My "friends" were round-eyed with excitement when I reboarded the bus. "Visa," I announced to the people on one side of the aisle, using the one word I knew was the same in both our languages. "Visa," I informed those on the other side. They nodded appreciatively. Since I hadn't been arrested, perhaps I wasn't a spy after all.

—

When I returned to Sarajevo in late 2004, the airport was functioning, and all travellers, including returning Bosnians, were required to show travel documents. But the city had barely recovered. Apartment buildings were studded with the same bullet holes, and plastic still stretched across gaping windows. My driver wanted me to see a new revolving restaurant; and, yes, it was a sign of change; but the bombed-out railway station had not been rebuilt and the Museum of the History of Bosnia-Herzegovina still stood broken and battle-scarred. How apt, I thought. In addition to being an attack on human beings, the war in Bosnia was an attack on history and culture, on the shared past of Yugoslavs who had lived together in harmony for half a century. It would take decades to repair the damage.

I had a friend in the city whom I was eager to contact. In 1997, F. had been understandably weary—traumatized by the struggle to survive—but she had expressed hope for the future. The fighting was over; surely real peace would come. My telephone call to her brought different tidings. She sounded jittery. Life was worse now, she said. She had a young daughter, but there was little to secure her future. Earlier hopes had evaporated, and no, there had been no reconciliation to speak of. The Dayton accords had turned Sarajevo into a "Muslim" city—divorced from the Serbs and Croats with whom her people had long intermingled in bonds of marriage and friendship.

No one in F.'s family had died during Radovan Karadžić's assault on Sarajevo, which was a miracle, since like everyone else they had had to forage for food under the guns of snipers stationed on the surrounding hills. They had survived largely thanks to her; yet this strong woman seemed to have lost hope. That F. felt so despondent struck me as an ominous beginning to my visit.

My guide and interpreter was Nidžara Ahmetašević, a young journalist with a local Sarajevan newspaper. Although still in her twenties, she too was bitter beyond words. She had recently written a story about the region of Prijedor, which had been the site of the infamous Omarska concentration camp. It was the pictures of emaciated prisoners standing behind the barbed wire of that camp that had first stirred international outrage; up to four thousand people from the area had been murdered in just three months. The ICTY's first conviction had concerned this event: in July 1997, Duško Tadić was sentenced to twenty years in prison for seizing, maltreating, and murdering these civilians.

The old Prijedor iron-ore mine, the locale of the Omarska camp, had been sold to a global company, Mittal Steel, which employed many locals, but there were still unrecoverable bodies in the shaft, and the families of the dead were demanding that a memorial be built at the centre of the mining complex.[1] Nidžara had talked to the survivors of the camp. She knew the names of the killers, some of whom still walked the streets, and she had published them—but there had been no response to her article, just as there was little response to other media stories about atrocities. "We live in a lawless, depraved place and no one is untouched by the degradation," she told me. Local women prostituted themselves to NATO soldiers: one village near a base not far from Prijedor consisted of twenty houses, of which ten were brothels.[2] "Our poverty runs deep," she said in a flat voice. "There is no future."

We are driving north of Sarajevo to the town of Tuzla, where the Mothers of Srebrenica have a central office. It is 5 a.m., dark, and November-cold as we leave the capital on a narrow mountain road flanked by a dense forest of snow-covered pine trees. Parts of Bosnia, like neighbouring Albania and Montenegro, occupy the wildest, most remote spaces of Europe: a land of untamed mountains where wolves and bears still roam. The shapes of destroyed houses emerge in the dawn light; they line the highway in mute testimony to the war waged against their inhabitants. "This was the front line. There was heavy fighting here," Nidžara reports. There is an edge of shock in her voice. She may not have ventured here before.

The Mothers of Srebrenica are the women whose sons and husbands were slaughtered by the Bosnian Serbs under the command of Ratko Mladić. They founded their organization in March 1996 out of sorrow and rage; their work was, in their words, "a campaign for truth and justice." Far away in The Hague, two of the men who were responsible for the Srebrenica tragedy had expressed remorse for the crimes they had committed against people who were their neighbours or co-workers, who had sat with them as children in school class-rooms. In the pre-war years, these future perpetrators and their victims (many of whom were related by blood and marriage) would have toasted one another's health with glasses of the local slivowitz and gossiped together over cups of aromatic Bosnian coffee.

The first to express remorse was Momir Nikolić.[3] During the three-year siege of Srebrenica, which began in 1992, he had served as chief of intelligence and security for the nearby Bratunac Brigade of the Bosnian Serb army. He was forty years old at the time, married, the father of two children and a graduate of the Faculty of Political Science at the university in Sarajevo, where he had studied defence and security. After graduation, he had settled into a solid career as a high school teacher. When the war began, his academic training had guaranteed him an important military post.

After the massacre at Srebrenica, in which he played a major role, he was named head of the Bratunac office of the Ministry for Refugees and Displaced Persons and the coordinator of that ministry for the greater municipality of Srebrenica. In other words, he became responsible for the well-being of the Muslims who were trying to return to the very places he and his fellows had forced them from. "War crimes are at the heart of this society," someone I met in Sarajevo had said more or less in passing. "The police, military, politicians—everything is infested with war crimes and corruption."[4]

On March 26, 2002, the ICTY issued a warrant for Nikolić's arrest. In the formal language of the indictment he was charged as a member of a "joint criminal enterprise," the purpose of which was "to forcibly transfer the women and children from the Srebrenica enclave . . . on 12 July and 13 July 1995; and to capture, detain, summarily execute by firing squad, bury, and rebury thousands of Bosnian Muslim men and boys, aged 16 to 60, from the Srebrenica enclave, from 12 July 1995 until and about 19 July 1995." He was arrested one week later and transferred to The Hague, where he became the first to plead guilty for the Srebrenica genocide.

On May 7, 2003, he signed an eight-page "Statement of Facts and Acceptance of Responsibility" in which he detailed the organizational plans for the attacks and how the operation against Srebrenica was carried out. He acknowledged that he had perpetrated acts against the civilian population that violated fundamental human rights; that these acts were committed on political, racial and/or religious grounds; and that he was aware of the wider political context in which his conduct had occurred. The court entered a finding of guilty against him with regard to "persecutions" (a crime against humanity in the statute of the tribunal). But there was also a quid pro quo arrangement that many of the survivors had trouble accepting: according to the plea bargain, the prosecution then dismissed all remaining charges.

On December 2, 2003, Momir Nikolić was sentenced to twenty-seven years in prison (later reduced on appeal to twenty); in its judgment, the court expressed the hope that his confession of guilt might jump-start a process of truth-telling and possible reconciliation within the estranged ethnic communities of Bosnia. Perhaps the judges were thinking about an "open letter" sent to them by the current (Bosniak) mayor of the Srebrenica municipality in October of that year, in which he wrote, "The admission of Momir Nikolić . . . [to] the crimes cannot alone compensate the families of the victims of genocide, but it is an encouragement and hope that finally the truth will come to light, reveal the criminals' monstrous plan, wake up the deluded Serbs and bring them to their senses. Momir Nikolić is the first officer of the Serbian Army who found the strength and courage to confess the crimes and his participation in them. I hope this is due to the pangs of conscience and there-fore I support his admission and appeal to the others to do the same. . . . Only by recognizing and admitting the real and whole truth about the crime of July 1995 and other crimes in BH can trust be rebuilt among the citizens of BH."[5]

That the Bosnian Serbs still denied taking any part in the massacres, up to that point, had been disheartening. In November 1995 Karadžić announced that "nothing happened" at Srebrenica. Others allowed that "something" might have happened, but suggested that the Muslims must have killed one another, or that perhaps they were murdered by outsiders who wanted to discredit the Serbs.

At his sentencing hearing on October 29, 2003, Momir Nikolić, struggling to control himself, publicly apologized to his victims. Emir Suljagić, a young survivor of Srebrenica, then later a journalist for the Institute for War and Peace Reporting in The Hague, was in the courtroom that day. His father had died early on in the conflict. Nikolić had been a family friend. "He knew my dad and my dad knew him, and one of them was not alive any longer," he told me bitterly when we met in a noisy smoke-filled Sarajevo café where we had to shout at each other over the din.

—

On the day Nikolić was sentenced, Suljagić heard him say, "I am aware that my admission cannot bring back the dead or ease the pain of their families, but I wanted the whole truth about Srebrenica to be known. . . . I want to express my sincere regret and repentance. I want to apologize to [the] victims, their families and Bosniaks [Bosnian Muslims] for my partici-pation in Srebrenica."[6] He said he was following orders (a defence that had been discredited a half-century earlier at Nuremberg) and stated that he too had been abused by extremists in the early days of the war when he objected to the violent turn of events. He said he had resigned from the army and moved with his family to Serbia but had returned to Bratunac when he was unable to find work. He spoke about his need to provide for his young children.

At this, Carmen Argibay, a judge from Argentina, who had been imprisoned by that country's military junta in the early 1980s, asked him a direct question. "Can you [also] think of the youngest sons of all those killed in the Srebrenica massacre?"

"The reason I pleaded guilty was the pain I carried with and within myself. I know I want to apologize once again to all victims, all children, all mothers. . . . I especially want to apologize to my students," Nikolić said tearfully. Appallingly, this man had been a teacher as well as a parent—a role model to the young.

Old friends testified on his behalf that he was not a nationalist before the war, that he had never involved himself in politics. (In this regard, he resembled Karadžić himself, a purportedly apolitical psychiatrist in his former life. During my earlier trip to Bosnia, I had met a colleague, Dr. Ismet Cerić, who confirmed that Radovan had demonstrated no interest in politics and had preferred the company of Muslims to his fellow Serbs, whom he denigrated as "untrustworthy, primitive peasants.")

By chance, Suljagić's path had crossed that of Nikolić back in 1993, a year after his father's death. Nikolić asked about the family. "He said, 'Hey, what's up with your dad?' And I said, 'He's dead.' He looked uncomfortable, like I shouldn't have said that. After that I began to see him on a daily basis [Suljagić had become a translator for the United Nations in Srebrenica], and most of that time he was a Serb officer busy with security and intelligence and that sort of thing. But on two occasions I saw him act in a humane way. One was when he asked about my dad. The other was when the brother of my colleague Hassan Nuhanović was taken away by the Serbs. When [Hassan] told Nikolić about this event, Nikolić put his hands over his face and said, 'Oh God, you shouldn't have let them do that!' It was crazy. I thought, What the fuck was he talking about? Was Hassan in a position of not letting anyone do anything?"

"Did it mean anything to you when you heard Nikolić confess?" I asked him over the din of the café.

"It *did* mean something to me, because for years after the war the only thing I heard was outright denial. This guy was the hardest of the hard core, but he came out and told the truth. That's why it was important to me. After his apology I remember running down the stairs of the ICTY building. I went into the toilet in the corner of the lobby and I cried and cried for half an hour. I couldn't stop."

"You believed him?"

"Yes, I did. I believed his remorse. It meant something to me that he came out and said it. Other people may not want to believe him when he said that thinking about his Muslim pupils upsets him. I'm not sure I do either, but I don't care. Whatever his motives, whatever his agenda, I do not care. The important thing for me was that he said it—on, and for, the record: yes, we did it. Yes, we killed over seven thousand people. Yes, it was a terrible thing."

The other perpetrator from Srebrenica to express remorse was Dragan Obrenović—a thirty-two-year-old Serb. He was indicted by the ICTY on March 16, 2001, arrested on April 15, and charged with complicity in genocide, persecutions and extermination. Like Momir Nikolić, he agreed to a plea bargain in which he provided details of his involvement in the carefully planned genocide.

From their factual statements to the court, it seems clear that the Serb perpetrators did not question their orders; nor, it appears, did they discuss what they were doing. In March

1995, Karadžić had issued signed orders to his troops: "By planned and well-thought-out combat operations, create an unbearable situation of total insecurity with no hope of further survival or life for the inhabitants of Srebrenica and Zepa." Like the Nazis, the men who massacred the civilian population of Srebrenica carried out their work efficiently. Their conversations concerned only logistics and manoeuvres, which is why one paragraph in the Dragan Obrenović transcript stands out from the rest:

> Sometime in August 1995 . . . I stood with General Krstić next to a trench where one of the soldiers was listening to a transistor radio. A survivor from one of the executions was giving an account of what happened to him over the radio broadcast from Tuzla. We stood there for about two minutes listening to the survivor and then General Krstić ordered that the radio be switched off and said we should not listen to enemy radio. He asked me if I had issued orders that enemy radio should not be listened to and I said that I had not.
>
> On the way back I thought about the survivor's story on the radio and this led me to ask General Krstić why the killings took place. I said that we knew the people killed were all simple people and asked for the reason why they had to be killed. I said that even if they were all chickens that were killed, there still had to be a reason. . . . Krstić cut me short and said that we would speak no more about this.[7]

Obrenović continued to think (he had plenty of time while awaiting his trial in The Hague); and at a hearing on October 30, 2003, he too expressed remorse. "I am to blame for everything I did at that time," he told the court. "My testimony and admission of guilt will also remove the blame from my nation because it is the individual guilt of a man named Dragan Obrenović. I am responsible for this . . . for what happened to the victims and their shadows."

He hoped his acceptance of responsibility would contribute to reconciliation, "if neighbours can shake hands and children play together again."

Chillingly, he also spoke of how "death moved into the vicinity and became our reality. . . . Surrounded by horrors, we got used to them. . . ." This pointed insight penetrated to the core of extremist behaviour, for people can indeed "get used to" just about anything, provided that those in authority, or those whom they admire, encourage and justify the shift. Obrenović told the court that the source of his greatest after-the-fact revulsion was that the atrocities were perpetrated in a community where people knew each other well: "[a community] that had lived almost as family. . . . We trampled on and forgot our best selves in hatred and brutality." It was within this context, he told the court, that "the horror of Srebrenica happened.

"Maybe decades have to pass before the wounds in the soul are healed. . . . It is too late for me, but not for the children in Bosnia."[8]

At Obrenović's sentencing hearing on December 10, 2003, the tribunal noted his "unqualified acceptance" of criminal responsibility and the help he had provided in establishing the truth of what took place in Srebrenica. Like Obrenović, the judges of the ICTY hoped his testimony would promote reconciliation. He was sentenced to seventeen years.

———

On August 2, 2001, the events at Srebrenica were defined as a genocide by the ICTY. That day, at the sentencing of General Radislav Krstić, the deputy commander of the Drina Corps (a division of the Republika Srpska army), the tribunal allowed that it was "convinced beyond any reasonable doubt that a crime of genocide was committed in Srebrenica," and that General Radislav Krstić was guilty of that crime. The thousands of men and boys were targeted because they belonged to a particular ethnic, religious, racial or national group, and for no other reason. Krstić was sentenced to an astonishing forty-six years, which was reduced on appeal to thirty-five.[9]

The facts of Srebrenica are well known, but they bear repeating, if only to expose the fragility of the post-Auschwitz mantra, "Never again." The "lessons" of Nuremberg and the Holocaust did not reach into the Soviet-controlled Balkans. Fifty years of multi-ethnic cohabitation quickly dissolved in the face of racist propaganda.

Briefly, the story of Srebrenica began in 1992, with the eruption of war. Tito had died twelve years earlier, and the old Yugoslavia was breaking up. Croatia and Slovenia had voted to become independent; so did Bosnia-Herzegovina, but this choice created difficulties. The Bosnian Serbs wanted to remain aligned with Serbia whose leader, Slobodan Milošević, dreamed of an expanded, ethnically pure state to be known as "Greater Serbia." In order to facilitate Milošević's plan, the Bosnian Serbs declared the existence of a "state" under the leadership of Radovan Karadžić, who then began to "cleanse" the territory of its Muslim population by expulsion, murder and rape. After the United Nations declared Srebrenica a protected "safe zone" in 1993, thousands of people fled north to take refuge in the enclave and its outlying villages. But the assault on Srebrenica intensified, in spite of the UN presence. On July 6, 1995, the Bosnian Serbs began their final attack. The Dutch UN commander, Thom Karremans, called for NATO air strikes, but his messages were lost in a bureaucratic maze, and help, when it came, was ineffectual. When General Ratko Mladić and his forces finally entered the town on July 11, approximately twenty thousand terrified people fled to the Dutch UN base, a large warehouse building in nearby Potočari. On July 12, Mladić arrived in Potočari with his men, where the latter mingled with the families—torturing, killing and raping.

That night and the following day, the world community abandoned thousands of unarmed men, women and children, just as it had abandoned the doomed Jews of the Nazi death camps. It was the old story: by 1995, the Bosnian enclaves, including Srebrenica, were thought to be already lost. The accepted political wisdom at the highest levels was that it would be unwise to antagonize the Serbs unnecessarily.

Making calculated use of the media, Mladić had a camera crew film him addressing the crowd. In the video he is seen speaking reassuringly to his victims. "Don't panic. Let the small children and women pass," he tells them. "Don't be afraid—no one will do you any harm." Some people thank him.

With the complicity of the Dutch peacekeepers, who chose to believe his soothing lies, an Auschwitz-style selection took place: women and girls to one side, men and boys to the other. The women, along with many of the elderly, were sent by truck to Tuzla, in Bosniak territory, while almost eight thousand men and boys were driven away, also on trucks, in the opposite direction. They were taken to several locations, ordered to descend and assembled in lines. One by one they stepped forward as commanded; one by one they were shot. The killings took many hours. Afterwards, the bodies were buried in shallow grave pits in the adjacent fields and forests, but in the days and months that followed, the killers returned frequently to the scene. They unearthed the dead with bulldozers for transfer to other places in the Serb Republic where they might be safe from prying eyes.

Only fifteen people survived the massacre. They had suffered non-fatal wounds and were left for dead.

Another twenty thousand men from Srebrenica did not go to Potočari but fled into the mountains in hopes of reaching Tuzla. Most did not make it. Either they were killed by Serb snipers waiting in ambush, or they died of exhaustion.

Unlike the Nazis, the Bosnian Serbs allowed females to survive, often for ulterior motives. Rape camps sprouted up across the "cleansed" territories. Many of the enslaved women became pregnant with the offspring of their violators, giving birth to what their torturers hoped would be a new generation of ethnic Serbs. That Bosnians of all groups had historically intermarried and produced children in loving families was an irony that mattered not at all in the new environment. The "other" had been reimagined, and not just as a wartime enemy: mirroring the earlier psychology of the Nazis, the Serbs configured a whole group as less than human. This was a necessary mental precondition for violent behaviour that a lifetime of social conditioning would otherwise have forbidden.

It is tempting to shrink from the details—from the knowledge that some of the people who murdered their neighbours and friends practised throat cutting on pigs, and that an elderly man was pinned to a tree then forced to eat the innards of his grandson.[10] But facts are facts. At the same time, the Bosnian Serbs were not "monsters," nor did they invent atrocity. At the end point on a continuum of dehumanization, such grotesqueries become possible. When the enemy is no longer a human being, the farthest reaches on the spectrum of untried behaviour may emerge as an unprecedented, perhaps liberating, fantasy.

—

Two rivers run through Tuzla, a city in northeastern Bosnia situated on the slopes of Mount Majevica, a site long known for its curative hot-water spas. Tuzla is large by Bosnian standards,

with a pre-war (1991) population of 100,000 people of all ethnicities, including a large Jewish component.[11] Since the Dayton
accords, it has been officially Muslim, or Bosniak.

The main square is built in the regal architectural style of
the Austro-Hungarian Empire, which governed this part of
the world from 1878 until 1917, and it looks entrancing, until
one reaches the central monument of the town. The event
commemorated there changed Tuzla forever. On May 25,
1995, as schoolchildren celebrated the end of the academic
year, a shell launched from the mountainside landed on this
square, instantly killing seventy-two of them, including a
three-year-old named Sandro Kalesić who happened to be
walking nearby with his parents.

The memorial stone that lists their names eulogizes their
lives with a verse by the twentieth-century Bosnian poet Mak
Dizdar:

> *Ovdje se ne zivi samo*
> *da bi se zivjelo*
> *Ovdje se ne zivi samo*
> *da bi se umiralo*
> *Ovdje se i umire*
> *da bi se zivjelo.*

> Here they do not only live
> to live
> Here they do not only live
> to die
> Here they also die
> to live.[12]

The house where the Mothers of Srebrenica meet consists of a
narrow sitting room with walls that are covered with snapshots
of the dead and the missing. Four women have been waiting

for us to arrive; there is much fussing and hospitality as they pour deliciously dark Bosnian coffee into small demitasses. In another era one might have called this drink Turkish coffee, but "Turk," with its echoes of Ottoman rule and religious conversion to Islam, has become a racial slur and is a word to be avoided.

Each of the women has a story of loss; each has pasted at least one picture of a disappeared husband or son on the wall.

Two of the women stand out in my memory. Hajra Catic was the president of the association, a fair-haired, articulate woman whose bitter voice silenced the others when she spoke. Both her husband and her son were murdered. Her son was a radio reporter: his smiling portrait covers an entire wall of the room.

On July 11, 1995, as Mladić's forces overran Srebrenica, the young man had hurled his last public words into the void: "If no one comes to help us, we are doomed," he cried. With no response forthcoming, he had escaped into the woods with a few friends, but was killed trying to reach Tuzla. His parents had sought refuge at Potočari, but Hajra's husband was taken away on a truck, never to be seen again.

It is she who replies to my questions while the others sit stiffly and listen.

"Are the trials that are taking place in The Hague important to you?" I ask her after the friendly introductions are over.

"They are important if something substantial is gained," she says. "I mean that every day we expect that the war criminals [who still live in Srebrenica] will be arrested, but nobody is doing that."

"But what about Momir Nikolić and Dragan Obrenović? They both confessed and expressed deep remorse."

"That means *nothing* to us! They just did it to reduce their sentences. We were offended that Obrenović only got eleven years [sic] and Nikolić got ten [sic]. Nikolić was my neighbour in Bratunac. He will still be a young man when he gets out. He'll be able to come back and keep on killing people."

I glance at the other women in the room, wondering whether they agree. Their expressions are flattened with shared pain as they listen.

"So you didn't believe him when he expressed remorse?"

"They excused him and gave him a light sentence. Lucky for him. But *I* don't have my family anymore," replies Hajra.

We pause. The room is silent because she has given voice to the only truth that finally matters: the murder of her family. Everything else is after the fact and possibly irrelevant.

I try again. "Did anything either of these men said to the court help you in any way?"

"We don't expect help from them or from anybody. We just want all war criminals to go to prison and to stay there for life."

I wonder whether I've reached the limit of this encounter. "Might a truth and reconciliation commission bring a sense of solace, if not justice?" I ask her.

"Lots of people mention this to us, but we don't have anyone to reconcile with. Only when all the perpetrators are jailed for life will there be some justice. Republika Srpska has just issued a report on Srebrenica and an acknowledgment of some kind, we know that, but they only did it under pressure from the international community.[13] Our question to them is, How many people has Republika Srpska jailed for committing war crimes? The answer is none."[14]

A majority of the Muslim survivors of Srebrenica had not returned to their homes, which were now located in Republika Srpska: their houses had been destroyed or taken over by former neighbours. The largest group among the displaced were older women; there were an estimated sixty-five hundred widows from Srebrenica alone. At the time of my visit in 2004, the economy was practically non-existent, and the only way to survive was to grow one's own food. Those who did return were obliged to interact with the very people who had killed members of their families—and they often knew exactly who they were. If a Muslim returnee needed to buy a litre of milk, she had to go to a Serb-run store, and the same was true of every other commercial dealing. "When some Bosniak people started to come back to their houses, the Serbs were angry," Hajra says. "Some of them actually told us, 'Why are you here again after what we did to you? Shall we do worse things to you now?' I know someone who was a policeman during the war. I *saw* him violently separating a friend of mine from her husband, and I *told* him I saw him. He just shrugged. Not one Serb in Srebrenica has said anything to us about what happened—just the ones who threatened us when we came back. Carla Del Ponte [the current prosecutor of the ICTY] came here and we gave her a list of names of war criminals, but she never did anything!"

At this I recalled my meeting with Louise Arbour when she was the chief prosecutor for the ICTY. She had said that for most of the victims, the most important perpetrators—those the court was most interested in trying—were mainly abstractions. She said, "The man whose daughter was raped and killed in a camp has in his mind the person who did it, but he is not the one we are likely to prosecute. In that sense the perpetrators have won. They took away the lives of their victims—that was the easy part—but they also took away their identity, their humanity. . . . In the sense that we cannot attend to every victim [or try every murderer or rapist], the perpetrators have won. . . ." As I listen to the woman sitting opposite me speak, I think that she was right.

The other standout in my memory from that day in Tuzla is Hajrija Selimović, a shy, soft-spoken woman in a tattered black coat with a kerchief tied around her head. She was fifty-six, but she looked twenty years older. Her home was in

Bratunac, but she had fled to Srebrenica in 1992 with her family—her husband, two sons, a daughter, a daughter-in-law and a small granddaughter. At the moment of crisis, the women and the child had escaped to Tuzla; the men set out through the mountains, and she had received no news about their fate. For nine years she had lived in a nearby refugee camp in a room too small to contain a bed or even a chair. A small pension of seventy-six euros per month must cover food, medicine and all utilities, such as electricity.

After a time her daughter-in-law remarried and moved to the United States, taking Hajrija's grandchild with her. The previous year, this generous young woman and her husband had paid for a trip so Hajrija could see the child once again, possibly for the last time. Her daughter had also married and had children; they lived nearby; but she and her husband were unemployed, and the entire family lived in one room. They could not take her in.

Of all those who died in her immediate family, she had only one picture of one son. Nothing more. She leads me across the room; there is the photograph on the wall, a small, blurred snapshot of a teenaged boy. We stare at it together. This is what is left to her. I gently touch her shoulder in sympathy. "I don't know why I lived," she whispers. "I will soon have to leave the camp and I have nowhere to go."

Once she was wealthy by Bosnian standards. The family owned a nice house and a cow, chickens and land. The house was razed to the ground— but still she saves her money to travel there to look at the place where it used to stand. She needs 5,000 to 10,000 Bosnian marks (2,500 to 5,000 euros) to rebuild something small there, she tells me. This is like wishing for the moon.

—

The Mothers of Srebrenica have become the most vocal organization of survivors in all of Bosnia. On the eleventh day of every month they and their surviving families walk in procession through Tuzla carrying banners and handmade pillowcases embroidered with the names of the missing. They have published a book, *The Fatal Summer of Srebrenica, 1995*, that includes survivor testimonials and created an archive, called the Srebrenica Documentation and Information Centre, for researchers; they have established a small fund that will, they hope, create a pasta-making business in Srebrenica that will employ ten to twelve returnees; they have set up a foundation to support the education of orphaned children; and fought for the acquisition of land for a cemetery and a memorial centre at Potočari. The centre opened in September 2003; by July 2007, 2,442 bodies, dug out of pits and identified by DNA analysis, had been buried there, across from the notorious barracks where the selections took place.

They have also launched several political and judicial initiatives. The first, which was submitted between late 2001 and early 2002 to the Chamber of Human Rights of Bosnia-Herzegovina (a body of fourteen members, including four from the Federation of Bosnia-Herzegovina, two from Republika Srpska and the rest nominated by the Committee of Ministers of the Council of Europe) consisted of nineteen hundred claims against Republika Srpska. In March 2003, the chamber accepted the first forty-nine of these and ruled that the Bosnian Serb government was to pay 4 million Bosnian marks (2 million euros) to the Srebrenica-Potočari Memorial and Cemetery Foundation, and provide information about the fate of missing persons and the locations of the mass graves. (They complied.) In June 2007, the Mothers of Srebrenica took bold action against the international community that ignored them in their hour of need, and sued for reparations from the United Nations and the Dutch government. In addition to these lawsuits they have collected evidence regarding the legal responsibility of persons in the employ of the international community who knowingly failed to prevent the killings.

In November 1999, UN Secretary-General Kofi Annan apologized. In a report titled "The Fall of Srebrenica," he spoke of "an institutional ideology of impartiality even when confronted with attempted genocide. . . . [There was] a massacre of a people who had been led to believe that the United Nations would ensure their safety." The moral damage to the UN was incalcuable, as Annan knew better than anyone. Given that the Serb attack had lasted for many days, there had been plenty of time for officials of the international community based in and around Srebrenica to intervene to stop the bloodshed. No one did.

In April 2002, the entire Dutch cabinet resigned after a damning independent report blamed the country's political and military leaders for giving their peacekeepers an "impossible" mission to protect the enclave.[15] The "Dutchbat" (the Dutch contingent) had watched passively as Serb forces separated the men and boys from the women. "Concern about their own survival in this hell meant more to them than the fate of the Muslim men," the authors concluded. But by December 2006, the humiliated Dutch government had turned aggressive. It gave medals to the members of the Dutch battalion that had failed to prevent the slaughter. Some of the former peacekeepers refused to attend the ceremony— but "Dutchbat" commander Thom Karremans (who was filmed at Srebrenica being cowed by the Bosnian Serb general Ratko Mladić) was not one of them. He was the first to be decorated. In April 2007, the government's message changed once again: it pledged 5 million Euros to rebuild Srebrenica. That same month a Dutch court instructed the Ministry of Defence to grant a Srebrenica widow access to confidential files. It seemed clear that the country that had long been known as a refuge for the downtrodden was still struggling to assimilate what had happened more than a decade earlier.

—

Reconciliation, one of the goals of the International Criminal Tribunal for the Former Yugoslavia, was not yet a part of the picture. In spite of the Serb Republic's formal acknowledgment of responsibility for what took place in Srebrenica, many ordinary Serbs, both in Bosnia and in Serbia proper, continued to deny the irrefutable facts. Mutual hatred still poisoned relations. In June 2005, ten years after the massacre, political leaders in Serbia snubbed an international conference on Srebrenica being held in Belgrade, prompting Nataša Kandić, the head of the Humanitarian Law Centre (of Serbia), to note that "the absence of representatives of the Serbian authorities is just another proof that there is no readiness in the institutions to face the past."[16]

On July 5, 2005, just six days before a formal ceremony marking the tenth anniversary of the genocide was to take place at Potočari, sixty-six pounds of plastic explosives were found planted in the ground at the site—"ready to detonate," according to the European Union troops that made the discovery. They were cleared away with alacrity, but their presence proved that in the minds of many, the war had never ended.

If there was justice for the victims, it was emerging from the remarkable work of the International Commission on Missing Persons, which was established at the 1996 G7 summit at the urging of former US president Bill Clinton. When the conflict in Bosnia-Herzegovina ended in November 1995, thirty thousand people in the region were reported missing. By August 2007, approximately thirteen thousand were still unaccounted for. Some lay in mass graves that had yet to be discovered; the bodies of others, already exhumed, waited in a special morgue for possible identification. Remarkably, more than eleven thousand individuals had already been recognized through the world's most advanced system of DNA analysis, in which bones and teeth were matched with blood samples donated by living relatives now dispersed across the globe.[17]

Before 2000, the process was much slower: dental and medical records, both traditional methods of identification, were often unavailable (Bosnia lacked a modern health-care system); but the development of new software for DNA extraction put the commission at the forefront of the emerging science. The first blood collection took place in June 2000, and by November 2001 there was a positive identification: that of a sixteen-year-old boy who had disappeared from Srebrenica in 1995.

Gordon Bacon is the director-general of the Sarajevo-based Missing Persons Institute, the successor to the original commission. He's an Englishman, a former policeman who came to Bosnia in 1994 as an aid worker and never left. He started by helping to feed refugees during the war, then continued his relief work through his efforts to find the dead.

"This is a human rights issue," he said the day we met in his Sarajevo office. "What people want and need is to know what happened to their son, their father or their husband. They need to have the body so they can bury it properly and begin to feel some closure."

First, they had to learn where the mass burial sites were located, and as the years passed, more information had become available; but the grisly reality was that the bodies were often in pieces, and in different places. Most of the dead had been moved at least once and sometimes twice; and occasionally only a fragment was found. This came as a shock to the surviving members of the family.

"When you think of how many people's lives are affected because just one person is missing, and multiply that number by thirty thousand, you begin to have an idea about how many people in Bosnia-Herzegovina are affected on a daily basis," Bacon said. "Finding the remains of a loved one is a massive step toward peace of mind and eventual reconciliation. The survivors are angry, they want justice, they want answers. They want the body back. Nothing ends when that happens, but it is a first step. *Then* they want to move on to the judicial process."

At first the survivors who came to the International Commission on Missing Persons for help sat separately in their little ethnic conclaves. They refused to talk to one another, or if they did, it was to mutter insults. That was changing, Bacon said. He and his colleagues had worked hard to gain the confidence of the Serbs in particular, to let them know that they were not all considered war criminals. "We've tried very hard to take the nationalism, the religion and the ethnicity out of it. It doesn't matter where the person was killed, or what group they belonged to. All that matters is being able to return a body to the family. Somebody they love is missing and they deserve to know what happened to that person."

"In your dealings with family members, have you a sense that the criminal trials in The Hague are of interest or benefit to them?" I asked.

"I think the problem is that the number of people being tried in The Hague is obviously small, while our work has a more direct influence on their lives. I'm not going to say they feel happy, but they do feel some justice when the burning question of what happened is answered and they can properly bury the remains. On the other hand, many, many thousands of people know that the person who killed their loved one is still walking the streets. They see them regularly. Many of these perpetrators have jobs with some authority.[18] I think that in the end the judicial process in The Hague is not going to satisfy the families. That is more likely to happen when the local court for Bosnia-Herzegovina starts to pick up the slack from the ICTY and tries more people.[19]

"I think that what has changed recently is the acceptance that a missing person is dead. They now accept that what we are doing is a body search, rather than looking for someone who is alive. Time has helped, but there are still so many missing people in this country. Reconciliation is a long way off."

—

Nidžara and I leave Tuzla for the short drive to the national mortuary and one of the four DNA labs that have been built across the territory, including in Belgrade and Zagreb. I am intent on seeing what I can of this extraordinary work. We stop before a large, barrack-like structure.

We are greeted by Zlatan Sabanović, the program manager, who offers to take us around. A climatized room contains rows upon rows of shelves divided by many thousands of cubbyholes, each one containing a numbered body bag. On the floor below each section lie paper sacks holding pieces of clothing and other personal markers of identity found near the remains. This is the after-the-fact reality of Bosnia's fratricidal war; awaiting identification are the remains of husbands, fathers and sons, brutally cut down in the prime of life, once living people who wore the sweaters, socks and wristwatches bunched below them in tagged bags. The clothes are often patched and well-worn, says Sabanović. Because no one had access to anything new during the war years, everything had to be repaired, sometimes making recognition easier for the wife or daughter who mended the garment. One piece of clothing had been made from the cloth of a parachute used for an airplane food drop. The attack on Srebrenica took place in July, but many of the men who fled through the high, forested mountains took sweaters and jackets to protect them from the night cold. These, too, were recovered from the grave pits.

Finally, after DNA analysis has attempted to make a connection between skeletal parts, a forensic anthropological examination of the post-mortem remains will try to determine age and sex, and to reconstruct the body, if possible. Only when there is an almost positive identification is the family contacted. This is the place they come to. The case manager who makes the difficult call was trained by that admirable organization, Physicians for Human Rights, an American group that has focused on creating a culture of human rights in the medical and scientific professions.

"Some families find it harder than others," acknowledges Sabanović, "especially if they have not been able to accept the death of the missing person. The most painful case we have seen was that of a woman who lost her husband and all five of her sons. So far we have found three sons and her husband. We are still looking for the two missing sons."

He tells me he is from the town of Brčko, the site of a notorious concentration camp where up to a thousand civilians were interned, tortured and exterminated during the war.

"How do you handle the stress of this work?" I ask him.

He pauses. "It's my job," he replies after several moments, "but the worst part is having to deal with the families. I suppose there is a certain satisfaction because you know that people desperately want to find the bodies of their loved ones and you are helping them a little, even though their lives are so terribly hard. They suffer. They are not able to go back to their homes. They still live in refugee camps. We have to try to understand them."

As we are leaving the mortuary, I notice a young woman working at a table in an adjoining room. I ask permission to enter. She is Laura Yezerdian, a Canadian forensic anthropologist from Victoria, British Columbia; and she is in the process of reassembling the parts of a skeleton that have been linked by DNA analysis. The job is almost complete, she says. The victim was eighteen years old. She knows his precise age from the look of his bones.

I look from her to the table. She is reassembling a murdered boy's humanity. Soon his name will be returned to him. And his mother will come to take him home.

———

The next day Nidžara and I head for the town of Srebrenica, close to the Serb border. Almost immediately, we are in Republika Srpska, now ethnically homogeneous, "cleansed" territory; before the war this region was mixed, with a majority of Muslims. The first town along the narrow road is Vlansenica, the site of the infamous Sušica concentration camp, which was set up in June 1992 at the start of the war. Over the next months thousands of people fled from the region; they walked along the road we are driving on (the *only* road through this remote mountainous terrain) toward Srebrenica, under hailstorms of grenades launched from the surrounding heights. In 1992 the population of Srebrenica was five thousand; by 1995, the time of the genocide, the numbers had swelled to forty thousand, until the supposed "safe haven" extended for approximately thirty square miles.

The name Vlasenica reminds me of something extraordinary that happened in 2003, during Dragan Nikolić's sentencing in The Hague. He was confronted by a witness who had spent three months in the Sušica camp—Nikolić's camp—along with her two sons. When she was released in July 1992, her sons were kept behind; she never saw them again.

She begged Nikolić to tell her what had happened to them—and, astonishingly, he did. "They were taken on September 30, 1992, to Debelo Brdo, and there they were liquidated," he told her, hanging his head. The camp was being closed down, he explained; the brothers were among a final group of about forty prisoners who had survived long months of torture. He knew her sons well. "As far as I can remember, one of them wore a denim jacket," he murmured. Then he told their mother exactly where to find her children's remains—on the slopes of a hill near Vlasenica.

He expressed remorse. "I feel ashamed because in the Sušica camp there was myself on one side, armed and uniformed. On the other side there were women my mother's age, children and friends I grew up with," he said. He told the court psychiatrist that he did not understand why he did what he did.

—

Srebrenica lies at the end of a two-lane highway that winds through villages where the living is subsistence at best: cabbages grow on hardscrabble lots; sheep and a few pigs snuffle about for food. Today is a religious holiday in the Serb Orthodox religious calendar, and in some places whole pigs are being roasted on spits in the village square. Signs of devastation soon appear. The houses in the town of Konjević Polje, an execution and burial site close to Srebrenica, are still roofless, although some of the buildings have been reoccupied by their original owners who are too poor to rebuild. Smoke rises from a partial chimney in a half-demolished structure; there is, apparently, one intact room that can be heated against the November cold. At the intersection of two streets is an Orthodox church that was recently constructed on the land of a former Muslim resident. Just weeks before there had been a violent clash at this spot: a group of Serbs had arrived with a priest to hold a service; a riot broke out; and approximately fifty Muslims and fifty Serbs had fought each other with fists, rocks and clubs.

We have reached Bratunac, Ratko Mladić's command centre during the Srebrenica siege. (The general was often rumoured to be hiding here under the protective wing of his sympathizers.) This municipality was also the place from which *Muslim* forces, led by Naser Orić, attacked twenty-two surrounding Serb villages in 1992, killing at least six hundred people.

The war in Bosnia was, above all, a war against civilians, a fratricidal war among former friends. The major difference was proportionality. The Serbs vastly outnumbered the Bosniak Muslims, and they were equipped with up-to-date armaments provided by Serbia and, to a lesser extent, Russia. The Bosniaks were under an arms embargo. But in no way did lack of proportionality excuse crimes against civilians. Naser Orić was arrested by NATO in April 2003 and transferred to The Hague.[20]

Close to Bratunac is the infamous Potočari warehouse. Its walls are still riddled with bullet holes. A now ironic-looking Red Cross sign sits forlornly in one of the windows. A UN poster decorates another. As a citizen of a Western country, I feel shame in this woeful place.

—

Srebrenica hugs the border with Serbia, which lies just over the next mountain. The town is largely destroyed; international money for rebuilding Bosnia seems not to have been directed here. Every wall has been shot to pieces; almost no one is in the streets.

Nura and Ahmet Begović used to own two houses, one in the centre of the town and another in a small hamlet a few kilometres away. He worked for a transportation company and earned a good living. They and their two daughters survived the siege and the killings, and now they have returned to live in the second home, which they have partially rebuilt.

They step outside to greet us as we pull up in front of their house. They're a couple in early middle age (he is fifty-two; she is forty-seven) and look relatively healthy: He is ruddy-faced from outdoor labour, although he is still thin nine years after his ordeal. They live in two rooms of what was once a large three-room house. I step into a tiny hall and kitchen; a small bathroom opens off this room, but there has been no water for several days. The weather is cold, but it's not much warmer indoors. The cooking stove is being used to heat wood; food is prepared in a microwave oven on the days when there is electricity.

Nidžara and I are ushered into an adjoining room furnished with a couch and a mattress that is stored against the wall during the daytime; on the floor is a striking, multicoloured Bosnian rug woven by Nura herself. I have brought them chocolates, a treat they probably cannot afford to buy. They, in turn, offer coffee and homemade slivowitz. The alcohol tastes deliciously of plums, but it is the strongest drink I have ever swallowed. My throat burns, seizes and contracts in violent complaint.

Nura and her two girls escaped to Tuzla at the end of March 1993, before the roads out of Srebrenica were cut off in April. The Serbs had been shooting from the hills above their home, and the children were waking at night, crying with hunger. They left on a UNPROFOR truck, but the presence of the United Nations did not deter the roadblocks in Bratunac and other Serb-controlled territory, nor did it prevent Serbian men from mounting the truck and removing people at will. Nura froze with fear for her daughters; rumours of rape camps had swirled though Srebrenica.

Ahmet stayed in the town. Why? I ask him. His reply echoes what I have heard others say in similar circumstances. Home felt as safe as anywhere—and he didn't really believe the worst could happen. I am not surprised. I have observed that when disaster looms, a wilful blindness sometimes seizes those in imminent danger. They think that because their family has lived in this ancestral place for decades, even centuries, it is the safest spot to be; they remember that they "belong" here; that their friends live here; that they love the earth that grows their food; and that their parents or grandparents wore uniforms in the service of the territory from which they are about to be physically, or psychologically, excluded. They remember the family graves in the cemetery just down the road. They find it impossible to understand the changes taking place in front of their eyes.

Ahmet's mother was killed by a grenade that landed beside her house; he buried her in his garden, next to his beloved plum trees. On July 10, 1995, his father went to Potočari and was subsequently trucked to a killing field. As for Nura, her father died in 1993 for lack of the medication he depended on. Her mother also went to Potočari, and survived, but her son, Nura's brother, did not. He and Ahmet escaped into the mountains along with almost twenty thousand other men. Only a third of them re-emerged alive.

"I thought I'd have a better chance in the mountains," Ahmet says. "I just didn't trust the United Nations." His fear was not misplaced. The survival rate of those who chose the mountain escape route may have been a mere one in three, but only a random few returned from Potočari.

Seven male members of the family set off around midnight on July 10, 2005. One of Ahmet's aunts had made five kilos of flatbread, to which they added a few cans of food. Naturally, they took slivowitz—for warmth, for comfort and because they had heard rumours that the mountain streams had been poisoned. The Road of Death was what they called it; the fugitives had to cross the front lines of the war zone twice, and their enemies knew the mountain paths as well as they did. The trail had been mined in places; there were even spies among them who led groups of unsuspecting Muslim men to the Serb positions, where they were killed outright. (When these agents were discovered, as they sometimes were, they were murdered on the spot.) When such a person was uncovered in Ahmet's small group, he was allowed to live in exchange for information on where the Serbs were waiting. With this help, the band survived.

Tuzla was 105 kilometres away by road, but infinitely longer by mountain forest path. The journey took six days and nights, most of it without food: a grenade had landed near the man carrying their provisions, and he lost the bag. Ahmet remembers the last piece of shared bread. He had put salt on it. After that the men salted the leaves from the trees.

He was unable to sleep when it was time to rest, and by the last day he could barely walk or see: the world seemed to be shrouded in a bluish fog. What he and the others did know was that they were travelling in the right direction, but before entering Muslim-held Tuzla, and safety, they would have to cross a road that was the front line. It was night and raining hard, but fortunately the rain turned to hail, and the shooters' visibility was reduced, their bullets often falling off the mark. Some in Ahmet's group were hit, but the others pushed on. "There was nowhere else to go; the rest of us could not stop," he recalls in a hoarse, emotional voice. "Tuzla lay on the other side of a final hill. We crawled on our bellies. There was shooting. Only a few of us made it over the top."

He was reunited with his wife and children in a Tuzla refugee centre.

His face is flushed with the strain of remembering this ordeal. "How did you keep going?" I ask.

"Jokes," he replies, laughing. "At least at first, when we had the most strength."

"Can you imagine a day when you will be friends again with your neighbours?" I ask them both.

"For the moment we get along by not talking much to each other," says Nura, "but I don't think we will ever be friends again. Personally, I will try to have a normal relationship with them as time passes, but it will depend on whether they can accept the reality of what happened here. It is not really possible for a tiny place like Bosnia to be ethnically divided; we are all aware of that, I think, and we know that we will eventually have to live together again. But we have no stable state institutions here, and you can still find people who are war criminals everywhere, even in the police force. If friendship is ever possible it will only be after the criminals are sent to prison. Especially Karadžić and Mladić.

"I knew Momir Nikolić from childhood, and I would never, ever have thought he was the sort of person who could kill somebody. I can only think that the propaganda from Milošević was in their heads—that they were promised they would live only with Serbs in an expanded Serbia."

"What do you think of Naser Orić? He's been charged with war crimes and taken to The Hague."

"I *know* he is not a killer, so I will protect him!" she replies with anger in her voice. "He was brave enough to stand up in front of us and say, 'Let's defend ourselves!'"

"So you don't believe he might have committed war crimes?"

"No, I don't believe it."

It is raining and getting dark again. Evening falls early in the shortened days of autumn, and Nidžara is anxious about the long night drive back to Sarajevo along the only road. We take our leave.

I think about how painful it is to admit that members of one's own group—one's defenders, that is—might have crossed the line, might have committed atrocities; but Bosnian Serbs and Croats also lost family members during the war, although the numbers of their dead were considerably lower. There would be no reconciliation until the Muslims also acknowledged that crimes were committed against others in their name.

My mind strays to an essay by Susan Dwyer, a professor of philosophy at the University of Maryland (Baltimore County), who wrote that before anything even approaching "reconciliation" can take place in the aftermath of war, the "narratives" told by former enemies must become compatible.[21] What she meant was that in order to understand, then to accept, the past, the peoples of this war-torn region would have to agree to a joint, truthful narrative about what had happened here. Historians and other researchers were grappling with this problem. Between 2001 and 2007, Purdue University history professor Charles Ingrao directed the "Scholars Initiative," in which 250 experts from the Balkans, Europe, and the US laboured to dispel the heroic patriotic myths that surrounded the Yugoslav catastrophe: the intractable historical misrepresentations that made it possible for one ICTY indictee, Simo Drljača, to say, "You have your facts. We have our facts. You have a complete right to choose between the two versions."[22] Perhaps the first glimmerings of shared understanding would emerge from a truth and reconciliation commission, when the time was right. This idea was currently being promoted by Jakob Finci, the president of the Citizens' Association for Truth and Reconciliation in Bosnia. Such commissions were quite successful at revealing the facts of a conflict, although reconciliation was far more complex.

Bosnians will certainly require multiple acts of "justice" to bring normality back to their lives. Justice, as a precursor to reconciliation, will mean confronting the impunity of the war criminals who still walk the streets and serve in public office; it means holding criminal trials in local, as well as international, courts—something that the ICTY was beginning to do by transferring some of its lower-level cases to a new tribunal in Sarajevo;[23] it means a possible truth and reconciliation commission with the right mix of carrot and stick incentives to produce salutary confessions from the perpetrators, which just might, in turn, lead to expressions of remorse—although for-giveness on the part of the victims may be too much to ask; it means discovering, then identifying, the thousands of bodies still lying in mass burial sites, for only when they have reburied a child or a parent with dignity will the families be able to grieve normally. Farther down the road, justice and reconcilia-tion may also come from grassroots initiatives such as the one being conducted by Branko Todorović, the head of the Helsinki Committee for Human Rights in Republika Srpska. A gentle, brave man (and a frequent recipient of death threats), he brings children from all the so-called ethnicities to play camps where they are taught basic principles of tolerance and rights. Justice and open mindedness may emerge, eventually, from an integrated school system where racist language and behaviour are declared to be off limits.

Realistically, it may be a generation or more before the peoples of Bosnia can be "reconciled"—before they trust one another again. The court in The Hague is but a tiny piece in the large, puzzling question mark that hangs over the future of Bosnia and Herzegovina.

—

I discovered Refik Hodžić by chance while browsing the Internet, where I found a transcript of a press conference he had held in Mostar, Bosnia, on November 27, 2002, in which he introduced himself to the people of the town. "I am the coordinator of the ICTY Outreach Program for the BiH [Bosnia and Herzegovina] Office," he told the people who came to hear him. "Our objective is to bring the work of the ICTY closer to the people. . . . We hope to be here every Wednesday . . . to give you an opportunity to find out what is happening at the ICTY and to answer all your questions regarding [its] work. . . . I have brought a small brochure with contact details about our office in Sarajevo. Let me also give you my cellphone number, at which you can contact me any time of day." Two years later, we would meet in a Sarajevo hotel. By then, he had quit his job with the ICTY out of frustration and was preparing a documentary film titled *Blind Justice*.

He was thirty-two and intense-looking—a man with an exceptional command of English and a lot to say about nation building in his native Bosnia. He thought it had been a flop. Elections were held before nationalist tensions had been defused, meaning that known extremists were voted into office. Police reform was a joke—corruption was rampant: war criminals, convicted or otherwise, often held top positions. The education system still favoured ethnic separateness: children from different groups made contact only when they insulted one another and fought in the schoolyard. There was no commitment to facing the past anywhere in the country. At the time of our meeting in late 2004 there had not yet been one local indictment of a war criminal to be tried in a local court.[24] Among the Serbs, there was outright denial of criminality; among the Bosniaks was razor-edged bitterness. And while it was true that hate speech had been outlawed by the international overseers (something to be thankful for), the country was still "at war"—not physically, perhaps, but psychologically.

Refik Hodžić's greatest disappointment was the ICTY's failure to communicate its work. For the first seven years of the tribunal's existence (between 1993 and 2000) there had been no formal outreach into the survivor communities of Bosnia, on whose behalf the court's proceedings were purportedly taking place. The victims were called as witnesses, then their usefulness ended. "It was the year 2000 before the first press release was issued in the language of the region," he says. "During those years the media from the different parts of the former Yugoslavia had a field day distorting the news and disseminating propaganda. They were controlled by people who had an interest in undermining the tribunal. On the Serb side, the favoured line was that the ICTY was anti-Serb, that its sole purpose was to punish Serb people and that it was a tool of the Americans, who wanted to subjugate small nations. The Croats under Tudjman were led to believe that the tribunal was there to undermine the legitimacy of their independence; and the Bosniaks believed the tribunal had been set up to prosecute only those who had committed crimes against *them*. They were convinced that the ethnic group with the largest number of victims could not be responsible for war crimes. How can you commit war crimes when you are defending yourself?"

By the time the Outreach Office got going, it was late. People already had a distorted picture of the tribunal's work, and there was no point talking to them about legal concepts such as "crimes against humanity." They couldn't care less. What mattered was "justice"—and as far as they were concerned, that meant seeing the incarceration of the neighbour who had raped, starved or tortured them in prison camps; who had murdered members of their families before their eyes, and who might now be a senior officer in the police force.

"The sentencing policy of the tribunal has also caused a lot of damage. People here don't understand plea bargaining. If someone is convicted of killing five people and gets eight years, they can't understand that. They think the ICTY is politicized."

I remember my conversation with Emir Suljagić: "There have to be standards!" he had shouted angrily over the noise in the café. "You cannot tell me that sentencing Obrenović to eight years for the five murders he pleaded guilty to is fair or just. First they sentenced [Timohir] Blaškić to forty-six years, then Krstić to thirty-five; then they reduced Blaškić to nine years and sent Biljana Plavšić away for eleven. What the hell is going on there? I'm confused, and I was *there* [at the ICTY] for two years!"

"Has the ICTY failed the survivors?" I ask Hodžić. He looks away for a moment. "That's the question of questions," he replies finally. "I think I must say, yes. Because of the tribunal's failure to communicate with them. Because they were never part of the process. I finally left the tribunal because it did not fulfill its mission in terms of contributing to reconciliation, even in terms of deterring further crimes. On the other hand it has been very successful in ending the culture of impunity. Until the tribunal was created, everybody in Bosnia believed that what happens in war just happens. If you really go overboard and kill, I don't know, maybe 300,000 people, then you may be arrested and tried; but basically that will only happen if you lose the war. If you win, you will never be tried.

"But the ICTY reversed that. You *can* be tried for war crimes. That is the tribunal's great achievement. The attack on impunity will be its outstanding legacy."

So the very existence of the court had had an effect. The *principle* of accountability could shift the culture of a lawless place even if some of the perpetrators still walked the streets of their towns. It was far from ideal, far from the vision of perfect justice that filled the dreams of some of the people who had worked so hard to build the international courts, including the International Criminal Court. It was the real world—and in that gritty place a little progress could be a lot.

ELEVEN

The Making of the ICC

T he framers of the International Criminal Court understood the concerns of Refik Hodžić. Never again would the survivors of atrocities be "used" (in Refik's charged words) as witnesses, then virtually ignored. It helped that by the mid-1990s, when the preparatory work for the new court took on a serious cast, human rights had become newly prominent. The televised faces of Bosnian prisoners; the failure of the United Nations in Srebrenica and in Rwanda; the visible pleasure of Slobodan Milošević as he toyed with international diplomats at the Rambouillet negotiations for peace in February 1999, and his subsequent attacks on the Albanians in Kosovo—these international embarrassments had culminated in the NATO bombings of Kosovo and Serbia in 1999, the first military intervention ever undertaken to save civilians from their own sovereign government.

A long, rocky path had led to the creation of the world's first permanent, international criminal court.[1] The first known trial for acts that would later be called "crimes against humanity" took place in the early 1470s after Charles the Bold, Duke of Burgundy (known to his enemies as Charles the Terrible) appointed his deputy, Peter von Hagenbach, governor of the Rhineland city of Breisach, with orders to subdue the population. Von Hagenbach was happy to comply, cheerfully imposing a regime of brutality that included murder, rape, the confiscation of property and a taxation policy designed to fill his personal coffers. Disturbingly, his instructions to his soldiers foreshadowed those issued at Srebrenica more than five hundred years later: "Kill the men in every house so the women and children will be at my mercy,"[2] he commanded. Still dissatisfied, he expanded his reign of terror to the bordering territories, carrying out bold attacks on Swiss merchants who happened to be passing through.

By 1474 a coalition of outraged warrior-knights from Austria, France, Bern and the Upper Rhine had had enough; they defeated von Hagenbach and his ambitious ducal patron in an ordinary-enough battlefield skirmish, but following this military victory, something entirely unprecedented took place. Sigismund, the powerful archduke of Austria, insisted that Peter von Hagenbach be tried in a court of justice for his crimes.

On May 9, 1474, twenty-eight stony-faced aristocrats from Alsace, the Rhinelands and Switzerland convened in a special tribunal that had been created for the occasion, and when all was quiet, Sigismund's judicial representative rose to his feet to face the accused. "Peter von Hagenbach has trampled under foot the laws of God and man," he thundered—charging the defendant with murder, rape, perjury and an assortment of other crimes.

Von Hagenbach didn't bother denying his offences: they were obvious to everyone. His only recourse was to "superior orders"—the plea that was adopted by the Nazi defendants at Nuremberg half a millennium later and is still heard today. He even had a lawyer, who stated archly, "Sir Peter von Hagenbach does not recognize any other judge and master but the duke of Burgundy! Is it not known that soldiers owe absolute obedience to their superiors?"

The defendant requested an adjournment so that the veracity of the duke of Burgundy's orders to him could be confirmed, but the tribunal refused. The defence of superior orders, they said, was "contrary to the laws of God." Furthermore, his crimes had been established beyond any doubt.

He was found guilty, symbolically deprived of his knighthood and quickly dispatched to the next world, but the judges took care to explain their verdict: Peter von Hagenbach had countenanced crimes that he had a duty to prevent, they said. Whether or not the governor had personally committed any of the crimes in question was irrelevant. He had ordered others to do so.

"Let justice be done," trumpeted the marshal of the tribunal as the prisoner was led away.

—

The trial of Peter von Hagenbach turned out to be an isolated event; as we have seen, it wasn't until the nineteenth century that attempts to codify war law began in earnest, and it was the mid-twentieth century before another international criminal trial took place. One can only guess whether there might have been other such tribunals, because in 1648 the Peace of Westphalia, the famous treaty that ended the Thirty Years War, determined that the sovereign nation-state would henceforth represent the highest level of international governance, subservient to no other. Few treaties have affected the world more profoundly; for more than three hundred years, the model of the absolutely sovereign nation-state ruled the international order with a ferocious, almost religious, intensity.

Until recently. After centuries of internecine strife interspersed with the occasional insight that life in Europe might be better all around if the many parts of the whole combined, at least concerning matters of trade, the first tentative sprouts of "supra-nationalism" appeared on the continent. Determined to redirect history, the ten founding signatories to the May 1949 Treaty of London—Belgium, Denmark, France, the Republic of Ireland, Italy, Luxembourg, Netherlands, Norway, Sweden and the United Kingdom—founded the Council of Europe, with the aim of achieving "a greater unity between its members for the purpose of safeguarding and realizing the ideals and principles that are their common heritage and facilitating their economic and social progress."[3] National defence was deliberately excluded: no one planned to surrender that option just yet; but the Council did oblige its members to protect human rights and the rule of law.*

The radical idea of "Europe" was an early signpost along a road that has, with twists and turns, bent away from the eternal verities of Westphalia. By the 1980s, supranationalism defined the interlocking spheres of economic globalism, where critical decisions affecting the financial life of nations were taken not by national governments but by international bodies, thus altering the traditional economic practices of many a bordered state. On the judicial front, supranationalism

---

* Everyone was wary of Germany (including many Germans who feared their own countrymen), but when the Federal Republic legislated a new constitution in 1949, which opened with a statement of unconditional individual rights and strictly curtailed the possibility of overly centralized power, it was admitted to the council, in 1951.

embedded itself in the legal details of the Rome Statute of the International Criminal Court. Political opposition to absolute sovereignty was also on the rise. In 1998, at a conference specifically convened to discuss the continuing relevance of Westphalia, NATO Secretary General Javier Solana struck a brazenly contradictory note: "Humanity and democracy [are] two principles essentially irrelevant to the original Westphalian order. . . . The principle of sovereignty . . . produced the basis for rivalry, not community of states; exclusion, not integration. Further, the idea of a strong, sovereign state was later draped with nationalistic fervour that degenerated into a destructive political force. The stability of this system could only be maintained by constantly shifting alliances, cordial and not-so-cordial ententes, and secret agreements. In the end, it was a system that could not guarantee peace. Nor did it prevent war, as the history of the last three centuries has so tragically demonstrated."[4] (It is worth noting that Solana delivered this startling epitaph in the past tense.)

Two years later, the German foreign minister, Joschka Fischer, announced that the system of politics set up by Westphalia had already become obsolete in Europe. "The core of the concept of Europe after 1945 was, and is still, a rejection of the European balance-of-power principle and the hegemonic ambitions of the individual states that emerged following the Peace of Westphalia in 1648, a rejection which took the form of closer meshing of vital interests and the transfer of nation-state sovereign rights to supranational European institutions," he argued in a speech at Humboldt University in Berlin.[5] For obvious historical reasons, Germany had passionately embraced the new Europe. Everyone in the audience that day understood what Fischer meant. His phrase, "the hegemonic ambitions of individual states," needed no elaborating.

This is not to suggest that the traditional nation-state, the repository of culture and national identity, was on the wane at the end of the twentieth century. The nation-state remained the core of the international system, and mistaking the power of nationalist loyalties could lead to serious errors in judgment (as Robert S. McNamara knew better than anyone). America was a powerful proponent of its own unbreachable Westphalian sovereignty—although not necessarily for others.

New ideas emerge over time like small ocean waves. At first they are more or less equal in size and importance; then, as the wind picks up, they may compete for prominence until one of them rises above the rest. In the early twenty-first century, the challenge to Westphalia was clearly visible, but the roiling epicentre was still well offshore. There had long been conflicting trends; for example, the crushing military defeat of Germany after the Great War had both strengthened the core of the nation-state (at the Versailles Peace Conference of 1919 national borders were so altered that large numbers of people born in one country woke up to find themselves living in another) *and* reopened the possibility of supranational criminal justice for the first time in centuries (although nothing came of a bid to try the German kaiser). In 1934, another political crisis rekindled the desire for an international criminal court to condemn individual perpetrators: King Alexander of Yugoslavia was assassinated by a Macedonian nationalist, reminding the world that the murder of Archduke Ferdinand by a Serb nationalist just twenty years earlier had ignited a global conflagration. France asked the League of Nations to draft an international penal code to properly criminalize such assassinations and to create an international court to condemn and punish "terrorists."[6] The league complied, and by late 1937 the two draft documents—the Convention for the Prevention and Punishment of Terrorism and the Convention for the Creation of an International Criminal Court—were ready. But the Terrorism

Convention received only one national ratification (from India), while the convention for an international criminal court received none. (After sober second thoughts, the member states of the league may have remembered that the jurisdiction of such a tribunal would also cover them.) Political crises also played a role in this failure: Hitler was elected German chancellor in 1933, Italy had invaded Abyssinia (now Ethopia) in 1935 and the Spanish Civil War showed no signs of abating.

—

Then there was genocide—Hitler's genocide—an act that was not new but had never before been named. When the United Nations approved the Genocide Convention on December 9, 1948, it borrowed the term from a Polish-Jewish lawyer named Raphael Lemkin. In the 1930s, wary of escalating anti-Semitism in his country, Lemkin had presciently explored Turkey's ruthless destruction of its Armenian minority between 1915 and 1917, struggling for a definition of this assault on men, women and children. He was not alone in his confusion: in August 1941, as millions of Russian Jews were being exterminated by German troops, Winston Churchill spoke of "[the] crime without a name."[7] In desperation Lemkin wrote a book describing the destruction of the Jews and other minorities in Europe as well as the subject that had been his obsession for more than a decade: What should one call such murderous events?[8]

   He decided on "genocide"—a neologism that combined the Greek word *genos*, meaning a people, or nation, with the Latin-based suffix "cide," meaning killing (as in "patricide" or "infanticide"). Genocide, in legal parlance, was "the planned annihilation of a people, in whole or in part," and/or "a coordinated plan of different actions aiming at the destruction of the essential foundations of the life of national groups, with the aim of annihilating the groups themselves."

Lemkin was laughed at when his book appeared in 1944; no one believed that the fate of the Armenians could ever be duplicated in the advanced societies of the West. But as the Second World War drew to an end and the opening of the landmark Nuremberg trials loomed, Lemkin knew his time-frame was short. What the Nazis had done to the Jews was, he believed, "genocide"—but he was only partly successful in having his concept included at Nuremberg. The crime of genocide was folded into "crimes against humanity" without being independently named in the lexicon of the tribunal's indictable offences.

Although the Genocide Convention was eventually added to the glossary of international law by the United Nations, the interest in Lemkin's breakthrough concept waned. As the freeze of the Cold War deepened, international priorities shifted—and the man whose exceptional contribution to our understanding of "the crime of crimes" was ignored. When Raphael Lemkin died in 1959, lonely and disappointed, only seven people stood at his graveside.

The Genocide Convention was just one of several determined attempts to prevent the rise of another Hitler. On December 10, 1948—just one day after the convention had been adopted—the United Nations General Assembly passed the Universal Declaration of Human Rights, a document that sprang directly from the philosophical *Weltanschauung* of the eighteenth-century German thinker Immanuel Kant, for whom every person has intrinsic value simply by virtue of being human. In 1946, during the first session of the United Nations General Assembly, the United States sponsored a resolution affirming "the principles of international law recognized by the Charter of the Nuremberg Tribunal and the judgment of the Tribunal,"[9] and in 1947 the world organization created the forerunner of the International Law Commission (ILC), a body mandated to prepare "a draft code of offenses against the peace and security of mankind" as well as a draft statute for a permanent international criminal court. The Nuremberg trials were still in session (they ended in 1949). They were in the news and on everybody's mind.

The very idea of an international law commission was radical, but because Nuremberg had codified new laws (and new crimes), the prospect of an international order based on global law now seemed possible. In 1950, the ILC duly reported to the General Assembly that an international criminal court *was* achievable, even desirable; however, the commissioners added, it was "not practicable." What did they mean? They were alluding to political reality. Translated into plain language, what they said was, Yes, it would be possible to create an international criminal court, and it might even be a good idea; on the other hand, there is a war raging on the Korean peninsula and Cold War politics, as well as Westphalian national sovereignty, will stand in the way.

The ILC committees went back to the drawing board, reporting to the General Assembly from time to time over the decade of the 1950s—but the end result was always the same. As the Cold War grew ever more intractable, the likelihood of an international court grew more remote. The time was never quite ripe. Among the permanent members of the Security Council, only France fully supported the creation of an international criminal court. Britain thought the idea was excellent, but only in theory. As for the superpowers, both Russia and America were virulently opposed. Stalin was preoccupied with internal purges, show trials and "disappearing" people into the gulag. An international criminal court would scarcely serve his purposes. The United States refused even to entertain the prospect of an independent criminal tribunal while glaring across the Cold War divide.

At the core of the hesitation (or, more accurately, the rejection) lay the problem of finding an acceptable definition of the crime of "aggression," since no power would agree to be subject to international law if that meant putting aside its perceived interests. Alarmed that an excess of enthusiasm for international criminal law and justice might affect their right to act as they pleased, the sovereign nations of the UN General Assembly repeatedly sent the drafting committees away with new instructions, only to rebuff them each time they reported back. What the committees included in their reports was always unacceptable; what they did not include *ought* to have been included . . . and so it went, until the dual process of defining a code of international crimes and establishing an international criminal court sank in the bureaucratic quicksand. It was 1974 before the General Assembly formally agreed to look seriously at a revised draft code of the same criminal offences that had initially been brought forward in the 1950s—and 1978 before it agreed to look again at a draft statute for an international criminal court.

In 1981 (after several more years of contemplation) the General Assembly once again invited the International Law Commission to study the proposed code of criminal offences for a possible international court—this time in the light of new developments in law over the preceding half-century. But without the intervention of Arthur Robinson a full eight years later (he who was lauded at the inauguration of the ICC), it is hard to imagine that the decades-long charade might have ended. Robinson, then the prime minister of Trinidad and Tobago, wanted the International Law Commission to explore something new. Would it be possible to create an international criminal court that could prosecute transnational drug running, he wanted to know. Narco-trafficking threatened to overwhelm his country. The United States perked up; its government was interested in the drug issue. The UN agreed. (Cherif Bassiouni thinks this, too, was a politically motivated gesture. "At the time Amoco Oil Company was negotiating with Trinidad and Tobago for an oil concession and Secretary [James] Baker did not want to embarrass Robinson," he recalled.)[10]

Other events contributed to the revived interest in an international court. The Berlin Wall crumbled in 1989 (the year Arthur Robinson made his critical proposal), signalling the imminent end of the long Soviet experiment—and, it must be added, the release of Pandora's myriad evils from their Cold War container. By 1993 it was impossible to deny that atrocities reminiscent of the Nazis' were once again being committed on European soil. That same year, the United Nations was virtually coerced into creating the ICTY: the world body had failed to stop the unfolding catastrophe in Yugoslavia and now had no other options. The same had happened for Rwanda: the UN created the ICTR in 1994, after having failed to pay attention to the signs of impending genocide. Both these dedicated tribunals had underlying statutes that clearly described the core crimes that came under their jurisdiction—and they were, in essence, the offences that had been defined at Nuremberg: crimes against humanity, including genocide; violations of the laws or customs of war; and "grave breaches" of the Four Geneva Conventions. The UN member states were aware (as was everyone who had suffered through the long-drawn-out farce of the continually rejected recommendations of the International Law Commission) that it would now appear absurd *not* to adopt a code of international crimes while two UN-mandated international courts were effectively prosecuting them, even as they debated the subject in New York.

Instead of limiting itself to the question of drug trafficking, the International Law Commission prepared a comprehensive draft statute for an international criminal court. It delivered its preliminary report to the General Assembly in 1992, then submitted more precise documents in 1993 and 1994—this time recommending that a conference to establish a permanent tribunal be convened. The General Assembly agreed to ask a legal committee to review the issues and a preparatory committee to carry the work forward. And so it happened that in 1997, after a half-century of waffling, prevarication and dedicated work on the part of the International Law Commission, the United Nations voted to hold a "conference of plenipotentiaries" in Rome to hammer out a formal statute for a permanent international criminal court. There had been no overreaching rational plan. The light had changed from red to green by pure serendipity after a coincidental confluence of political events finally drove the world body to act.

William Pace, the head of the NGO Coalition for an International Criminal Court, has his own theory about this unanticipated success. "I suspect the General Assembly thought nothing much would come of the International Law Commission's 1994 draft statute," he told me when we met in his New York office. "The legal committee is the place you send things when you want them to disappear on a shelf or behind polite words. The permanent members of the UN were pretty sure that the differences between the civil law countries, the common law countries, the Arabs and the Asians, *and* the realization that this was a court that could theoretically arrest your political leaders, would become so obvious that the idea would go nowhere. Everyone expected the legal committee to back off and defend sovereignty. Instead, the draft statute for an ICC actually caught fire in that committee. I think what happened is that a bunch of young legal advisers with no instructions from their governments, and a few senior legal advisers who were at the end of their careers, came together . . . and said, 'Let's see if we can't make this work.' My personal theory is that this was a reflection of ongoing globalization in terms of democracy and justice and the rule of law in the world. So instead of pulling the draft statute apart, they started putting something together, and somehow their work went under the radar of the political powers who were sure this would go away." (It was true that politics was never far from view. In 1995 the United States and China still thought the political climate in support of an international criminal court had not sufficiently "matured.")

The preparatory committee, expertly chaired by Adriaan Bos, a lecturer at the Hague Academy of International Law and a legal adviser to the Netherlands Ministry of Foreign Affairs, met six times between 1996 and 1998, trying to resolve contentious issues in the draft ICC statute. How far would the court's jurisdiction extend? Would its reach be confined to perpetrators who were citizens of countries that had joined the ICC as States Parties? Or would it be "universal," meaning every nation in the world would be covered? Under existing international law, as we have seen, states already had the theoretical right to prosecute any perpetrator of the core crimes who was arrested on their territory, although some needed to make changes in their domestic legislation so this could happen. As if these questions weren't tricky enough, the committee also had to grapple with what would, or could, "trigger" an ICC prosecution. Would investigations be launched by a request from a particular government, say, that of an African country with an out-of-control insurgency? By a referral from the Security Council? By an autonomous, independent ICC prosecutor? Or by a referral from an NGO? There was also the sticky question of the Security Council itself. Should its members have a veto over individual prosecutions? (This was a key demand of the Americans since it would allow them to reject cases.) And what about "complementarity," which would allow a state to try an accused perpetrator on trial at home, thus avoiding an ICC indictment altogether? Finally, what about the old bugbear of "aggression?" There had never been agreement on the definition, for obvious reasons: powerful countries did not want to be hamstrung.[11]

Between 1995 and 1998, a coalition of middle and small powers known as the "Like-Minded" helped pave the way.[†] Spearheaded by Canada—a country with a history of backing multilateralism—and informally headquartered at the Canadian UN mission, the Like-Minded countries initiated critical discussions with other states and with the international non-governmental organizations (NGOs), who played an important role in the creation of the court.[12] But the central issues in the ICC statute remained controversial, at every level. "There was no real agreement on any of these subjects," recalled Jon Allen, a career diplomat in Canada's foreign service who headed the Canadian delegation to the preparatory committee. "There was a tug-of-war between the military types, who were the people most likely to be prosecuted [for war crimes], and the human rights types, who were pushing for universal jurisdiction and law that applied equally to all. When the process ended, there were still lots of unresolved issues in 'square brackets.'"[13]

The preparatory committee and the Like-Minded states went as far as they were able: the next step would have to be a diplomatic conference to hammer out the language of the treaty. It was hard to believe that the efforts to consolidate and anchor the work of the Nuremberg Tribunal in a permanent international criminal court might bear fruit at last.

—

[†] Australia, Austria, Argentina, Belgium, Canada, Chile, Croatia, Denmark, Egypt, Finland, Germany, Guatemala, Hungary, Ireland, Italy, Lesotho, The Netherlands, New Zealand, Norway, Portugal, Samoa, Slovakia, South Africa, Sweden, Trinidad and Tobago (representing twelve Caricom states), Uruguay and Venezuela.

Had it not been for the *fin de siècle* re-emergence of "international civil society"—an unplanned offshoot of globalization—the entire enterprise might still have come to nothing. In its original market-oriented incarnation, globalization had already changed the world. There were economic advantages to borderless trade, but the demands of supranational bodies such as the World Trade Organization, which provided help with debt relief and restructuring, often interfered with the ability of weaker states to provide economic and social justice to their own citizens on their own terms. Global civil society—loose networks of activists who lobbied in the service of their respective interests—had emerged as a partial antidote to the top-down fiat of the older international bodies by promoting rights, especially human rights. Like their counterparts in global commerce, they operated in cyberspace. Ideas were transmitted across continents with a click of the index finger, organizational plans bypassed the formal structures of states, and policies that might have taken years to implement using conventional routes and institutions were effected in record-breaking time.

Non-governmental organizations had been making headlines since the 1992 Earth Summit in Rio, the first international meeting to address urgent problems of environmental protection. The conference had accredited fifteen hundred separate groups, and their proposals had breathed life into what might have been a staid event attended by cautious diplomats. Three years later, no fewer than thirty-five thousand NGO representatives attended the Fourth World Conference on Women in Beijing, where a landmark decision was taken to define rape and other forms of sexual violence committed during warfare as crimes against humanity. The most stunning success to date has been the global campaign to ban the use of anti-personnel land mines. When the 1997 UN Conference on Disarmament failed to reach an agreement to ban the production, sale and use of these devices, a coalition of NGOs and interested states had banded together. The result was the Ottawa Process, the most quickly negotiated treaty in the history of international diplomacy.

So it happened that in June 1998, Pace's Coalition for an International Criminal Court helped to midwife the birth of the institution that had been talked about for almost a century and thwarted for almost as long. Of the tens of thousands of international NGOs then operating in the world, few were more effective than his CICC, a network of eight hundred organizations spanning the globe. Pace had once been the president of the World Federalist Movement, an organization whose very name dismayed sovereignists. The WFM had been calling for world government based on international law and accountable global institutions since 1937. Its members had rejoiced in 1945 at the foundation of the United Nations, and again at the federative experiment of the European Union, which they saw as a signpost to the future of the international order. They had been marginalized as woolly-headed idealists during the years leading up to the Second World War and throughout the Cold War standoff, but in the reconfigured, globally wired world of the 1990s they had started to come into their own.

It was worry that drove Pace to put together his coalition. When the draft statute for an international criminal court was dispatched to the legal committee of the General Assembly in 1994, he began to be alarmed. The World Federalists had been monitoring the issue: they understood that the legal committee could make or break the ICC and that any plans that emerged might be dumped on the "unwanted" shelf and sit there for years. "We wanted to prepare ourselves for the upcoming debate in the General Assembly, so Christopher Hall from Amnesty International in the UK, myself and a handful of other people organized our own meeting on February 10, 1995, right across from the

UN building. We had representatives from about thirty interested groups, and by the time we finished talking we had formed our Coalition.

"But *none* of us predicted that this [the creation of the ICC] would happen so quickly. We were thinking ten years at the earliest, maybe twenty or fifty or even a hundred years! When I agreed to take on the directorship of the coalition, dozens of people said to me, 'Bill, this is important, keep doing it, but you know, it's not going to happen in your lifetime or your children's lifetime or your grandchildren's lifetime.'"

—

On June 15, 1998, five thousand representatives from 160 states gathered in Rome for a diplomatic conference that would, they hoped, bring a permanent international criminal court into existence. The meeting was sponsored by the United Nations (although the future court would be independent of the world body); the mandate of the delegates was to negotiate a multilateral treaty. The time allotted (for financial reasons) was just five weeks—an exceptionally short period, considering the daunting level of detail that needed to be distilled and debated, the need to coordinate different legal systems and the fact that many of the participants were diplomats with little if any background in law.

UN Secretary-General Kofi Annan was the first to speak at the opening session, and he did not mince words. "Our own century has seen the invention and use of weapons of mass destruction and the use of industrial technology to dispose of millions upon millions of human lives," he told the delegates in his unique soft voice. "Gradually the world has come to realize that relying on each state or army to punish its own transgressors is not enough. When crimes are committed on such a scale, we know that the state lacks either the power or the will to stop them. Too often [the crimes] are part of a systematic state policy, and the worst criminals may be found at the pinnacle of state power."

He was equally blunt about the roadblocks that had delayed this historic moment. "Humanity had to wait until the 1990s for a political climate in which the United Nations could once again consider establishing an international criminal court. . . . People all over the world want to know that humanity can strike back—that wherever and whenever genocide, war crimes or other such violations are committed, there is a court before which the criminal can be held to account; a court that puts an end to a global culture of impunity; a court where "acting under orders" is no defence; a court where all individuals in a government hierarchy or military chain of command, without exception, from rulers to private soldiers, must answer for their actions. . . ."

Then he addressed the apprehension everyone felt. "I do not underestimate the difficulties you have to overcome in the five weeks ahead. . . . Some small states fear giving pretexts for more powerful ones to [challenge] their sovereignty. Others worry that the pursuit of justice may sometimes interfere with the vital work of making peace. You have to take those worries into account. . . . But the overriding interest must be that of the victims, and of the international community as a whole. I trust you will not flinch from creating a court strong and independent enough to carry out its task. It must be an instrument of justice, not expediency. It must be able to protect the weak against the strong. . . . [Succeeding generations] will not forgive us if we fail."

There was a stunned silence in the room as the secretary-general stepped down from the podium, followed by sustained applause. All those who spoke on behalf of their governments and constituencies that day noted the historic nature of the moment. Some, like Dullah Omar, then the justice minister for South Africa, referred to the deadly conflicts ravaging the African continent and the urgent need for justice.[14] His own country had only recently emerged from the darkness of apartheid, and like every non-white who had lived under that system he had personal knowledge of human rights violations. (In 1996, he had told me about a botched, state-instigated plan to poison him.)

Tony Lloyd of the United Kingdom, who spoke on behalf of the European Union, noted that 1998 marked the fiftieth anniversary of the adoption of the Universal Declaration of Human Rights and the Genocide Convention. Lloyd Axworthy, Canada's minister of foreign affairs, observed that the priorities of international relations had expanded in recent years to include the security needs of citizens—of civilians: a welcome outcome of the discussions that began at the famous nineteenth-century conferences where the laws of war were debated. (Axworthy inspired Canada's strong support for the ICC.) But it was William Pace who articulated the jitteriness that pervaded the room: the fear that the United States might try to subvert the process. "The issue is whether the majority of nations will galvanize the political will to resist those nations not ready for this court, who will attempt to block the adoption of a strong treaty, or who will attempt to create a weak and powerless court which would be subject to the control or veto of the most powerful nations . . . ," he told the delegates (who included David Scheffer, the chief negotiator for President Bill Clinton). "Will we replace the centuries-old rule of impunity with the rule of just law? . . . We cannot fail!" he finished passionately.

The caucus of Like-Minded nations was committed to ideas that might have been at odds with the general view the permanent members of the Security Council held of the court, reflected William Schabas in a later interview. The Like-Minded wanted the ICC to have *universal* jurisdiction over the core crimes of genocide, crimes against humanity and war crimes—wherever in the world they were committed; and they wanted the prosecutor of the ICC to be independent, with the power to initiate cases against individual perpetrators, rather than being a passive recipient of referrals. What they did not want was a Security Council veto on prosecutions, which would have allowed any council member to reject any case. ("You wish to arrest General Justcause from *my* law-abiding country? How absurd!") If the ICC was to become more than a showcase stage, more than a puppet theatre with strings pulled in the service of powerful state interests, it would need to resist this sort of political oversight.

There were also technical problems. Because of translation difficulties (six official languages were in play), the final text from the UN preparatory committee had not been distributed to the delegates until just weeks before the opening date. "So you've got a window of about thirty days for a lot of people in Foreign Affairs ministries and Justice ministries all over the world who may have never *heard* of this before!" Cherif Bassiouni thundered from across his desk the day we met. Bassiouni was chairman of the conference's all-important drafting committee, the person ultimately responsible for the precise wording of the statute, which described every aspect of the workings of the court and the crimes over which it held jurisdiction. "My guess is that of the five thousand delegates who came to the opening of the conference, a maximum of six hundred had read it, and maybe three hundred understood it!" he said.

Who could blame them, I wondered. With its thirteen parts and 128 articles dealing with the creation of the court and its relation to the United Nations, the statute was a challenge even to specialists in international law. To explain and negotiate in multiple languages in the hope of creating a treaty that would be acceptable to the majority of the delegates, almost all of whom were acting according to instructions from their governments, was daunting, to say the least. The twenty-five delegations that made up Bassiouni's hardworking drafting committee carried the brute weight of the conference; they translated from language to language, comparing texts to ensure that the meaning remained the same. During the final two weeks of the conference the members of this committee worked up to twelve hours a day, preparing material being submitted to them on a daily, sometimes hourly, basis.

By the end of the first week, many of the delegates were feeling pessimistic. The less informed were asking questions that had already been debated (and sometimes settled) by the preparatory committee years earlier. In the second week, a rumour that there would have to be another Rome conference, sometime, somewhere, made the rounds. Failure seemed imminent.

Philippe Kirsch was the one who turned things around. A Canadian career diplomat, he had not been involved with the ICC in its early preparatory stages, although he had had plenty of experience directing international negotiations. Just days before the conference was to open, Adriaan Bos, who was slated to chair the proceedings but had fallen ill, telephoned. Would Kirsch take over the job? Kirsch was startled; he wasn't sure it was a good idea since he hadn't been involved in prior negotiations. But Bos thought he might be the only person whom everyone would willingly accept as a substitute. Kirsch was in the middle of pleading a case between Canada and Spain before the International Court of Justice in The Hague. He thought about it; then he accepted, handed the remainder of the Canada-Spain file to his deputy and boarded the next plane to Rome. En route he studied the background and the issues.

He was concerned, to say the least. "When I saw the [draft] Statute with the 1,400 square brackets, it was . . . rich, but impossible to use as the basis for negotiations. So I thought, 'We can't work with that [text] and we can't work with square brackets, because if you try to undo each square bracket, it is impossible to do in five weeks.' So, in my first meeting in Rome with all the twelve or fifteen coordinators, I said, 'What I am really insistent on is that you . . . do the drafting yourself. You listen to what [the delegations] have to say and consider written proposals . . . , but you don't ever table a paper with square brackets.'"[15]

As rumours of impending disaster distracted the delegates from their work, Kirsch made a critical decision. He called a halt to the large sessions that were bogging down in irrelevant speechifying and opted instead for small working groups. Although this meant that a few states, or even one state, could theoretically hold up the proceedings by refusing to join a consensus reached in the smaller workshops, his judgment effectively saved the day. By the end of the second week the working groups were sending positive progress reports to what was called the Committee of the Whole, the "control centre" of the conference.

With only two weeks to go, Kirsch circulated a statement of possible options on each of the difficult outstanding issues:

• the extent of the Court's jurisdiction;

• what would, or could, "trigger" a prosecution;

• the question of a Security Council veto;

• the precise definition of the "core crimes";

• the principle of "complementarity," which would allow the home state to try an accused perpetrator, thus avoiding an ICC indictment.

Alarmingly, the list still covered just about everything. The problem was consensus. Some delegations were happy with a few of the proposals and unhappy with others; several delegates had adopted inflexible positions. The looming issue was that the draft statute would need a two-thirds majority to pass in a plenary session vote.

Back room, front room . . . the intensity escalated hourly. Some delegations had been mandated by their governments to make decisions; others had to check constantly with their bosses at home. There were major compromises over the content and language of the text, largely reflecting the desire to bring the United States on board. David Scheffer allowed that his government had major concerns: would the ICC investigate after every US military mission? The US wanted the prosecutor's reach limited to planned or large-scale war crimes. (They were successful on this front.)

On July 17, the last day, Philippe Kirsch took a calculated risk: he issued a "compromise package" in all six languages. As William Schabas later put it, he donned the cloak of "a skilled blackjack player [who] had carefully counted his cards but had no guarantee of success."[16] He hoped to sidestep deadly procedural hurdles during the final hours. His "package" would make or break consensus.

It was already evening—and at midnight (as at Cinderella's ball) one of two things would happen: the gala would end in a rousing success, or the glittering trappings of hope would fade away, perhaps for another generation. It was then that the delegates of the United States and India proposed last-minute amendments. The US insisted that the ICC's jurisdiction had to depend on whether or not the defendant's home state agreed that he or she should be indicted—a suggestion that would have effectively neutered the court's independence. For its part, India wanted two changes. First, that the use of "nuclear, chemical and biological" weapons be defined as war crimes. (It had already been agreed that these terms would not be included, but might be added by amendment at a later date.) Second, that the already established consensus to allow the

Security Council to refer situations to the ICC (though not to veto) be annulled.‡

Surprise stilled the room. Both these interventions were clearly last-ditch efforts to scuttle the adoption of the statute. After what seemed a long silence, the delegate from Norway introduced a motion to leave consideration of these two requests for a later day. This vote passed—with a massive majority.[17]

As the implications of this unexpected ballot became clear— the statute had been adopted—the delegates rose spontaneously in a standing ovation. Sophisticated men and women with years of diplomatic experience cried with joy. The "impossible" seemed to have happened—albeit in a startling way.

The clock registered 9 p.m. when Philippe Kirsch ended the session. The Committee of the Whole would meet, he said, then the delegates would reconvene for a formal confirmation.

It was not quite midnight when they reassembled, only to be confronted with yet another surprise. David Scheffer now demanded yet another vote on the statute, hoping to rally latent opposition. This time the consensus in favour was stronger still: 120 delegations voted for adoption, 7 voted against and 21 abstained.

"No one knew what was going to happen in those last hours," William Pace recalled. "When India presented a motion to amend the statute to outlaw the use of nuclear weapons, everyone knew this was not their true intent. They had just set off a nuclear weapon a few weeks before! It was an effort to wreck the treaty. When the United States proposed a motion to say that in order for a case to go forward you had

‡ The right to refer cases already gave the Security Council a role within an independent ICC; the Indian proposal would have marginalized the ICC by isolating it entirely from the core decision-making body of the United Nations.

to have the permission of the government of the nationality of the person accused, that, too, would have gutted it. When both those motions were defeated . . . I think at that moment we knew that we had won, that the governments of the nations represented in that room were going to go ahead against the United States, China, India and some other powerful countries and say, 'We're going to set this up even though they are opposed.' I've never been in an intergovernmental meeting where people started clapping and crying. The emotion was quite unbelievable, and then Philippe Kirsch, who himself was crying, just hammered it together.

"I said to my wife, who was there with me, 'My God, we've done it!' I think everyone there understood that this was one of the most important treaties ever agreed to by the international community—and that we simply had to make it work."

Hans-Peter Kaul, who headed the German delegation (and was later elected to the bench of the ICC) also recalled the moment, when he and I met in The Hague. "In the German delegation, we had a *Leitmotiv* which we quoted to one another at difficult times: 'Nothing is stronger than an idea whose time has come.' Victor Hugo wrote this 150 years ago, but it was never so true as at the moment of the vote that created the International Criminal Court. The time for this idea had come. That was the historic meaning. "

Philippe Kirsch underlined the unique nature of the process. "The court was created democratically, by treaty," he later told me. "It was not imposed on the international community. It was not created by the Security Council. It was created by the states themselves, and they agreed on its features in a very difficult exercise.

"There were 120 positive votes in Rome, but by December 31, 2000, 139 countries had signed the treaty. Nothing like this had ever happened in the history of international legal negotiations—that a treaty acquires more signatures than it had [original] votes—because it's a lot easier to vote for something than to say yes after the fact and be committed to do what is necessary to make it work. I'm convinced that within a few decades the International Criminal Court will be as natural a part of the international landscape as the UN is today."

—

One has only to read the preamble to the Rome Statute to feel the emotion of the delegates who voted the International Criminal Court into being that July night.

> *Conscious that all peoples are united by common bonds, their cultures pieced together in a shared heritage, and concerned that this delicate mosiac may be shattered at any time,*
>
> *Mindful that during this century, millions of children, women and men have been victims of unimaginable atrocities that deeply shock the conscience of humanity,*
>
> *Recognizing that such grave crimes threaten the peace, security, and well-being of the world,*
>
> *Affirming that the most serious crimes of concern to the international community as a whole must not go unpunished . . .*
>
> *Determined to put an end to impunity for the perpetrators of these crimes . . .*
>
> *Determined to these ends and for the sake of present and future generations, to establish an independent permanent International Criminal Court in relationship with the United Nations system, with jurisdiction over the most serious crimes of concern to the international community as a whole,*
>
> *Emphasizing that the International Criminal Court established under this Statute shall be complementary to national criminal jurisdictions,*
>
> *Resolved to guarantee lasting respect for, and the enforcement of, international justice,*

[The States Parties to this Statute]
Have agreed as follows . . .

Thus began the text that would underpin the twenty-first century's first steps toward permanent global justice. The world was changing rapidly, becoming more frightening, more anarchic. The creation of the International Criminal Court was a triumph of the rule of law over impunity.

—

Postscript USA

David Scheffer is eager to defend his record when we meet in Washington in September, 2004. He is out of government and teaching international law at George Washington University.

"Somehow there's an assumption out there that I was opposed to the ICC under the Clinton administration," he says somewhat defensively. "The United States was *not* opposed. In fact we were strong supporters of the court from the very beginning. The question was, what kind of court would it be? Our position was that we wanted this court, but we wanted the Security Council to be responsible for triggering the cases."

"But this would have condoned impunity, would it not?" I say. "If the council could veto cases that were referred to the ICC by other states, you'd have politics as usual."

"I hear the argument," he counters abruptly. "Look, we were basically saying that there should be some backstop approval by the council so there is no conflict between what it might be trying to achieve in a situation and what the ICC might impose."

He looks downcast. He was, he tells me, under strict instructions from Washington regarding possible wiggle room. He simply didn't have any.

"I was dealing with the National Security Council and the White House, but I wasn't talking to the two top guys, the president and his National Security advisor Sandy Berger. So there was gridlock, because no one under them is going to make a decision. And I'll tell you something that's just my instinct. I think what happened to us in Rome was one of the casualties of the Monica Lewinsky debacle of that summer. I don't think the president was as engaged as he should have been. Life was tough in the White House in those months. I *can* tell you that I did have a meeting with Hillary Clinton before I went to Rome and it was clear that she was distraught and frustrated and it was going to be tough getting her on board to help prevail with the State Department. I'll never forget her saying to me, 'What went wrong? [with the preliminary ICC negotiations to that point]. I thought when we got into this thing with a permanent court that cases would be triggered by the Security Council, but now we've got States Parties referring cases and we've got this provision for an independent prosecutor. How did this happen?' So I said, 'There's not much support in the rest of the world for having the Security Council run the show.' But, you know, I realized that when *she* thought about an independent prosecutor, she was thinking about Kenneth Starr!

"The recommendation of the Pentagon was always, don't sign. Period. I was on the phone from Rome every night trying to nudge the system, and I *did* get this in front of the Joint Chiefs of Staff. That was important because if you negotiate something that the Joint Chiefs then oppose, you're dead meat in Washington, and so is your court. So in the fifth week of the five-week Rome conference I was finally able to get the Joint Chiefs to approve a new proposal. It was to create a transitional period whereby you could sign on to the treaty, but you had a ten-year period at the end of which you could opt out of coverage for crimes against humanity and war crimes—but not genocide. The Joint Chiefs approved that position. But in

Rome no one wanted to buy into that. They wanted it all up front. So we lost our battle then and there . . ."

"So why did you call for a vote you knew you would lose?"

"I *told* Washington that we're going to attract a lot of criticism if we call for a vote, and we're going to lose the vote, there's no question. But the decision, and I think it was out of the Pentagon at that stage, was, no, you call for a vote so we can register our disapproval of the final draft. So I carried out my instructions and Norway was able to defeat us . . . It wasn't a formally recorded vote, but people knew who had raised their hands in favour of our proposal. The countries that raised their hands were the rogue states of the world and the United States."

"What were your thoughts at that moment?"

" I felt sick . . . I'll be blunt with you. We have lost our leadership role in international justice. We have sacrificed that on the altar of an ideological aversion to international law. Other countries are assuming the mantle—the United Kingdom, Germany, Canada, Italy, Argentina . . . People in Europe no longer trust the US on issues of international justice or even on the broader scale of foreign policy. But I have to say that everything we hoped for regarding the integrity of the court has been demonstrated in terms of the [later] selection of the prosecutor, the judges, and the overall staff. And the prosecutor's choices of initial investigations, which have come from State Party referrals, speak to his and the court's competence. I don't think the ICC has done anything yet that validates the critics' fears or is disturbing in terms of America's sovereignty."

"Can the ICC succeed in the long run without the US?"

"I think it probably can. It's just that the full potential of the court will never be realized without the US on board, with our financial contributions, our expertise, our ability to use the clout of the Security Council and our own government to compel cooperation."

He is quiet for what seemed to be a long time. "How much do you think about all of this," I ask him.

"Oh, quite a lot . . . The irony is so many of my negotiating colleagues from around the world are now on the staff of the ICC as judges, in the Prosecutor's staff, in the Registry, and so the old negotiating crowd is actually there and so it's kind of, you know, I'm in touch with them and I see everything evolving and it's very, very sad for me not to see the United States part of it. So, yes, I think about it . . . I wonder how history will view all of this."

TWELVE

History and Justice

I n February 2003, the eighty-eight members of the Assembly of States Parties¹ met at the United Nations headquarters in New York to elect the ICC's first panel of eighteen judges. Each member country was allowed to put forward one person, using its own national procedures for nominating candidates to high judicial office, or the procedures of the International Court of Justice in The Hague (the UN tribunal that adjudicates disputes among states). The nominees needed to have established competence in criminal law and procedures, or in relevant areas of international law.

After four days and thirty-three rounds of voting, the new tribunal had its first judges: eleven men and seven women. One-third of these were selected by lot for a term of three years; another third drew lots for six years; the remainder would sit for nine years. The staggered system promised change as well as continuity. There would be elections every three years, but enough "institutional memory" to keep the wheels of the court oiled and in motion.

Then in April, the assembly reconvened to elect the court's chief prosecutor—the putative ogre of John Bolton's nightmares. Their choice was Luis Moreno-Ocampo of Argentina, a man renowned for having prosecuted members of the Dirty War junta that had held sway over his country starting in the 1970s. His role would be crucial to the success of the new institution; it was he who would choose the court's first cases, which would either make or break the reputation of the tribunal. Everything he said and did would be watched closely and critically, especially in the United States. Well aware of this, he made his first statement to the Assembly of States Parties an attempt to reassure his critics. He acknowledged the "apprehension and concern" that his office aroused in some quarters. He pointed out that the principle of "complementarity" protected state sovereignty because it allowed countries to conduct trials of their own nationals; and he alluded to the overarching control the States Parties held over his office. So far, so good. There were no complaints in the US media.

The Nuremberg Tribunal had held fair trials for all its defendants, including those who had committed unprecedented atrocities, and the International Criminal Court could do no less. Its judges needed to be persons of blameless reputation who could be counted on to uphold the rules of due process, even in the worst cases. As it happened, a majority of the newly appointed judges were citizens of countries that had endured— or inflicted—major human rights abuses. Their election had sent out a message about the textured layers of understanding the court would be privy to. Even the ultramodern, white-facaded, fifteen-storey headquarters of the ICC on the outskirts of The Hague suggested a break with the past.

As I am shepherded through multiple levels of bag searches and passport perusals, I am reminded of the dangers that the judges and prosecutors of this institution will live with every day as they confront the impunity of some of the world's worst perpetrators.

A private secretary leads me through more locked doors. I have scheduled meetings with a few of the judges, and with Moreno-Ocampo. I have been frankly curious about these people—especially about the role that the past, both personal and national, may have played in their commitment to this judicial experiment. Now I'm about to meet the German judge Hans-Peter Kaul. He and his country were central to the ICC from its beginnings in the years of preparatory meetings. In the light of twentieth-century history, this is hardly a surprise. Contemporary Germans still wrestle with the knowledge that the generations of their parents and grandparents were participants in the Nazi project. Shame still taints the collective national identity.[2]

A fair-skinned blond-haired man of medium height stands politely as I enter his office and indicates two seats at a small round table. Kaul was born in 1943 near Dresden, in what would soon be Soviet-controlled East Germany. Early in life he dedicated himself to resisting tyranny, by *legal* means, of course. I ask him about this and he replies with a smile, "Oh yes, my family escaped to West Germany in 1952, and when I was seventeen I decided to defend the Western world against the Russians. So I joined the German Federal Army. The Cuban missile crisis had just happened, and I had seen the Russian tanks in action. I was very frightened." Later, it occurred to him that he might resist tyranny more usefully by studying law. In one of the speeches he had recently made about the International Criminal Court, he had explained that even as a very young man he realized that countries that were ruled by global law in their foreign affairs were far less likely to commit crimes.

He is modest, but his accomplishments in the fields of international law and diplomacy are legendary. He entered the German foreign service in 1975, working his way through the ranks until 1984, when his interest in German history, and his deeper than usual knowledge of the recent past, made him his government's choice for one of its most difficult postings: press counsellor and spokesperson at the German embassy in Tel Aviv. "I'm going to talk openly with you," he tells me suddenly and earnestly. "To go to Israel was something I truly wanted to do, but it was also significant because it meant [I] was seen as being able to withstand the, um . . . the burdens and the pressures . . . , that [I] was able to cope with our wonderful past, in Israel itself, and to do it in public."

After two years, he was posted to the embassy in Washington, where he was responsible for the German reunification file; and by 1993 he was a high-ranking officer in Germany's permanent mission to the United Nations. He was Germany's lead negotiator during the years of ICC preparatory meetings, and at the Rome Conference, and today, he is one of the world's foremost authorities on the International Criminal Court. But what he pointedly wants me to understand are the underpinnings to his lifelong commitments: his early exposure to violence—and Germany's murderous past.

He was eighteen months old, he tells me, when the Allied firebombings of Dresden in February 1945 killed approximately forty thousand civilians, including his paternal uncle.[3] When the war ended in the spring of that same year and the Soviet army entered the city, his father, who had been a major in the Wehrmacht, was taken prisoner. He returned home after four years of forced labour in Siberia, at the age of fifty-two. "I still remember the day he came home, when I saw him consciously for the first time," he recalls in a soft voice. "It was Christmas 1949. My father was a man of six feet, but he was a skeleton. He had jaundice and all the sicknesses you get from malnutrition. He died young. His constitution had suffered too much. But this is nothing special. He shared his fate with hundreds of thousands of others."

And so, from his earliest childhood, Hans-Peter Kaul knew violence, havoc, family disruption and loss. "My childhood was heavily marked by the destruction, by the suffering, by the misery, by the hunger that the crimes committed by Adolf Hitler and his followers brought to many countries in Europe, but also to the German people. Our favourite playgrounds were the ruins of bombed-out houses. In our neighbourhood you had parts of cellars and balconies that were still intact. You can imagine how wonderful it was to play on these things . . . but I became politically aware very early.

"One day when I was still a teenager I came across a book that talked about the mass murders. It was called *Der SS-Staat: Das System der deutschen Konzentrationslager* by Eugen Kogon. [The book was translated into English as *The Theory and Practice of Hell: The German Concentration Camps and the System Behind Them.*] I was quite terrified by what I read. That too was why I joined the army. Maybe I was a little bit naive, but I thought that I could contribute my share in defending our *new* Germany." (Kogon's groundbreaking book was published in 1946, when German newspapers were still reporting daily testimony from the Nuremberg Tribunal.)

"Nuremberg is still very much alive in Germany," he says. "I think that the excellent reporting at the time helped people to face what had happened. Today, national support for the ICC is universal, from the far left of the political spectrum to the far right. For obvious reasons Germans understand the need for a universal court with the capacity to set legal and moral standards for the entire world."

Because he thinks historically about the umbilical cord that links the Nuremberg Tribunal to the International Criminal Court, he wants to talk about an extraordinary event that took place on October 27, 2000, the day the German parliament adopted the Rome Statute. It was a signal moment for every living German, he says, and especially for him. Several weeks before, he had received a letter from the American Nuremberg prosecutor Whitney Harris, asking if he could come to Berlin to witness this historical moment in the Bundestag. Kaul was thrilled and made arrangements for Harris to occupy a prominent seat.

"I was sitting on the government bench behind the chancellor when one of the members leaned over and said, 'I just learned that Professor Harris, one of the Nuremberg prosecutors, is here. I propose that at the moment the Rome Statute is adopted, we all rise in his honour.' And that is what happened. The entire Bundestag stood and applauded him. He witnessed the moment when—with 528 yes votes, only one no vote and two abstentions—Germany adopted the ICC Statute, legislation that would allow for the extradition of German nationals accused of major crimes."

His voice betrays an edge of emotion as he speaks about this stunning moment in the history of the nation that had once pursued total war and genocide.

"I know the International Criminal Court will never be able to try large numbers of people; yes, we will have to concentrate on those who bear the greatest responsibility. But we *will* establish an authentic historical record. We will warn future perpetrators and pay attention to the victims of major international crimes whose suffering has not been sufficiently recognized. Sometimes I think of the court as being like those billboards they have in Times Square in New York City. Do you know what I mean? Like a signpost for the rule of law in the world."

A man of abiding principle, he considers his own children and feels happy. "I think it is unhealthy when a young person accepts the exercise of power as a reality against which one can do nothing. So I am glad that my children are a little bit rebellious against the generation to which I belong, and are critical. Nobody can claim that he or she will always live up to high principles, but I believe the principles must remain intact, despite constraints and occasional concessions. This is the way I have tried to live my life."

The apex of his lifelong personal defiance of the crimes of Hitler was the International Criminal Court, whose birth he had helped to midwife. The future of the tribunal was as yet unknown; all the same, Hans-Peter Kaul numbered himself among the happiest of men.

—

There is something satisfying about the fact that the office of Justice Claude Jorda of France is close to that of Justice Kaul. For the first half of the twentieth century, Germany and France were mortal enemies. They fought a war of mutual annihilation between 1914 and 1918, and a mere twenty years later the former had occupied the latter, leaving a knotty legacy of resistance and collaboration that was still not entirely untangled after six decades. From his high perch in France's legal bureaucracy, Jorda had lived close to this legacy as several government-initiated war crimes trials challenged the country's postwar myths. He was director of legal services at the French Ministry of Justice from 1982 until 1985 during the period when the Nazi war criminal Klaus Barbie was captured in Bolivia and returned for trial in France; and attorney general (chief prosecutor) in Bordeaux as the government prepared its long-overdue case against the Vichy-era civil servant Maurice Papon, a man who had been blanketed with national honours prior to being indicted, tried and convicted of complicity in crimes against humanity for deporting Jews from the region. In 1992 he was attorney general of the Appeals Court in Paris just as the Bousquet affair began to heat up (René Bousquet, the head of the French police during the wartime Vichy regime, had negotiated his forces' collaboration with the SS in the arrest of Jews and Communists, yet he was acquitted of any crime by a French court in 1949. In 1991 he was finally arrested by the French police and charged with crimes against humanity. He was shot dead by an assailant just before his trial was to begin). And in January 1994 Jorda was appointed to the newly created ICTY when Richard Goldstone was prosecutor-in-chief.

He is waiting for me in his office, a pleasant, friendly-looking man with a hint of the reserve that well-bred Frenchmen of his generation reveal in their bearing. His complexion is Mediterranean, possibly reflecting his family's origins in the south of France, near Perpignan—though he was born (in 1938) in the French colony of Algeria. I am intrigued to learn that like Hans-Peter Kaul, he chose a career in law after having been introduced to violence early in life. The Allies engaged with the Axis forces on the Algerian front, and his hometown, Bône, was bombed by the Allies in November 1943. His elementary school was closed for an entire year, and there was very little to eat.

Knowing the Vichyist tendencies of the French in wartime Algeria (the colony was a bastion of ultra-rightist sentiment), I ask about his family. Yes, he replies, his father was a hard-line supporter of Marshal Philippe Pétain. "When Admiral [François] Darlan was assassinated at Algiers, my father insisted on taking me there for a visitation of the body.* I was just three

---

* François Darlan was Pétain's deputy in Algeria and his designated heir.

or four years old." Young Claude was intended to perpetuate his father's right-wing tradition, but he did not. "I was lucky to have an education that instilled a respect for diversity. My mother was very Catholic, very pious; my father was agnostic; so I was sent to a public high school, but I also had a religious education. It was because I had these two aspects to me, and because of the war, that I became interested in social and political issues early on.

"I was still young when the violence of the Algerian war for independence swept France and Algeria in the late 1950s and early 1960s. I was always *for* independence because it struck me as being historically inevitable. It was very painful. I was at law school in Toulouse at the time, and the battle among students, the Algeria liberationists against the extreme right, was terrible and violent. Students today cannot imagine what it was like, this terrible quarrel over decolonialization.

"The other formative aspect of my development was the fact that I spent my first years in a multicultural environment. I grew up with Arab children. They were my playmates, and I think this also created in me a basis of acceptance of others that sent me in a different direction from my father. I often think about this today when I see the difficulties Arabs living in France are experiencing."

The cultivated blindness the French maintained with regard to their wartime collaboration was long summed up for me by a comical scene in Eugène Ionesco's play *Amédée*, in which a charming young couple hides in a cupboard a corpse that proceeds to grow and extend grotesque members during unlikely "dinner-party" moments. In the real world, this "corpse" became gradually (and controversially) more visible with the trial of Klaus Barbie (1987); the indictment of René Bousquet (1991); the trial of the French perpetrator of crimes against humanity, Paul Touvier (1994); and that of Maurice Papon (1997). I have often wondered whether this late-century judicial activism underscored France's strong support for the International Criminal Court, just as Germany's twentieth-century history propelled that nation toward international justice.

I ask Jorda the question. He replies, "I do think the French position vis-à-vis the ICTY, the ICTR and later the ICC was very much strengthened by the knowledge that public opinion was by then strongly in favour of criminal justice in war crimes cases." France, he reminds me, played a significant role in the creation of the UN courts for the former Yugoslavia and Rwanda.[†]

In 1999 Jorda was elected president of the ICTY by his peers, a position he welcomed. "There is an ethical dimension to bringing justice to the victims and to fulfilling a duty to the collective memory," he once said in a speech about the ICTY. But he became increasingly critical of the court's slow workings, and in January 2000 he introduced large-scale reforms to improve efficiency. "I fought with my colleagues about this. I exhausted myself talking about efficiency, and I still believe the trials have to go faster, to be closer to the events. Look, if we finally bring Karadžić to trial in 2025 that is completely unacceptable, counterproductive. . . . I came to *this* court [the ICC] saying to my colleagues, 'Be careful because we will be judged according to how efficient we are.'"

"Are you suggesting that the ICTY may be poorly regarded by history?" I ask him.

---

† But not without being accused of blatant hypocrisies. The French had been allies of the Serbs since the First World War, and later, in December 2001, a French army major would be jailed in France for having warned the Serbs about the imminent NATO bombing of Kosovo. There were also allegations that French diplomats and military personnel had helped the Serbs, including facilitating the escape of Radovan Karadžić.

"No, not at all. The ICTY was the first dedicated [ad hoc] court, so it had to create everything from scratch. . . . I believe the ICTY has judged slowly but conscientiously. The accused have nothing to complain about. They have all necessary rights; everything is open and transparent; anyone can watch the trials in The Hague, or at the ICTR in Arusha. I am convinced that these courts will leave a mark on the history of humanity. But the work of the International Criminal Court is even more important. We are a *permanent* tribunal—and we must learn from the experience of the ad hoc courts for the former Yugoslavia and Rwanda."

His professional life has spanned the political earthquakes of the Barbie and Papon trials in France and the beginnings of the movement for international criminal justice. "You are now in your sixties," I say. "What thoughts have you now about your career?"

"I will finish my working life as a judge," he replies, after what seems a long silence. "I like it, though in my heart I think I am still something of a prosecutor. But when I think long term, I honestly believe that nothing could please me more than to have been a part of these critical early years of international justice."[4]

———

Judge Anita Ušacka occupies an office down the hall. Tall, blond, slim and reserved, almost shy, she is a citizen of Riga, Latvia. Her presence in The Hague speaks to the transition in her region from Soviet Communism to European democracy, which included the adoption of Western justice. Once, back in the mid-1990s, the Belgrade lawyer Nicola Barović had guffawed aloud when I asked him about the possibility of fair trials in Serbia, or anywhere in the post-Communist East, for that matter. Anita Ušacka appreciates the joke. She used to be

a law professor at the University of Latvia, specializing in constitutional law—that is, the law of the Soviet constitution of
1936. Theoretically, this was one of the world's noblest
humanitarian documents: it established universal direct suf-
frage and guaranteed the right to work; it recognized collective social and economic rights, including health, housing and
education; it provided for the direct election of all government bodies. Although there was no connection whatever
between these high sentiments and reality, Stalin's constitution was taught to young lawyers throughout the Soviet
Union. "It was abstract," she says with notable understate-
ment. "We were teaching these ideas of good governance, but
none of it meant anything in the real world."

The real world operated with something called "telephone
law," she explains, with a look of embarrassed chagrin. "That
was when the leaders of the Communist Party telephoned a
judge and said, 'You need to decide this case this way.'"

The road she had travelled was a metaphor for the yearning
for change in Latvia itself; in fact, her personal transformation
and that of her country had begun the moment the latter broke
free from the Soviet Union on August 21, 1991. Less than three
weeks later, parliament banned the Communist Party of Latvia (a
branch of the Communist Party of the Soviet Union) and dis-
carded the Soviet constitution in favour of the former (amended)
Latvian constitution of 1922. The European Commission (the
executive body of the European Union) quickly recognized
Latvia and the other Baltic States as independent countries.

That same summer, she attended a course at the
International Institute of Human Rights in Strasbourg,
France. It was her first trip "outside," as she puts it—to a
"capitalist country." There she met Thomas Bürgenthal, the
author of a useful little work titled *International Human Rights
in a Nutshell*. Ušacka says she was amazed as much by the sys-
tematization of such rights in international agreements as by

the nature of the rights themselves. On her return to Latvia she applied to the Soros Foundation for the funds to translate the book into her language; and with this important effort she became instrumental in establishing the teaching of human rights where there had previously been none.

She became a full professor of constitutional law at the university where she directed projects on law reform and the protection of human rights, both of which were integral to her country's transition to democracy. And when the Latvian Constitutional Court was created in 1996, she was immediately elected a judge.

She confides that she is "obsessed" with the tangled skein of Latvia's twentieth-century history. I sympathize. Who wouldn't be? In 1939—on August 23, to be exact—the small Baltic state fell prey to the Hitler-Stalin non-aggression pact, which allowed the Soviet Union to annex the territory. Within a year, more than fifteen thousand people had been deported to the Soviet gulag, most of them free-thinking intellectuals. The pact lasted until June 22, 1941, when Germany invaded the Soviet Union. Three short weeks later, Latvia was reoccupied, this time by the Nazis. Now, thousands of prominent people who had strategically collaborated with the *Soviets* were either killed outright or sent to concentration camps.

A significant minority of Latvians collaborated wholeheartedly with the SS in the destruction of more than 90 percent of the country's pre-war Jewish community (as well as tens of thousands of foreign Jews, whom the Nazis had transported into the country from elsewhere in Europe). Altogether, about ninety thousand people were murdered: seventy thousand Jews, eighteen thousand ethnic Latvians and two thousand Roma. At the war's end, the Soviets reoccupied the country, and in March 1949 a second mass deportation effectively ended all resistance. For the next fifty years, Latvia and its Baltic neighbours, Estonia and Lithuania, "were erased from the map of Europe," in the words of Latvia's president, Dr. Vaira Vike-Freiberg, in a speech delivered in Riga on January 14, 2005.

On May 1, 2004, Latvia became a full-fledged member of the European Union, but no one could pretend that the roots of democracy and human rights were anything but shallow. In March 2006 rumours of a fascist resurgence prompted a pointed question at a meeting of the European Parliament.[5] The official denial was predictably robust; however, just weeks earlier the Latvian foreign minister had felt it necessary to declare that his country "categorically denounce[d] the Holocaust and genocide and the activities of the continuators of these ideologies."

Like many states that look upon their own history with dubious fascination, even fear, Latvia viewed the International Criminal Court as a means of self-preservation. The government signed the Rome Statute on April 22, 1999, less than a year after the ICC founding conference. It had refused to sign an Article 98 immunity pact with the United States, and the US had withheld promised military assistance as punishment. To be well regarded in their regained European home had outweighed the need for American aid. The hope was that Europe's values of democracy and the rule of law would help to prevent the resurgence of totalitarian thinking, even as a minority political opinion. For these reasons Latvians were exceptionally proud that one of theirs had been elected among the first judges of the court.

"How much do your compatriots know about the ICC?" I ask her.

She looks doubtful. "They know something, but they misunderstand. People write me letters about the Soviet and Nazi deportations. They want to call them genocide. After all these years they still want to know what happened to members of their families, and they still want justice. Naturally, we will not be dealing with those issues here. Our own national courts can take up those cases, should they wish to do so."

"Would a truth and reconciliation commission help Latvians understand one another and the past?"

"I don't think it would be in our tradition," she replies slowly. "It's politics, you know. You see, Russia is so close. We would need their co-operation in order to know the full truth and be reconciled." She implies that Latvians may be years, even decades, away from reaching a consensus about their shared history. They are confused and divided about what is true and false, and about who should assume responsibility. There is no agreement about what should be taught to the next generation of children.

The International Criminal Court points to a cleaner future—to the democratic values of global justice *and* to its domestic implications. The very existence of the ICC might head off emerging problems. Hans-Peter Kaul had voiced the same thought when he said that passing the Rome Statute in the Bundestag meant that Germans could be deported and tried in The Hague, if it ever came to that. The ICC was a protection. That was the dream in tiny Latvia—a hope personified by Anita Ušacka, whose election as a judge had honoured the nation.

—

Finally, there was Navanethem (Navi) Pillay of South Africa, a woman of Indian background. She, too, had to learn about human rights and fair justice outside her country of birth. Her presence in The Hague was a miracle of sorts, for she had been born into a society that thwarted her every effort to become properly educated. As a child she was angered by the blatant injustice in her world—by the shabby way that her parents were treated outside their home. She openly acknowledges that she studied law as an alternative to pursuing violence. "There was so much injustice that you felt you could kill the judge in question," she says quietly, as we talk about her early career, when she represented clients who were accused of anti-apartheid activism or breaking apartheid rules. "Naturally, you wouldn't; you worked through the law even though the system itself was unjust. I became a lawyer because I thought I could fight injustice that way. I thought it would empower me to know what my rights were."

Pillay is tall and elegant; friendly, yet appraising in her regard—and direct about her struggle to survive in a society that held her in contempt. She speaks about the internal discipline she had to foster and about her commitment to human rights, which began with an effort to understand her own status as a human being and was now epitomized in her election as a judge at the ICC.

She was born in Durban, Natal, in 1941, to a bus driver father and a mother who cared for her seven children at home. As a young couple, her parents lived in a tin shack, scavenging bricks from army dumps in the hope of building something better. "Mother would say, 'You have to be educated so you never become a slave to a man,' and Father would say, 'I want my girls educated because the last thing I want is for them to come home crying, saying they were beaten by their husbands.'"

At six she already knew there was a world close by where she was not welcome; but one day, something life-transforming occurred. She was carrying a pouch of money to her father, when a man grabbed the bag from her hands. Everyone had to go to court, and it was there that she saw her father publicly humiliated. "I was terrified of the police and the magistrate because of the way they treated him. My father was an important person to me, but they didn't respect him; they treated him like a boy." She remembers feeling sick for him. "Why did the magistrate shout at you?" she innocently asked him afterwards. Her mother intervened. "She said, 'The magistrate was just asking him to speak up.' But I knew that wasn't true. It was a terrible thing for me to see."

She was just seven years old in 1948 when the National Party first came to office and wove the suffocating cloth of apartheid around the lives of non-whites. Over the subsequent decades, the everyday acts of dark-skinned South Africans were managed by regulatory legislation that established what their official colour was. The category they were placed in determined where they could live, whom they could marry or have sex with (agents were assigned to investigate the crime of interracial sexual intercourse) and where they were allowed to work.

Although the segregated Indian community of Clarewood had built its own elementary and high school with money saved by the sugar-cane workers, advanced education was a remote dream. But Pillay was a brilliant student, and when she was about to graduate the school principal was so chagrined at the probable waste of her talents that he went from house to house urging people to contribute money to send her to university. He raised enough, and more: Pillay and two other students from her class became the first in their community ever to receive a post-secondary education.

"When did you become aware of the anti-apartheid movement?" I ask.

"In high school. Some of the boys distributed leaflets for meetings, but my parents kept us out of politics. They said, 'Concentrate on your education and don't try to be equal to the white man. You are not equal.' But you learned to think about these things from your friends and from the teachers. Sometimes the security police came to the school and lined us up and questioned us. They even came to our elementary school and called us 'subversive elements.' The principal and the teachers were helpless. To see their powerlessness was a lesson in itself."

In 1959, the year she completed high school, the government passed the Separate Universities Act. Pillay applied successfully for permission to do a BA at Natal University, but when she tried to enter law school she was refused on grounds of race.

Then, coincidentally, a Ministry of Indian Affairs was added to the infrastructure of government bureaucracy, and in the short honeymoon period that followed, she was allowed to enter the faculty.

In 1967, Navi Pillay became the first woman in the province of Natal ever to open a law practice. She and her lawyer husband, Gaby, acted on behalf of people who were accused of breaking the apartheid laws. In the courtrooms where they represented their clients, everything was segregated. "You entered from separate entrances. All the magistrates were white, and they yelled at you in public. There was no treatment of us as professionals." Their law office was bugged. Plainclothes security agents sat in cars parked outside their home. The couple learned to speak in code. Then one day in 1973 Gaby was arrested and held in solitary confinement under the Terrorism Act.

Knowing he would almost certainly be tortured, she applied to the court, bringing affidavits from other detainees who had been physically abused. Remarkably, she obtained an order preventing the police from using "unlawful methods of interrogation." (The judge was moved, she says, by his personal experience as a prisoner of war.) After five months Gaby Pillay was released. But he was never the same again.

For twenty-eight years Navi Pillay practised law. Then in 1994, apartheid formally ended. And in 1995, she was appointed a High Court judge to the court of Kwazulu-Natal, the first woman (of any colour) to be so honoured. Until that moment she had never been permitted to step into a judge's chamber, let alone occupy a chair. She remembers the day with vivid clarity. "The telephone rang and someone said, 'Please hold for the president.' Nelson Mandela was on the line. He said, 'I phoned to express my personal joy.' I couldn't believe he would take the time to make that call. Perhaps he knew of me because I had visited Robben Island. I was, I think, the first female lawyer to set foot there."

In May 1995 she was elected to the bench of the International Criminal Tribunal for Rwanda; and in 1998, she and her colleagues made history by condemning the former Rwandan prime minister, Jean Kambanda, for genocide. Kambanda (who pleaded guilty) was the first head of state ever to be convicted for the crime of crimes (Slobodan Milošević might have been the second, had he survived).

In the first case of its kind since the trial of the Nazi propagandist Julius Streicher at Nuremberg, Pillay and her colleagues also convicted three Rwandans for using radio broadcasts to incite genocide. Over the national airwaves, the infamous journalists of Radio-télévision libre des mille collines had called for the destruction of the Tutsis. When they summoned Hutus to "stamp out the cockroaches," what had been sporadic attacks exploded into genocidal blood lust.

Finally, she helped to convict Jean-Paul Akayesu, the Hutu mayor of the Rwandan town of Taba, who was tried for inciting murder, torture and rape. The Akayesu decision marked a turning point for international criminal law. Rape, when employed as a weapon of war—when intended to destroy a target group through pregnancies and the birth of new members of the "victor" class—was henceforth a crime against humanity.

The Rwandan tribunal was plagued with problems. Its physical location was in Arusha, Tanzania and not in Rwanda (for security reasons) and the court's slow workings consigned people to prison for unconscionable lengths of time before their trials. Furthermore, the Western-styled procedures of the tribunal were foreign to Rwandan culture. Eventually these were augmented by local forms of justice, a shift Pillay supports. "It's important that Rwandans see that those who ordered the genocide and carried out the killings are being brought to justice, but I readily acknowledge that because we were not situated inside Rwanda, people were alienated from the process."

In 1999 she was named president of the ICTR. "What can the International Criminal Court learn from the Rwandan tribunal?" I ask her.

"I think the ICC will face some of the major difficulties that the ICTR and the ICTY faced, in that they totally depend on the co-operation of governments. I also think we are likely to face difficulty in getting state co-operation in the investigations, arrests, transfer of information, and witnesses. On the other hand, the Rome Statute obliges the ICC to pay attention to the victims of serious crimes. For the first time they will have a right to representation in the courtroom as a group, or as individuals, and there will be a right to reparations, although I really don't know how this will pan out. . . . Clearly, they can't be providing compensation to millions of people."

She had encountered injustice at the age of six and had determined, before the age of twenty, to fight back through legal means. She had seen her husband's life irreparably altered by the racist apartheid regime. Her uniquely contoured background had sensitized her to violence against women—domestically and during wartime. She knew the meaning of crimes against humanity in her bones.

There were few in the world better suited to sit on the bench of the International Criminal Court than Navi Pillay.

—

Many of the other judges had biographies to match. As Bolivia's minister of justice, René Blattmann had single-handedly effected massive judicial reforms in the mid-1990s, establishing the rule of law across the institutional spectrum. He created a constitutional court and introduced controls to enhance the civil rights of citizens vis-à-vis the state. Akua Kuenyehia, another colleague, had been dean of the faculty of law at the University of Ghana before her election to the ICC, and a barrister on her country's Supreme Court. An expert in criminal law and international human rights, she had coordinated a study on women and the law in anglophone West Africa. Georghios Pikis had been president of the Supreme Court of Cyprus and a judge at the European Court on Human Rights. From 1996 to 1998 he had served on the United Nations Committee against Torture; and in 2004 he had chaired the Twelfth Conference of European Constitutional Courts.

They were a formidably impressive group. And although I wasn't able to meet all eighteen, I was struck by the frank transparency of the several conversations I had. Cynicism is often an easy option, I thought as I left the ICC premises; to hold hope demands courage. In their weathered maturity, seasoned by their personal and national histories, these individuals from across four continents were, as they understood better than anyone, pioneers in an emerging era of accountability.

—

I have an appointment to meet Luis Moreno-Ocampo, the chief prosecutor, the following day. He had played a leading role in the 1984–1992 prosecutions of the top military commanders of Argentina's Dirty War—the first criminal cases brought against senior officers for mass murder since the Nuremberg Tribunal; and for this he became wildly famous throughout the country. To bring these cases to trial, he had to analyze more than ten thousand instances of alleged abuse. Seeking to understand the roots of his country's problems, he established a private law firm that specialized in "corruption control" programs for large firms and organizations. As a major player in law cases involving political bribery, the protection of journalists and freedom of expression, he worked closely with Transparency International for Latin America and the Caribbean, an NGO dedicated to reducing corruption in business, and served on the board of its global arm, Transparency International. He was the founder and president of Poder Ciudadano (Citizens' Power) and an adviser to the international Project on Justice in Times of Transition, which helped "recovering" states foster reconciliation, economic development and effective governance. In April 2003, at the time of his election to the ICC, he was the Robert F. Kennedy Visiting Professor at Harvard Law School. He lectured internationally on justice and human rights. He was, in other words, a star candidate for the star job at the International Criminal Court.

He is only six months into his nine-year mandate when we meet and the work of the court is still preparatory; no investigations have begun. I am searched once again, ushered anew through the series of electronically locked doors, then accompanied to a large windowed office that overlooks one of The Hague's many canals.

Moreno-Ocampo's feet are resting comfortably on his desk as I enter the room, and a friendly smile spreads across his face as he waves me toward a chair on the other side of the wooden expanse. We are immediately on a first-name basis—at least he is. He looks fiftyish; his eyes sparkle with intelligence and humour. I am soon pressed to follow the effusive rush of his speech, which seems barely to keep pace with the speed of his thoughts.

He is immediately at pains to help me understand the philosophical dimensions of his thinking. "Justice," he says, "is not merely what happens in a courtroom." He believes in justice "as a way of creating consensus," by which he means "the rules people live by, an agreement about justice and peace." In the developed world, he explains, sounding a little like the professor he once was, nations with well-functioning institutions such as the police and the judiciary try *breaches* of established law, isolated cases of murder, for example; but the calm that characterizes consensual agreement even in these societies is relatively new, and behind it lie centuries of war. On the other hand, in places like the Democratic Republic of the Congo where there is no functioning state to control violence, "You may have eight or ten militias killing each other for reasons of race, economic problems or a security vacuum; and if you jail one leader of a militia you are not changing the culture." Justice then becomes "a consensus about how to solve conflict—something that does not yet exist in my own country," he is quick to add.

He takes a deep breath and smiles. "I used to say that in Argentina we're a lot better off now than we used to be. In the 1970s the state was killing us; in the 1980s and 1990s it only robbed us. That was a positive evolution! I know the North and I know the South, and my feeling is the world is a lot more like Argentina than Canada."

He appears to feel confined by the traditional tasks of a prosecutor: investigating crimes, collecting evidence, making arrests, then deciding whether a suspect should be brought to trial. He is vastly more ambitious. Years of fighting corruption and prosecuting crimes committed against the innocent have sensitized him to social consequences of violence, and from this he has fashioned a key to understanding the broad impact of the rule of law on society.

"Courts are important and you have to protect them, but they are technical." He clarifies: "The analogy is this: if you have cholera, the operating room is not a solution: you need clean water, proper nutrition and good hygiene. It's the same with justice. When basic social conditions exist, the court system may be the key to stability, but when these conditions are absent, it is not sufficient in itself."

In other words, courtroom justice is only one element of the larger process of building a functioning society where there is consensus about the rule of law. "How can you entertain such grand ambitions?" I ask him. "Doesn't the kind of transformation you are talking about depend on elements beyond your control as a prosecutor?"

"That's the problem!" he counters enthusiastically. "These social transformations don't [just] happen! Of course I will investigate the very worst cases when countries are unable or unwilling to undertake their own prosecutions. But my vision is larger. I'll try to accomplish more by means of my cases. Let's take the DRC (Democratic Republic of the Congo). Thirty years of Mobutu, who was supported by some Western countries, produced a huge conflict. The country has diamonds and gold, so whoever controls the territory becomes rich. . . . You cannot stop the crimes [committed there] simply by putting people in jail. You need a functional system around you, a different environment. So when I talk about consensus, I'm not talking about utopia. I need this just to do my job.

"I will try to make sure that I am not working alone in the Congo. There must also be efforts from the national system, the neighbours, the regional leaders, donors, the UN and the big companies that do business there. We need new ideas. In these countries, 60 percent of the soldiers are kids under the age of fifteen."

Given what he has just said about the Congo, I ask if his first case will concern that woebegone place. This he refuses to confirm.

"Where does your interest in human rights come from?" I ask with growing curiosity.

"From my country."

"How old were you when the Dirty War was happening?"

"I was the age of the guerrillas and the killers. The Dirty War started in 1970, when I was eighteen, and it ended when I was twenty-eight. But I wasn't involved; I was finishing high school and starting law school. My family had once had money, but had lost it, so I was also trying to organize a small business to make a living. I got married at twenty-three, had kids at twenty-five and was divorced by twenty-eight—so you see, I was busy. My only connection with what was going on was an employee who was killed by the army and a family friend who was kidnapped. Because there was no reliable public information, you only knew what you knew directly."

Having lost interest in his business venture, he became absorbed by current events. Eventually he took up the practice of criminal law. But it wasn't easy. "When I began my cases against the generals, my own mother was opposed to what I was doing," he confides. "Her entire family was in the military: two of her brothers were colonels, and her father had been a general. She *loved* General [Jorge Rafael] Videla, who was the president [of Argentina] and the head of the junta; he was like a close relative. One day she called me. She asked me, 'How can you do this?'

"It was very difficult for her; every day the papers were filled with what was happening in our hearings. But at some time over the next weeks my mother read about a pregnant woman who was kidnapped and gave birth in a car, alone, in handcuffs. She completely understood what that meant. She changed her mind. Then she called me again and said, 'I feel very sad, but Videla must be jailed. Even though I like him personally.'

"For me this was critical; my most important goal was to have people like my mother change their minds—upper-class people who had supported the military."

It occurs to me, as I listen to this profoundly admiring story about his own mother, that her willingness to pay attention to the facts and subsequently change her mind may have helped to shape his view that it is as possible to create public consensus through the dissemination of truthful information as through disinformation and propaganda; and that the factual evidence that emerges in a courtroom from questioning by a determined prosecutor can help to establish a true and credible historical record.

"How did someone like you emerge from this kind of family?" I wonder.

Unlike his mother's side of the family, the Morenos were modern and liberal. Luis has a view: "Moreno is a common Jewish name," he says. "There have never been practising Jews in our family, as far back as we can know, but we believe we are of *converso* background.[6] Truly, I believe we were Jewish. The Morenos have always been non-traditional and open-minded. So my family had both traditions going at the same time: courage and loyalty from the Catholic Ocampos and liberal openness from the Morenos. This allowed me to understand things more clearly when I was prosecuting the military."

Suddenly changing the subject, the complex man seated across from me speaks about the psychology of denial that sometimes comes into play at times of extreme stress. "Everyone denied what was happening in Argentina. My mother denied it until she understood the reality; even the *victims* denied that what was obviously happening *could* be happening! You know, when you live under such conditions you have to believe that if you are doing nothing wrong, nothing bad will happen to you. You can't live if you think that the state can arrest you at any moment for no reason.

"I remember when the head of the association of psychologists disappeared, one of the members of the same association tried to explain what had happened. She said, 'I advised her to stop trying to protect people, but her attitude was "I don't *care* if they did something wrong, I have to protect them, I need to know what the charges against them are."' She was working on the assumption that the state would only attack you if you were doing something wrong, but the truth was that simply by asking a question of the military, you were seen to be attacking the military. Exactly the same thing happened to a nurse who simply informed a family that their daughter was having a baby in the hospital. She disappeared.

"But the worst case was a guy who was kidnapped and kept for five months in a secret detention cell before he and a friend managed to escape. They were naked and they had no money. They tried to steal a car, but they had no experience and the alarm went off and a neighbour called the police. So they hid in the garden of the house until one of them took the risk of ringing the doorbell. The woman who answered took pity on them. She gave them clothes. They again hid in the garden and successfully eluded the police.

"Afterwards, this man went to his own house. Then, at the end of a year, he actually went to the police to renew his passport. When he realized there might be a problem, he ran away, went to Sweden, got asylum and stayed there until the dictatorship ended. Then he came home and began to work with us.

"One day I said to him, 'Claudio, how could you even *think* of going back to your own house after you escaped from the detention centre?' He said, 'It was my house! I had done nothing wrong!'

"This was key. Law-abiding people had enormous difficulty understanding that they were under attack from the state and not from a few crazy people."

Moreno-Ocampo is quiet for a moment. "This is why consensus is central," he finally says. "When people talk about torturers, they have the bad guys in mind; but in my country the torturers were not bad guys: they were ordinary citizens. That's the problem. They thought that to torture the opponents of the state was a public duty."

The prosecutor-in-chief was a man of intellectual and emotional complexity whose life, like those of the ICC judges I had met, had been coloured by the violence of the twentieth century. Like Claude Jorda, Luis Moreno-Ocampo had been raised in a dual tradition that allowed him to understand the world from more than one perspective. His was the most difficult job of all: his choice of first cases, and the way they were subsequently handled by the trial judges, would shape the reputation of the International Criminal Court.

THIRTEEN

The Moral Landscape

—————

P ower, law and justice. Although these ancient
aspects of world order usually co-existed more or
less comfortably (although not without upsets),
the first years of the twenty-first century altered the
normal balance. At one pole was America's mili-
taristic response to the terrorist attacks of September 11, 2001,
and its pre-emptive invasion of Iraq. At the other pole was the
inauguration of the International Criminal Court. Rarely had
contrasting philosophies been opposed with such clarity.

By 2007 the superpower was facing unanticipated hurdles. The US-led War on Terror had not gone well. Early on,
Osama bin Laden had simply vanished from sight—in spite
of an edict by President George W. Bush that he was to be
captured "dead or alive." The October 2001 attack on the
Afghan Taliban was declared a success that same year, but by

early 2003 the former protectors of al-Qaeda were back in force. The March 2003 invasion of Iraq, which was sold to the American people as critical to their survival, would be exposed as a house of cards built on a duplicitous foundation. Iraq did not have weapons of mass destruction. Nor was there a link between the Iraqi dictator, the militantly secular Saddam Hussein, and the religious fanatics of al-Qaeda.

Long-settled ideas about the rule of law had fragmented into unfamiliar shards. Did the "War on Terror" fatally pre-empt the international rules of armed conflict that had been hammered out by generations of rulers and diplomats? Had the world really entered a new phase, destined to last for generations, in which the supreme leader of the supreme country would decide what was, and was not, legal?

As books and articles detailing the Bush administration's falsehoods spilled off the presses, and as the post-invasion anarchy in Iraq devolved into sectarian war, the American people lost faith in the president whose language featured "winning," "freedom" and "democracy" long after the killings in the streets of Baghdad had metamorphosed into slaughter. By 2005 many of the surviving neo-conservatives who had planned the Iraq adventure were leaping off the listing ship of state. Paul Wolfowitz, the chief strategist of the disaster, had decamped to the safety of the World Bank (from which he would be forced to resign in 2007). Douglas Feith, a former undersecretary of defence (who had provided manipulated intelligence to Vice-President Dick Cheney) also left his post. So did John Bolton, who now also had an unlikely forum as the United States ambassador to the United Nations—an institution he had once claimed did not exist. (Bolton lost his ambassadorship in December 2006, when Congress refused to reconfirm him. He returned to his former home at the American Enterprise Institute, from which he issued bulletins advising President Bush on foreign policy, including a recommendation that the United States attack Iran.) By 2007 the list of disgraced acolytes was even longer. Alberto Gonzales, the United States Attorney General—the man who had used his senior position to rule that torture could be justified in the "War on Terror"—was forced to submit to an humiliating interrogation in the US Senate, then to resign his position. I. Lewis Libby Jr., formerly the chief of staff to Vice President Dick Cheney, was convicted of obstruction of justice, giving false statements to the FBI, and perjuring himself during the investigation over the exposure of a CIA operative (he was subsequently pardoned by President Bush). The controversial secretary of defense Donald Rumsfeld was ousted by his pre- viously loyal boss after the rout of the Republican Party in the mid-term elections of 2006. Only Dick Cheney appeared to be entirely safe. He was, after all, the closest to the president, and as Cherif Bassiouni had pointed out, the office of the president was sacrosanct.

The most surprising attack on the Iraq war came from Francis Fukuyama, the author of the triumphalist book *The End of History and the Last Man*, which celebrated the "winning side" after the massive failure of the Soviet experiment, and *After the Neocons: Where the Right Went Wrong*. Fukuyama, as usual, was in a class of his own. He was appalled, he said, by America's free fall in world opinion, which he blamed on the illusions of a few ideologues who had been allowed to shape foreign policy; and he called for an immediate U-turn to emphasize international development and global institutions. Had he perhaps happened across Mikhail Gorbachev's rueful comment during a state visit to France in October 1986, I wondered. Reflecting his growing recognition that military confrontations were expensive and ultimately unproductive, Gorbachev had famously acknowledged that "ideology" was not a suitable basis for foreign policy.[1]

—

The American president appropriated exceptional powers to himself, with which he claimed the authority to ignore, or alter, the rules to suit his purposes—but not without a challenge from constitutionalists and civil libertarians. The dispute over the controversial military commissions (in which "enemy combatants" could be tried without legal protections) entered the American court system through the auspices of the Center for Constitutional Rights, and as early as November 2004, a US Federal Court judge ruled that the Geneva Conventions *did* apply to the detainees being held at Guantánamo Bay. The military commissions violated not just the international laws of war, but the US Constitution, said the judge.[2] The Bush administration appealed, and on July 15, 2005, a higher court overturned the earlier decision.[3] Now the Third Geneva Convention did *not* apply to the prisoners at Guantánamo Bay.

Confusion reigned at high levels; then on July 27, 2005, a judge in a US federal district court offered a spirited defence of established law after he sentenced the Algerian national Ahmed Ressam to twenty-two years in prison for plotting to bomb Los Angeles International Airport. "I would like to convey the message that our system works," said John Coughenour. "We did not need to use a secret military tribunal, detain the defendant indefinitely, or deny the defendant the right to counsel. . . . Our courts have not abandoned the commitment to the ideals that set this nation apart."[4]

The judge's words pierced the heart of the controversy, but his allusion to the creed of American exceptionalism merely deepened the cultural battle lines (a cohort of bloggers responded with articles such as "The Terrorists' Little Helper").[5] However, the Ressam decision did stiffen backbones. On October 3, 2005, three distressed Republican senators,[6] led by John McCain, introduced a small amendment into the trillion-dollar Defense Appropriations Bill, in which they sought to outlaw the use of torture with regard to all detainees in American custody.[7] Predictably, Vice-President Cheney leaped into the fray: the proposed amendment would interfere with President Bush's ability to fight terrorism, he claimed; furthermore, it was unnecessary because the detainees were terrorists, not prisoners of war.

The Cheney-McCain confrontation laid bare the essence of the home-front battle over values, law and rights. The debate is "not about who *they* are, it's about who *we* are," retorted McCain. "We are Americans and we hold ourselves to a higher standard than those who slaughter the innocent in Iraq or Afghanistan, or in London, or on 9/11 here at home."

On October 5, the United States Senate voted 90 to 9 to support the McCain amendment. But there was a catch. The legislation contained a second, late-hour amendment that denied the Guantánamo Bay detainees the right to ask a court for help, if the mistreatment continued.[8] The McCain amendment stated that the United States outlawed the torture of detainees. But by blocking legal recourse, the second amendment made the enforcement of the McCain law difficult, if not impossible.

President Bush was obliged to consent to the new law (although the second amendment made the bitter pill considerably easier to swallow), and he gave his formal approval on December 30, 2005. Then he immediately issued a "signing statement," a document allowing him to *interpret* the newly minted legislation. The signing statement was an outright disclaimer: "The executive branch shall construe [the part of] the Act relating to detainees in a manner consistent with the constitutional authority of the President to supervise the unitary executive branch and as Commander in Chief and consistent with the constitutional limitations on the judicial power which will assist in achieving the shared objective of the Congress and the President . . . of protecting the American people from further terrorist attacks."

The language may have been convoluted, but the meaning was clear. The president, not Congress, would have the final say on the use of torture.

—

On June 29, 2006, the juridical pendulum that had swung the fate of the proposed military commissions wildly back and forth finally came to rest. That day, the US Supreme Court announced its decision in the case of *Hamdan v. Rumsfeld*. The planned military commissions to try "enemy combatants" were unfair, illegal under US law and contrary to the Geneva Conventions, the court determined.[9]

Michael Ratner was relieved. "This decision vindicates our five-year legal struggle," he wrote in a press release. "Now the President must act: try our clients in lawful US courts or release them. The game is up. . . . People must be treated humanely and the administration cannot put itself above the law."

Yes, the Supreme Court decision was a triumph for established law, but whether "the game [was] up" remained to be seen. In his strongly worded dissent, Justice Clarence Thomas expressed the opposing view. The court's judgment would "sorely hamper the president's ability to confront and defeat a new and deadly enemy," he said. Furthermore, the Supreme Court sent the entire package back to the elected legislators in Congress, where they would be free to rewrite the law in favour of the president's policies, should they wish to do so.

Ratner sounded less confident in a private email exchange.[10] "To overrule the president regarding the application of the Geneva Conventions was pretty remarkable, particularly regarding the laws of war, but I don't know what the future will bring. We have many current and former military who want to see compliance with the international laws because of the harm that could come to [captured] American soldiers, so in this area I do perhaps see a better future. But as far as Congress is concerned, our options look terrible. The only question is which of the bad deals we will get. . . ."

He was right. Barely a month later, the *Washington Post* confirmed that the White House was asking Congress to amend the very law on which the Supreme Court had based its judgment: *American* war crimes legislation that incorporated Common Article 3 of the Geneva Conventions.[11] Common Article 3 is viewed as the core of international humanitarian law—a "treaty in miniature" that sets out minimum standards and protections. The Bush administration wanted this "clarified." Still on the torture track, the president wanted the removal of the prohibition in the law against "outrages upon [the] personal dignity" of a prisoner.

When the senators who had drafted the original McCain Amendment against torture resisted, and when other Republicans joined them in opposition (including the former secretary of state Colin Powell), the president and his advisers found themselves in sudden, unexpected trouble.* In a parallel effort, they had also been trying to ensure that the defendants in any future military trials (should Congress agree to rewrite the law the Supreme Court had ruled on) would remain ignorant of the allegations against them. The stakes were now exceptionally high. Should the president's proposed revisions to American law pass, there would be no further legal challenges to his administration's intended program for detainees.

If the United States "revised" the Geneva Conventions to suit its purposes, what would stop other countries from doing

---

* On July 20, 2007, President Bush issued an executive order as part of his ongoing attempt to "intercept" Common Article 3 regarding CIA interrogations.

the same, asked John McCain? He and his supporters quickly
proposed alternative legislation, in which detainees would be
allowed to see a "summary" of the evidence against them. But
their efforts only illuminated how low the bar had dropped. A
"summary" of the evidence? This compromise, should it
pass, would push the United States off the international legal
map altogether.

The dispute ratcheted up in volume. "The Military
Commissions Act of 2006 will allow the continuation of a CIA
program that has been one of America's most potent tools in
fighting the War on Terror. . . . Information we have learned
from the program has helped save lives at home and abroad,"
stated the president.[12] But he now had another opponent:
Patrick Leahy, the veteran Democratic senator from Vermont.

"Passing laws that remove the few checks against mistreatment of prisoners will not help us win . . . the generation
of young people . . . being recruited by Osama bin Laden and
al-Qaeda. Authorizing indefinite detention of anybody the
Government designates, without any proceeding and without
any recourse is what our worst critics claim the United States
would do, not what American values, traditions and our rule
of law would have us do."[13]

By now, everyone knew the script and where they stood.
Patrick Leahy failed. On October 17, President Bush signed
the United States Military Commissions Act of 2006 into law
during a special ceremony at the White House. Four weeks
later, the US Department of Justice cited the new act when it
declared that a detainee named Ali Saleh Kahlah al-Marri
would be tried as an enemy combatant in a military tribunal.[14]

The Al-Marri case is worth noting because it clarified the
meaning of the new law. He was a Qatari citizen living legally in
Peoria, Illinois, on a graduate student visa. In December 2001 he
was arrested as a "material witness"—meaning that he was suspected of having information relating to a criminal proceeding

against another person. In 2002 he was charged with credit card fraud. In 2003, just before his criminal trial was to begin, he was arbitrarily reclassified as an enemy combatant and transferred to a naval brig in South Carolina. In 2004 he was allowed to see a lawyer. In 2005 his lawyer asked the federal district court in South Carolina to declare his incarceration unconstitutional. This petition was dismissed in August 2006. When the lawyer appealed, he was told that the new Military Commissions Act had stripped the court of its jurisdiction over his client.†

—

Torture is condemned under international law at all times and under all circumstances. It is a crime contained within the framework of *jus cogens*—the legal principles that express the universally understood laws of human intercourse.¹⁵ Torture is taboo—a moral breach that degrades both the abuser and the abused. Yet a poll conducted in November 2001 indicated that 32 percent of Americans condoned the practice.¹⁶ The numbers were high, but the September 11 attacks had just happened, and there was great anger in the country. However, four years later another survey (by the respected Pew Center) found that 63 percent of respondents justified physical and mental abuse.¹⁷ How had this happened? Rationally speaking, there was, and is, ample evidence that information obtained in this way is intrinsically unreliable. Notoriously, a person being tortured will admit to anything to stop the pain.¹⁸

The growing support for what had earlier been unthinkable illuminated the power of propaganda, especially when it

† A subsequent appeals panel ruled that the federal court did have jurisdiction over the case, that the president lacked the authority to detain Al-Marri as an enemy combatant, and instructed he be released from military custody.

emanates from official sources. And when respected public figures such as the lawyer Alan Dershowitz and the human rights expert Michael Ignatieff defended this radical policy (with caveats), the public grew ever more accepting.[19] The taboos surrounding racist discourse faltered. In the name of free speech, the evangelical leader Franklin Graham (the son of Billy) described Islam as "wicked, violent and not of the same God"—and got away with it. The Reverend Jerry Falwell called Mohammed a "terrorist." Not to be upstaged, the Baptist pastor Jerry Vines of Jacksonville, Florida, branded the sixth-century founder of Islam a "demon-possessed pedophile."[20] John Ashcroft, then the United States attorney general, opined that "Islam is a religion in which God requires you to send your son to die for him [while] Christianity is a faith in which God sends His son to die for you."[21] There were no apologies or retractions.

During the years that separated the opinion polls of 2001 and 2004, every official utterance had characterized the prisoners at Guantánamo Bay as "guilty," although substantive evidence was rarely, if ever, provided. They were simply evil people who "hated America," as the president liked to put it.

Deprived of human rights and legal protections by an invented status definition (enemy combatant), the detainees at Guantánamo Bay and in the myriad other camps around the world were effectively non-persons. Helpless and without rights, they had been dehumanized. The sole agency still attaching to such diminished creatures was the hunger strike or suicide, yet even these were denied them.[22] At Guantánamo, the hunger strike was countered by forced tube feedings; and when three prisoners did succeed in hanging themselves, this last act was derided and impugned.[23] Rear Admiral Harry B. Harris, Jr., who commanded the prison, said, "They have no regard for human life, neither ours nor their own. I believe this was not an act of desperation, but an act of asymmetric warfare against us."

—

On May 25, 2005, the Nobel Prize-winning organization Amnesty International called the prison at Guantánamo Bay "the gulag of our times." The United States government, they wrote, "thumbs its nose at the rule of law and human rights."[24]

Shocked and appalled, President Bush, Vice-President Dick Cheney and Donald Rumsfeld took to the airwaves to express their outrage. Leading American newspapers, including the *Washington Post*, attacked the Amnesty position.

"Absurd!" retorted President Bush when questioned at a May 31 press conference. "The United States promotes freedom around the world and fully investigates allegations of improper behavior towards prisoners in a transparent way. . . ." [The report was based] on allegations by people who were held in detention, people who hate America."[25]

Dick Cheney was "frankly offended." "For Amnesty International to suggest that somehow the United States is a violator of human rights, I frankly just don't take them seriously. I think the fact of the matter is the United States has done more to advance the cause of freedom, has liberated more people from tyranny over the course of the twentieth century and up to the present day than any other nation in the history of the world."[26]

Donald Rumsfeld called the accusation "reprehensible." The gulag, he said, was the place where the Soviets kept millions in forced labour concentration camps, and also possibly life in Iraq under Saddam Hussein. "To compare the United States and Guantánamo Bay to such atrocities cannot be excused. . . . Those who make such outlandish charges lose any claim to objectivity or seriousness."[27]

In a second-tier effort at damage control, five members of Congress were invited to tour the camp. They were prevented from talking to the inmates for alleged security reasons; and perhaps it was delicacy, or discomfort, that prevented them from asking about the Amnesty International investigations that had led to the "gulag of our time" accusation. On his return, Republican Jon Porter declared that the detention camp compared favourably with prisons in his own state (which may have raised a few eyebrows in Nevada); he thought many of the captives were "happy" to be in a place where they could get medical and dental care. "I would only wish that my loved ones or anyone's loved ones could be treated as well if they were captured by [Osama] bin Laden," he added.[28]

Informed readers of the *Las Vegas Review Journal* may have cringed at an unbidden reminder of other similarly staged visits, such as Grigori Aleksandrovich Potemkin's minutely detailed, entirely fake villages, which he constructed for Catherine the Great's tours of the Ukraine and the Crimea. Another was the Nazi concentration camp of Theresienstadt (Czechoslovakia), which the Germans prettied up and invited dignitaries to visit so they might report on the well-being of the inmates, who were, as it happened, en route to Auschwitz. Others may have heard echoes from their own national history, for the "medical and dental care" argument was once a mainstay of slavery apologists: they, too, were given to describing their human chattels as "happy."

William Schulz, the executive director of Amnesty International USA, held his ground. "What is 'absurd' is President Bush's attempt to deny the deliberate policies of his Administration, which has detained individuals without charge or trial in prisons at Guantánamo Bay, Bagram Air Base and other locations," he countered. "What is 'absurd' . . . is the Bush Administration's failure to undertake a full independent investigation, and that completed reports into human rights violations in these prisons remain classified and unseen. The network of secret detention centers operated by the US around the world must be opened to scrutiny by independent human rights groups, and those responsible for torture, no matter how senior, must be held accountable . . ."[29]

The provocative use of the word "gulag" to describe the American detention camps was an open publicity stunt.

("I wouldn't *be* here if we hadn't used that word," Schulz acknowledged on Fox News.) Without that shocking analogy, Bush, Cheney and Rumsfeld might have skated across the surface of Amnesty's criticisms, the media might not have noticed, and the American public would never have heard of it.

But beyond the noise and the scandal lay a different reality. The gruesome Soviet-era camps were infinitely worse, but Guantánamo and its sister camps in Afghanistan and elsewhere belonged to the same genus and could reasonably be called by their right name. Arbitrary indefinite imprisonment in defiance of both international and American law; detention without charge in an environment beyond scrutiny, established rules and protections; self-serving redefinitions of what acts constitute torture; the existence of "ghost detainees"—prisoners being held incommunicado in secret locations; the "extraordinary rendition" (secret transportation) of detainees to third countries known to practise torture in their domestic prisons; proposed trials by military commissions that mocked every rule of due process; guard-inflicted homicides; sexual and psychological humiliation, including the deliberate breaching of Islamic religious mores and the desecration of Koranic texts.

The president's dismissal of the Amnesty International report as based "on allegations by people who were held in detention, people who hate America" rang hollow: the rampant abuses against inmates in both Iraq and Afghanistan were well documented and in the public domain. No one expected the man in charge of the policies to concede the point, but what was peculiarly jarring about the president's response, which effectively blamed the victims, was its quality of schoolboy recitation—rote speech disconnected from thought. Faced with the evidence of torture and sanctioned lawlessness in his country's detention camps (the US army investigation into the deaths of two Afghan prisoners had been published just ten days earlier), it was possible to hope that the president might have grappled with the extraordinary accusations being levelled at his government instead of countering them with diversionary clichés. His empty words about the human beings being held indefinitely by his government recalled the suffering endured by Jewish Holocaust survivors when the deniers of the Nazi enterprise attacked their credibility. Those Holocaust deniers—the Ernst Zundels and the David Irvings of late-twentieth-century notoriety—were eventually marginalized by the force of indisputable historical fact, by public opinion and by the courts. Now, the president of the United States was blaming the victims of his own grey-zone politics.

On the day of President Bush's press conference, 520 men from forty countries were being held in the Guantánamo Bay prison. Only four had been charged with a criminal offence. If the gathering public relations storm were to result in their eventually being released, as Gary Solis had predicted,[30] and if their stories then became known, as they surely would, the unsavoury denials of George W. Bush and his colleagues would enter the history books in the same chapter as those of David Irving and his cohorts.[31] With one difference. Irving and his friends were liars, to be sure, but they were only commentators. President Bush and his White House entourage were perpetrators as well as propagandists.

Central to the gathering storm of disenchantment and moral confusion was the recurrent theme of law: broken law, subverted law, bent law, invented law and the flouting of international law. Rising from the ashes of genocide, the postwar "free world" had been founded on individual rights, national law and global law, including the Geneva Conventions, the Anti-Torture Convention, the Genocide Convention and the Charter of the United Nations. Although these rules had been breached during recurring storms of shifting sovereign interests, the foundations remained undisturbed until September 11, 2001. No postwar Western leader had so disdained the rule of law as George W. Bush.

The arrogance of his administration recalled the pithy repartee in Robert Bolt's play *A Man for All Seasons*, first performed in London on November 22, 1961.

> WILLIAM ROPER: So, now you give the Devil the benefit of law!
>
> SIR THOMAS MORE: Yes! What would you do? Cut a great road through the law to get after the Devil?
>
> WILLIAM ROPER: Yes, I'd cut down every law in England to do that!
>
> SIR THOMAS MORE: Oh? And when the law was down, and the Devil turned 'round on you, where would you hide, Roper, the laws all being flat? This country is planted thick with laws, from coast to coast, man's laws, not God's! And if you cut them down, and you're just the man to do it, do you really think you could stand upright in the winds that would blow then? Yes, I'd give the Devil benefit of law for my own safety's sake!

—

The Bush administration's policies in the aftermath of 9/11 affected civil liberties at home, the international rules governing conflict abroad and human rights in the world at large. But one of them, the rendering of terrorist suspects to countries that practised torture in their domestic prisons, also impinged on the laws of other countries. There was, for example, the cautionary tale of the Syrian-born Canadian engineer Maher Arar. On September 26, 2002, he was arrested at John F. Kennedy Airport in New York as he was changing planes after a family vacation. He was questioned for thirteen days about a Muslim acquaintance in Ottawa. Then, without being charged with an offence, he was deported to Syria. Arar was held in a notorious torture facility centre, known as the Palestinian Branch detention camp, in a windowless cell three feet wide and six feet deep.‡ A "grave," he later called it. His companions were rats that urinated and defecated on him as he lay in his dark container. He was regularly beaten with shredded cables until he "confessed" to being a terrorist in order to stop the pain. Through the walls of his cell he could hear the screams of others undergoing torture.

In October 2003 Canada managed to secure his release, and when he was safely back home Arar mounted the public stage. He proclaimed his innocence. He accused American officials of sending him to Syria knowing that country practised torture. He initiated a lawsuit in the United States through the Center for Constitutional Rights in which he accused US Attorney General John Ashcroft of violating the International Convention against Torture, to which the US is a signatory. This effort came to nothing. In February 2006, a Federal Court judge dismissed the case on grounds of national security.[32]

For three months after Arar's repatriation, the Canadian government refused to open an inquiry into the bruited involvement of Canadian officials in his deportation. Then Paul Martin, the newly elected prime minister, bent to public pressure and ordered a fact-finding commission in January 2004. "It's about his deportation and detention and it is about . . . the actions of Canadian officials, if any, in relation to those events," explained Anne McLellan, then the deputy prime minister. The head of the commission, Justice Dennis O'Connor, would be allowed to see classified documents and call witnesses. The government of the United States was invited to participate in the inquiry. It refused.

---

‡ The Palestine Branch detention camp has repeatedly been called a torture centre by Amnesty International and Human Rights Watch.

In spite of official denials, claims of ignorance, buck passing and the provision of government documents with sec-
tions blacked out for reasons of national security, a picture of
Canada's complicity in the deportation of Maher Arar
emerged over the next three years.[33] In April 2005, Justice
O'Connor released more than two thousand pages of internal
government correspondence—emails and memos suggesting
strongly that not only had senior Canadian officials failed to
prevent Arar's deportation, but they had also been openly
interested in the results of his interrogations, although they
suspected he was being tortured. In the fall of 2005 the
inquiry heard that Canada's admired national police force,
the Royal Canadian Mounted Police, had shared discrimina-
tory and faulty intelligence with Syrian and American officials. Superintendent Mike Cabana testified that after the
September 11 attacks his superiors had told him to disregard
Canada's traditional safeguards on the transfer of sensitive
information.[34] The new policy was called "the caveats are
down." Normal protections were no longer relevant.[35]

In October 2005 a fact-finder appointed by the inquiry concluded that Maher Arar had been tortured while in Syrian custody. On September 18, 2006, Justice O'Connor reported that
there was no evidence Arar was ever linked to extremist groups
or was a threat to Canada's national security. He confirmed that
the RCMP had long-standing rules to determine the kinds of
intelligence information they routinely exchanged with their
counterparts in the US, and that in this case the regulations were
disregarded. US security officials were given an inaccurate and
unfair picture of Maher Arar—information that "very likely led
to his deportation." O'Connor also found that the RCMP had
deliberately omitted important facts about Arar's case when
briefing senior government officials.[36]

On September 20, 2006, the Parliament of Canada issued
a unanimous apology to Maher Arar for his detention and

torture. Eight days later, Giuliano Zaccardelli, the commissioner of the RCMP, apologized to Arar for the contribution of the national police agency "to the terrible injustices that you experienced." On December 6, 2006, after denying that he would leave his post, Zaccardelli submitted his resignation to the prime minister. Finally, on January 25, 2007, Prime Minister Stephen Harper apologized to Maher Arar and his family on behalf of the Canadian government and offered more than $11 million in compensation for his suffering.

Still, the US government refused to clear Arar's name, claiming (still without evidence) to have information that had not been brought forward. The reason for this reluctance was monetary as well as political. To admit Arar's innocence would have obliged the Bush administration to acknowledge the existence of its policy of extraordinary rendition, which (although widely known) was officially a secret. It would also have triggered legal liability for wrongdoing and opened the door for Arar and others to sue for financial compensation for illegal arrest and detention, and other abuses. Unfortunately, until the United States admits that it sent an innocent man to be tortured in a third country, Maher Arar's reputation can never be fully restored.

The larger issue was that the American-led War on Terror had brought about the subversion of law in a neighbouring country. So eager were Canadian officials to please the Bush administration after 9/11 that they had "flattened the law," to paraphrase Robert Bolt's Sir Thomas More. And Canada was not alone. More than any other world leader, Britain's prime minister, Tony Blair, was from the start a full partner in the Bush administration's War on Terror. Among other collaborative acts, MI-5 intelligence officials had rendered two British residents into the hands of the American Central Intelligence Agency in late 2002. In November of that year, they were transferred to Guantánamo Bay. No charges were ever laid against them.[37] Events, as they rolled out in Britain, resonated like an echo from across the sea. The British government approved the March 2003 invasion of Iraq, although it knew that "the intelligence and facts [had been] fixed around the policy."[38] Britain's defence secretary, John Reid, called for the Geneva Conventions to be "redrawn" in order to expedite future military actions. (The rules were "out of date," he explained.)[39] But in a legal battle similar to that being played out in the US courts, a British high court judge called the Blair government's "control orders" against people suspected of terrorism "an affront to justice."[40]

Britain had a long-standing "special relationship" with the United States that went back decades. On the economic front, each favoured the other in its foreign investments. And the strong personal relationship between the previous prime minister, Margaret Thatcher, and the former American president Ronald Reagan had brought the two countries closer in their underlying ideologies. This was the legacy Tony Blair brought to the table in the post-9/11 world, and it made him vulnerable to US blandishments. But Blair did not back down in his defence of the reconfigured world order. On February 23, 2006, he told critics of his foreign policy and human rights record that they misunderstood the international situation: they had "the world the wrong way round"; he reconfirmed this position at the time of his resignation, in May 2007. Although he had assumed power as a social progressive, Blair would leave the government as the leader who had effectively completed the foreign policy shift initiated by Mrs. Thatcher. How history will judge his contribution to the American-led War on Terror is an open question.

On February 23, 2006, while the Arar Commission was still hearing witnesses, the news agencies Canadian Press (CP) and the Associated Press (AP) reported that CIA planes had refuelled in Canada seventy-four times since September 2001.[41] The information was contained in a report from Canada Border Services Agency (stamped SECRET) that had been released under Canada's Access to Information Act. The file revealed that senior intelligence officials from six federal government agencies had met in late November 2005 to discuss the flights—and what to say about them—since the government had issued a statement the previous January in which it claimed that a review of the purported landings had exposed no evidence of "illegal activities." The meeting was almost certainly precipitated by an open letter from Alex Neve, the secretary-general of Amnesty International Canada, dated November 22. Neve had asked for precise information about the purpose and destination of the flights. As everyone involved knew, to be complicit in the secret transportation of detainees to a third country was illegal under Canadian and international law.

Although Maher Arar's ordeal had begun with just such a flight, and although the commission exploring his case was still in session, the stonewalling continued. A memo in the file dated November 28, 2005, instructed officials to tell the media that there was "no credible information to suggest that these planes were used to ferry suspected terrorists to and from Canada, or that illegal activity took place."[42]

Alex Neve wrote again on January 18, 2006; then again on April 5. On July 27, 2006, he received a reply from a minister in the Conservative government of Stephen Harper assuring him that Canada "strongly values the human rights and fundamental freedoms that have made our country a model for the world."[43] A review had found "no information that would indicate irregularities or illegal activities with respect to aviation, immigration, customs, or applicable international rules." Had the government's review looked beyond aviation to human rights standards, Neve wrote back. He also inquired about the status of his recommendation that safeguards be established "to ensure that Canadian airspace and airports are not used by foreign governments in the course of international, illegal activities such as extraordinary rendition." There was no further reply.

"To be complicit in torture is a criminal act," said Neve in a telephone interview in early 2007. "We remain concerned that the government of Canada is not taking the question seriously."[44]

Canada's lack of interest contrasted with efforts by the Europeans to uncover similar breaches. The first report of CIA detention and torture centres in Europe was published by the *Washington Post* on November 3, 2005; and immediately following this exposé, Human Rights Watch confirmed that CIA prisoners had been flown from Afghanistan to Poland and Romania. That same month, the Council of Europe, a forty-six nation human rights group, appointed a special investigator to conduct public hearings—a Swiss politician and former prosecutor, Dick Marty, who had been a member of the council since 1998.

On January 22, 2006, Marty reported that CIA landings were being investigated in several countries, including Britain, France and Germany; and that Muslims had been kidnapped in Bosnia, Italy and Germany and sent to Guantánamo Bay.[45] What surprised him, he said, was that these rendition flights had been going on for several years before the media in any country explored the story. In his preliminary analysis, Marty reported that hundreds of CIA-chartered flights had passed over European territory, and that it was "highly unlikely" that the governments in question were unaware of this. He also mentioned Canada, signalling that Amnesty International had made many efforts to acquire information about CIA extraordinary rendition flights refuelling on Canadian territory and that no serious governmental investigation had taken place. "We have no doubt that Canada, a permanent observer to the [Council of Europe's Parliamentary] Assembly, will shed full light on the allegations," he wrote.[46]

As for the secret detention camps in which unnamed ghost detainees were tortured, there was enough "coherent, convergent evidence" to believe that they existed. And, he added, this seemed to be acceptable to certain governments (he mentioned the US and Germany) as long as *their* democracy was not doing the torturing. Human Rights Watch had already identified Poland and Romania as countries that housed detention camps. Marty also pointed to Bulgaria, Greece, Kosovo, Chechnya, Macedonia and Ukraine. In June 2007, Dick Marty confirmed that "high value" detainees had been held in secret CIA prisons in Poland and Romania between 2002 and 2005, without ruling out that secret detentions may also have occurred in other Council of Europe member states, including Italy and Germany, that had invoked "national security" concerns to thwart his investigations, and that "partly secret decisions" among NATO allies in October 2001 had created the framework for these illegal activities.[47]

The European Union warned its members that any country found to have operated secret CIA prisons could lose its voting rights and demanded answers from the US State Department. But the US government had already taken note of the gathering storm in Europe. In December 2005 the sites in Poland and Romania were closed and the inmates transferred to North Africa.

Both Poland and Romania had been seeking US aid and were eager to please. Poland had joined the US-led Coalition of the Willing in 2003 and sent two hundred soldiers to Iraq. Romania had offered the United States basing rights and signed an Article 98 agreement in which it agreed never to send a US citizen to the International Criminal Court. So there were interests at play. But was it a coincidence that Poland and Romania were countries in which human rights and democracy had only recently been introduced? After decades of totalitarian rule, the presence of secret state-run prisons would not have seemed unfamiliar. The same was true for Bulgaria, Kosovo, Chechnya, Macedonia and Ukraine—

all countries with relatively new (or still absent) democracies. The outlier was Greece.

Senator Marty called attention to the many investigations that were initiated after the story first broke in the *Washington Post*. He noted that several US government officials, who were now vying with one another to speak to researchers and the press off the record, were people who were well aware of the facts and could not, in conscience, accept such methods in the "war" against terrorism. "These officials face two contradictory imperatives: official secrecy and the ethical duty not to collude in acts infringing [on] human dignity," Marty said. "In this context, whistle-blowing is the expression of civic commitment and courage, rather than an act of denunciation or betrayal."[48]

It is disturbing to observe how quickly laws and rights slip away before the demands of a powerful state—and marginally reassuring to realize that the truth about abuses will eventually come to light and that countries with well-rooted institutions can usually recover. Canada's formal apology to Maher Arar was an acknowledgment that high-ranking officials had failed to respect Canada's laws. The resignation of the RCMP commissioner who held "command responsibility" for the breakdown marked a similar acceptance. When the head of the Arar commission recommended a new body to oversee the national police, and the federal government accepted his recommendation, that too was a righting of the balance. Canada went further still, setting up a second independent inquiry to explore the possible collusion of government officials in the cases of three other Canadian Muslims who had been imprisoned in Syria.[49] But the government's unwillingness to take a stand against the United States by seriously investigating its complicity in allowing secret CIA flights transporting prisoners to refuel in Canada was a major blot on its self-proclaimed human rights record. So was the scandal that broke in late

April 2007 over the transfer of Afghan detainees, to the Afghan authorities, by the Canadian military operating in southern Afghanistan. In a series of articles that helped to remind readers about the importance of on-the-ground investigative reporting, Graeme Smith of the *Globe and Mail* wrote that Afghans initially detained by Canadian soldiers were regularly "beaten, whipped, starved, frozen, choked and subjected to electric shocks during interrogation," despite assurances from the Canadian government that the rights of captured prisoners are always protected.[50] Since torture is a war crime under the Geneva Conventions, such transfers made Canada complicit under international law. Almost immediately, two experts in the field sent a letter to the ICC prosecutor Luis Moreno-Ocampo. William Schabas and Michael Byers (who holds the Canada Research Chair in Global Politics and International Law at the University of British Columbia) said the following: "We write to draw your attention to possible war crimes committed with respect to the transfer of detainees from Canadian custody in Afghanistan. In particular, we request that you open a preliminary examination . . . to determine whether there are reasonable bases to investigate Mr. Gordon O'Connor, the Canadian Minister of National Defence, and General Rick Hillier, the Canadian Chief of the Defence Staff . . ."[51]

Now Canada was the subject of a formal complaint to the very international institution it had worked so hard to found.

The ensuing commotion in the country would have been comical if it had been less serious. For an entire week the Harper-led government denied, stonewalled, made counter accusations and tried to discredit the reports. Taking a page from the political handbook of George W. Bush, Stockwell Day, the minister for public safety, suggested that the detainees (he called them "the Taliban") deserved no better because "these people . . . want nothing more than to kill [Afghanis] and their children."[52] In another echo from Washington, Prime

Minister Harper said that Canadians who worried about detainee transfers lacked respect for the troops in the field. As for the minister of defence, Gordon O'Connor couldn't get his story straight. One day Canada had a working agreement with the Red Cross; the next day it did not. Then he announced that Canada had an arrangement with the Afghan Independent Human Rights Commission to safeguard the rights of prisoners; but the commissioners quickly countered that they were not allowed entry into the prison.[§]

Finally, a new contract was drawn up, bringing Canada closer into line with standing agreements between the Afghan government and other NATO countries. Among other considerations, it required the Afghan government to investigate allegations of abuse by reference to international standards of justice, and in consultation with the Canadian government and human rights monitors. But without the pressure from the media, the letter to the International Criminal Court, and a court case brought by Amnesty International Canada and the British Columbia Civil Liberties Association seeking to halt Canada's transfer of prisoners, there would have been no effective oversight of the detainee situation by the Canadian government.[53]

Whether the new agreement worked remained to be seen, but the signs appeared dubious. Just months later, General Rick Hillier refused to release all documents pertaining to detainees captured in Afghanistan, citing reasons of national security.[54] The fracas that surrounded the treatment of prisoners was further evidence of the ethical slippage brought about by the War on Terror. Detainees had been tortured in known and secret places around the world for almost five years. Some of them were undoubtedly guilty of crimes, but others were not. Unfortunately, it was impossible to know

---

§ The beleagured minister was removed from his post on August 14, 2007.

who was who because established laws had been dismantled and just procedures no longer applied.

In Europe, quick action by the European Union effectively helped Romania and Poland to rid themselves of the American detainee camps. Alone, neither of these countries would have carried sufficient heft to take such steps.

Cherif Bassiouni had said it would take a long time before the rule of law re-established itself. He expressed shock that the legal foundations to society had proved to be so shallow, even ephemeral. He was right: the struggle over law was far from over.

—

On November 16, 2006, Senators Christopher J. Dodd, Russell Feingold and Patrick Leahy proposed the Effective Terrorists Prosecution Act of 2006, a bill they hoped would narrow the definition of "unlawful enemy combatants" by "excluding evidence obtained by coercion and allowing defendants to review evidence used against them."[55] Then on December 5, 2006, Senator Leahy (the incoming chairman of the Judiciary Committee) and his colleague Arlen Spector (the outgoing chairman) introduced the Habeas Corpus Restoration Act of 2006 "to restore habeas corpus for those detained by the United States."[56] Leahy berated his fellow lawmakers. "We have eliminated basic legal and human rights for the twelve million lawful permanent residents who live and work among us, to say nothing of the millions of other legal immigrants and visitors who we welcome to our shores each year. We have removed the check that our legal system provides against the Government arbitrarily detaining people for life without charge. . . . We have removed the mechanism the Constitution provides to check Government overreaching and lawlessness. This is wrong. It is unconstitutional. It is un-American. . . ."[57]

Leahy's language was passionate and heartfelt, but the Effective Terrorists Prosecution Act died at the end of the 109th congressional session before it reached a vote. The Habeas Corpus Restoration Act of 2006 also disappeared from the books at the end of the 109th session, but it was reintroduced by Senators Leahy and Spector on January 4, 2007, at the start of the 110th session. At this writing, the reintroduced bill has just begun its long trajectory though committees (it successfully passed the Senate Judiciary Committee and is on the Senate Legislative Calendar); however, should it succeed in both Houses of Congress, it will almost certainly be vetoed by the president. The Pentagon has already designed new rules for the military commissions that open the door to convictions and executions based on hearsay testimony as well as coerced statements. Suspects would be allowed to see only summaries of the evidence against them.[58] The deputy assistant secretary of defence for detainee affairs, Cully Stimson, has called on American corporations to boycott law firms whose attorneys represent suspected terrorists held at Guantánamo Bay. George Bush may be in his last term as president, but he is not giving in to pressure.

The first trial by a military commission opened in Guantánamo Bay on March 26, 2007, and closed the same day. The defendant was David Hicks, an Australian who had been held at the prison for five years. Many Australians were outraged by his incarceration and Hicks's case had become a political irritant in US-Australian relations. Given the lower standards that adhered to the military commissions, and given the US government's obvious need for a guilty verdict in its first hearing of an enemy combatant from Guantánamo Bay, Hicks was unlikely to be found innocent. But a long prison sentence would exacerbate the difficulties with Australia.

The solution was pure politics. On March 30, 2007, Hicks was sentenced to seven years, but there was a deal—a plea bargain. He agreed to plead guilty to "providing material support to a terrorist organization" (al-Qaeda), which allowed the Bush administration to justify its policy of incarcerating enemy combatants. And though he had previously accused his jailers of abusing him mentally and physically, he now signed a statement saying that he had "never been illegally treated" while being held by the United States, and that his detention was lawful pursuant to the laws of armed conflict. He also agreed that he would not talk to the media for a year. In return, his sentence was immediately commuted to nine months, which he was allowed to serve at home in Australia.[59]

Gary Solis thought that all the prisoners being held at Guantánamo Bay would eventually be released for lack of substantive evidence, an inevitability that would embarrass the United States for years to come. The David Hicks plea-bargain solution looked like a shrewder choice, one in which everyone seemed to win.

The cynicism was breathtaking. Beyond the transparency of expedient politics masquerading as justice, the absence of a real trial with real evidence meant that no one would ever learn the truth about David Hicks and al-Qaeda. More than five years after 9/11, the public deserved to know what was fact and what was fiction. Real trials provided that kind of information. Pretend trials did not.

In August 2007, Britain negotiated the release of five UK residents who were imprisoned at Guantánamo Bay (after having long refused to help them because they were not citizens). One of them, a former law student, immediated issued a dossier detailing the abuse he had endured and witnessed.[60] But the most unsettling case was that of the young Canadian, Omar Ahmed Khadr, who was accused of throwing the grenade that killed American soldier Christopher J. Speer, in Afghanistan in 2002, and of aiding al-Qaeda. Khadr was fifteen years old when he was arrested and transported to the

Guantánamo prison, where he became one of approximately two dozen children in the camp under the age of eighteen (including three who were thirteen). Omar Khadr was a prize because there were actual charges against him. He was scheduled to become the second detainee brought to trial under the Military Commissions Act.

The Khadr case was complicated. In May 2007, he fired his US lawyers, saying he wanted to be defended by Canadians. This created consternation: his demand ran counter to the rule that only American lawyers could represent the detainees in war crimes trials. Second, Khadr's age at the time of his purported crime became a legal *cause célèbre*. The disturbing issue of child soldiers was furrowing legal foreheads around the world. Youngsters as young as seven and eight were being recruited into the civil wars that raged in Africa and indoctrinated to kill. The question was whether a child, including a fifteen-year-old teenager, was capable of making a mature, deliberate choice for which he should be judged and possibily incarcerated for the rest of his life. (The US had decided not to seek the death penalty in this case.) Some thought, yes—including the widow of Sergeant Speer. Others argued that children who wage war are the victims of their kidnappers and recruiters. Soon after David Crane, the former chief war crimes prosecutor for Sierra Leone, was appointed to his post by UN Secretary General Kofi Annan, he announced that he would not try anyone under the age of eighteen. He thought younger warriors did not have the intellectual and emotional maturity to be prosecuted for war crimes.[61]

The Bush administration was determined to go ahead. Whatever the result, the Khadr hearing would set a legal precedent.

Like that of David Hicks, Omar Khadr's trial ended before it began, but in Khadr's case the manoeuvres played out by each side resembled a strategic chess game. During Khadr's first appearance before the Military Commission on

June 4, 2007, a US military judge dismissed all the charges against him on grounds of "lack of jurisdiction." Congress had created the military tribunals to try only so-called *unlawful* enemy combatants for war crimes or murder, said the judge, and the ruling on Khadr's status designated him only as an enemy combatant. Never had a missing adjective been so important: the Bush administration had been momentarily checkmated. The government made the next move: Omar Khadr would not be released. In fact, he might be held as a prisoner until the end of the War on Terror.

On June 29, a US military judge declined to revive the charges against Khadr. That same day the US Supreme Court agreed to hear the appeals of Guantánamo Bay detainees who were seeking a habeas corpus review of their cases. Not to be outdone, government prosecutors filed an appeal with the Court of Military Commission Review on July 4.[62] On September 24, they won. Now Khadr could be tried as a terrorist.

The case of Omar Khadr was controversial in Canada. The David Hicks case was resolved because the government of Australia had assumed the cause of one of its citizens. The Canadian government, on the other hand, showed little interest in repatriating Khadr for trial in Canada, even after the Bush administration announced that he would remain incarcerated—possibly forever—should things not go its way. Prime Minister Stephen Harper chose to stand by Washington, in spite of his obligations to a Canadian citizen. Perhaps he believed that he had enough public support to neglect this duty, for the Khadr family had been widely reviled since two of its members defended their suppport for terror in the cause of radical Islam on the public airways. With the exception of the occasional newspaper article demanding his return and a strongly worded letter to the government, signed by forty-five indignant Canadian and US lawyers,[63] Canadians had evinced little sympathy for Omar Khadr. This was a pity in a land that enjoys a strong commitment to human rights and the rule of law—a blight on its international reputation.

—

In late 2006, the Center for Constitutional Rights launched a new effort to indict Donald Rumsfeld for war crimes, after he was forced to resign following the midterm elections of November 2006. Although the German prosecutor had rejected the CCR's first attempt to create a case on the grounds that the United States was perfectly capable of conducting its own war crimes trials, the CCR now argued that because the US had refused to carry out its obligation to try senior officers, including Rumsfeld, for the many documented war crimes perpetrated during the Iraq war, the former defence secretary had to be brought to trial elsewhere. Such offences could not be ignored under international law, they argued.

The Center for Constitutional Rights charged Rumsfeld, Attorney General Alberto Gonzales and former CIA director George Tenet with command responsibility for torture and war crimes committed at Iraq's Abu Ghraib prison and at Guantánamo Bay. The plaintiffs in the case included eleven Iraqis who had been prisoners at Abu Ghraib, as well as a Saudi detainee from Guantánamo, Mohammad al-Qahtani, who had undergone a "special interrogation plan," including sexual humiliation and other forms of abuse. Had the case gone forward, none other than former Brigadier General Janis Karpinski (of Abu Ghraib infamy) had agreed to testify. "It was clear the knowledge and responsibility [for what happened at Abu Ghraib] goes all the way to the top of the chain of command to the Secretary of Defense Donald Rumsfeld," she said in a written statement. Other government lawyers were charged with facilitating, aiding and abetting torture by drafting erroneous legal opinions that justified the abuse.[64]

The case was complex, but not impossibly so. Scott Lyons, the project manager for the American Bar Association's Rule of Law Initiative, wrote that "the purpose of universal jurisdiction prosecution is to 'close gaps in punishability' and ensure criminal accountability. However," he added, "a State's interest in combating impunity must be balanced against the fundamental principle of non-interference in the affairs of foreign States."[65] True enough, but there was a major precedent for prosecuting lawyers for war crimes. The Nuremberg Tribunal indicted nine officials of Hitler's Ministry of Justice for participating in the drafting, and carrying out, of unlawful orders, which allowed war crimes to be perpetrated under the pretence of law. The Nazi lawyers also had decreed that the Geneva Convention on the treatment of prisoners of war did not apply to German actions. "While the allegations stemming from Iraq and Guantánamo Bay are in no way comparable to those relating to events in World War II, the [Nuremberg] 'Justice Case' forms an instructive precedent [for attaching] criminal responsibility to lawyers who provide legal justification for the commission of war crimes," added Lyons.

It seemed unlikely that the German federal prosecutor would indict the former defence minister of the world's most powerful nation even after a second invitation to do so—and on April 27, 2007, the case was formally rejected.

Had the lawsuit proceeded, the Military Commissions Act, and the suspected culpability of President Bush's advisers, might have been "clarified" outside the United States. By 2007 the "outside" mattered. The strong-arm go-it-alone defiance that characterized the presidency of George W. Bush was being undermined by a loss of support at home and the failures of his foreign policy.

President Bush would leave office after the US elections of November 2008, but it would take years, perhaps decades, to reverse the damage he and his advisers had caused.

—

Accountability. For five decades after the end of the Second World War, the International Law Commission of the United Nations quietly tried to draft a code of international criminal law and create a permanent international criminal court. That they finally succeeded was due largely to happenstance—to the genocidal wars of the 1990s in Bosnia and Rwanda. But few would have predicted the success of the new courts. As William Schabas put it in 2003, "Ten years ago, if you committed a human rights violation, a major atrocity, you had as much chance of being caught as you did being struck by lightning. I don't think that's quite so true anymore."[66]

Those who believed that sustainable peace is achievable only within the rules of international law were determined to push forward. The alternative, they said, was to stoke endless cycles of anger, revenge and violence. It was anger over criminal impunity that had so enraged the mothers and wives of the Srebrenica dead: the brazen visibility of blood-stained neighbours who still walked the streets of their towns and often held high positions in the community; the slow realization that only the "big fish" would be tried by the ICTY in The Hague; and the eventual understanding that no one would ever stand in that distant prisoner's dock for the murder of their loved ones. However, by January 2005 they had a modicum of hope: a special "hybrid" court to deal with violations of local, as well as international, law, with a staff of prosecutors and judges from inside and outside the country, opened its doors in Sarajevo. It would try low and mid-level perpetrators, leaving the ICTY to concentrate on its major cases.

It was anger over impunity that had compelled the mothers of "disappeared" children to parade around the Plaza de Mayo in central Buenos Aires for twenty years, carrying placards with

pictures of their missing sons and daughters, demanding justice—but here, too, there were signs of change. In June 2005
the Argentine government revoked the previous amnesties for
the Dirty War of the 1970s, thus opening the way for charges to
be brought against hundreds of people for torture, disappearances and baby kidnapping.

It was anger over impunity that drove thousands of demon-
strators into the streets of Santiago, Chile to demand that their
country's former leader, General Augusto Pinochet, be tried for
his crimes against his people. Although there had been several
inconclusive attempts to bring him to justice, the general died
peacefully on December 12, 2006, at the age of ninety-one,
thus adding his name to the list of twentieth-century tyrants
who expired in comfort at the end of their long lives.

Just as the exercise of unmitigated power had created
unexpected problems for overly confident leaders, so the
international courts had encountered obstacles. Although the
ICTY and the ICTR were dispensing justice fairly and creating new law for use in future trials, the physical distance from
the sites of the atrocities they were prosecuting, and their
failure to reach into the communities of the survivors, diminished their achievements in the minds of many. By 2005 there
were, or would soon be, hybrid courts in Bosnia, East Timor,
Sierra Leone and Cambodia. These were an intelligent half
measure between the fully international courts, such as the
ICTY, the ICTR and the ICC, and locally run tribunals.
The latter were often suspect. Unless a country had a record
of conducting trials according to internationally accepted
standards, the judgments rendered by its courts would be
seen as unfair.

The trial of Saddam Hussein was a case in point. Although
human rights organizations and international law associations
had urged the Iraqis and the Americans to prosecute the former dictator outside Iraq, or inside the country with a mix of

local and international judges to ensure standards, they were rebuffed. The result was a flawed trial. The defendants were allowed to grandstand and march out of the courtroom in protest. Saddam's half-brother Barzan Ibrahim wore pyjamas and sat with his back to the judges. The prosecution was permitted to present documents without previously advising the defence of their existence. And the presiding judge engaged in snide repartee with Saddam. Outside the courtroom, Iraqi politicians were indifferent, or oblivious, to the idea of judicial independence. The chief judge was forced to step down after being accused of softness with regard to the defendants. Security was almost non-existent. Three defence lawyers were murdered. A fourth escaped to save his life. Thirty witnesses were too frightened to testify.

The Saddam Hussein trial was a poster case for *not* prosecuting major international crimes in countries that lack the administrative, political and judicial capacity to do so fairly. This caveat had been written directly into the Rome Statute of the International Criminal Court. The ICC would take over when the country in which the suspected perpetrator held citizenship was unwilling, or unable, to fulfill its obligations according to international standards of justice.

—

One of the questions facing the new international courts was what ought to happen when a war winds down. Should critical peace deals include amnesty for the perpetrators of atrocities? Amnesty is the carrot that's dangled before suspected war criminals to entice them to lay down their arms. It is a trade-off: we'll forget about your crimes if you agree to stop the bloodletting.

But amnesty allows major perpetrators to escape justice. It means that people who have committed murder, rape and child abduction among other offences do not face consequences. It blocks accountability. It deprives the victims of their need—indeed, their right—to see justice done. Although amnesty may feel familiar to people living in Judeo-Christian cultures because it is often presented as an expression of Christian forgiveness, few remember that it is a cynical transaction. Or that it can block long-term stability because, without justice, the prospect of social reconciliation between previously warring parties is diminished. Furthermore, amnesty is altogether illegal under international law in major cases of crimes against humanity, genocide and war crimes.

The tables of peace conferences past are littered with the detritus of naive amnesties that failed. Take the case of Sierra Leone. Diamonds put that African country on the map. By 1970 yearly production was two million carats; by 1996 mined diamonds were worth approximately US$15 billion a year at an average price of US$270 per carat. Then the DeBeers company of South Africa, which had received exclusive mining and prospecting rights in the 1930s, was nationalized. Production dropped, and a frenzied free-for-all ensued.

First among the pillagers was a rebel warlord named Charles Taylor—the future president of Liberia. During the anarchic, almost decade-long civil war that began in 1991, Taylor's militias hacked off limbs, lips and ears from unfortunates who happened to cross their path. Taylor personally sponsored Foday Sankoh, a Sierra Leonean associate who set up his own Revolutionary United Front. Their "friendship" centred on the diamonds. Sankoh would keep Sierra Leone in turmoil while Taylor maximized his profits, which he shared with the RUF leader. Sankoh's barbarity knew no bounds. The RUF specialized in mass rape and hacking off limbs. They were also accused of cannibalism.

As a condition of the 1999 Lomé Accord between the government of Sierra Leone and the Revolutionary United Front,

Foday Sankoh was pardoned and amnestied. So were all the members of his gangs pardoned and amnestied "in respect of anything done by them in pursuit of their objectives," which was as broad a "condition" as could be imagined.[67] Sankoh was rewarded by being named head of a powerful government commission, after which he immediately restarted the conflict.

Not until the Sierra Leone hybrid court was established in January 2002 and both Sankoh and Taylor were indicted for their crimes was there a glimmer of justice in the ravaged country. Sankoh happened to be already in custody (he was arrested in 2000, after his soldiers gunned down protesters), but he died of a stroke while awaiting his trial. Taylor, by contrast, disappeared into Nigeria after being offered sanctuary by the president of that country. Such was the impunity of the powerful. Seeking refuge from a welcoming country was a time-honoured tradition . . . although Taylor was, as it happens, eventually delivered to the Sierra Leonean court.[68]

Cherif Bassiouni had said, "Peace and justice are not necessarily exclusive." He believed that amnesty should never be offered to "decision makers and senior executors," or to anyone at a lower lever who has engaged in torture; but amnesty might be allowed for certain categories of persons, such as "nominal members of a ruling party," and "identifiable categories of low to mid rank officials . . . whose involvement . . . in the particular atrocity was not something that, under the circumstances, that category [of official] could have acted against."[69] But these limited amnesties always had to take into account the ultimate goal of reconciliation; in other words, the victims must not feel that they had been denied justice. Nor should such qualified amnesties exclude other remedies, such as the payment of compensation, the removal of perpetrators from government positions or the establishment of truth commissions.

The rest was trickier. If the negotiator cannot promise amnesty, "it can nonetheless be understood that prosecutions may not be imminent," Bassiouni said. "When I was chairman of the Security Council commission to investigate war crimes in the former Yugoslavia, I did not publicize the investigations, which meant that the senior perpetrators with whom [Cyrus] Vance and [Lord David] Owen were negotiating were not embarrassed by being publicly branded as subjects of a criminal investigation. Nor did I come out and make claims that they might be indicted as war criminals. . . . I could have kept the evidence in the file . . . until a peace deal was signed. This is what I mean by saying that there is a question of timing. [On the other hand] a 'realpolitician' could take this one step further and hint at an amnesty or a pardon, and even put some words to that effect in the peace agreement as a way of inducing a particularly fractious leader to sign, as was the case with [Charles] Taylor in Sierra Leone. Then things may change—again, in the case of Taylor, after he obtained refuge in Nigeria." (Liberia's new leader, Ellen Johnson-Sirleaf, demanded Taylor's extradition so he could stand trial.)

Bassiouni's explanation was subtle, complex and practical—although it might depend on one's tolerance for the *realpolitik* solution of proposing the possibility of amnesty while knowing it would not be granted. On the other hand, attaching qualified amnesties to peace negotiations could mean saving the lives of innocent people, at least in the short term.

—

By July 2007, 105 countries had ratified the Rome Statute of the International Criminal Court: twenty-six Western European states (included in this category were Canada, Australia and New Zealand); twenty-eight African states; twenty-two Latin American states (including the Caribbean); fifteen Eastern European states; and thirteen Asian states.[70] Few would have imagined this level of support on the eve of the 1998 Rome conference that gave birth to the tribunal. More surprising still, the International Criminal Court was gaining acceptance in the United States, now that the neo-conservative project was faltering. As David Scheffer noted, the ICC member states had made no mistakes when they elected the judges and the prosecutor. And the court's first indictments in Uganda and the Democratic Republic of the Congo (DRC) had not raised anyone's hackles over national sovereignty.

The turning point in the United States was the deteriorating situation in Darfur. In January 2005 a UN commission headed by Antonio Cassese, a professor of law at the University of Florence, recommended to Kofi Annan that the perpetrators in that conflict be turned over to the ICC;[71] and on March 31, 2005, the Security Council complied with a referral. The US agreed to abstain from the vote, a compromise that permitted the resolution to pass.[72] It was not in the interests of the US to cast a veto after the Bush administration had proclaimed that the violence in Sudan had to end. On September 9, 2004, then-Secretary of State Colin Powell had called the situation in Darfur "genocide," a designation that can trigger intervention under international law. Nine months later, on June 1, 2005, President Bush used the same potent word.

The referral from the Security Council marked a coup for the International Criminal Court and a diplomatic U-turn for the Bush administration, since the resolution allowed the ICC to conduct investigations in a sovereign state (like the US) that had not signed the Rome Statute (like the US).

On May 19, 2006, a new opinion poll shed light on changing public attitudes in America. Although the United States' refusal to join the International Criminal Court remained controversial, 74 percent of respondents favoured US participation. When the same people were asked a longer version of the question, which included the government's argument that "trumped-up charges may be brought against Americans, for example US soldiers who use force in the course of a peace-keeping operation," bipartisan support dropped slightly, but only to 68 percent. "The American public continues to show strong support for having international courts and tribunals and does not feel that the US should have any special treatment," concluded Steven Kull, the editor of WorldPublicOpinion.org and the principal investigator for the study.[73] In another endorsement of the tribunal, Jendayi Frazer, the top US diplomat in Africa, announced that same month that Washington wanted to "get rid of" Uganda's Lord's Resistance Army by the end of the year. "There's this nasty little group . . . in northern Uganda which is just creating havoc, killing kids, kidnapping people and we have to take care of that problem. . . . As ICC indicted war criminals, they need to be captured and turned over to the court," she remarked. This seemingly casual acceptance of the place of the International Criminal Court in the firmament of global institutions spoke for itself. So did the fact that no one in Washington rushed to contradict her.

Weeks later, John Bellinger, the State Department's chief lawyer, said in an interview, "Divisiveness over the ICC distracts from our ability to pursue . . . common goals" in the fight against genocide and crimes against humanity. . . . We do acknowledge that it has a role to play in the overall system of international justice."[74] And in November 2006 the Council on Foreign Relations posted a report in which military personnel argued that "the US government needs to inform the military about the ICC to reduce military anxiety, address US interests directly by participating in the Court's proceedings, and close any gaps between US law and the crimes within the ICC's jurisdiction."[75] A shift seemed to be taking place at the top. Months earlier, on March 10, 2006, Secretary of State Condoleezza Rice had lobbed a small torpedo into the administration's ICC policy during an official visit to Chile. We should not be "shooting ourselves in the foot" by cutting off aid from nations that co-operate with the US in the drug wars or the War on Terror, she said. These remarks were echoed just four days later by the head of the US Southern Command in a statement before the Senate Armed Services Committee. "Although well-intentioned, ASPA [the American Service Members Protection Act] continues to have unintended consequences," reported General Bantz J. Craddock.[76] "Eleven partner nations in our area of responsibility are unable to attend US international military education and training programs. . . . The fact is, foreign military financing is gone. . . . Other nations are moving in. The People's Republic of China has made many offers."

One could be certain that neither John Bolton nor Senator Jesse Helms had considered the possibility that they might be hindering "military education programs" and "foreign military financing"—both long-standing features of US strategy in Latin America. In the race to prevent China and possibly India from overtaking the US in influence, ideology (as Gorbachev had astutely noted) had turned out to be a poor foundation for policy.

—

The ICC's first cases were all in Africa—in the troubled, post-colonial hot spots where strongmen and anarchical wars over power and mineral resources had hijacked the potential for good governance.[77] In December 2003, the tribunal received its first referral from a member state when the Ugandan president, Yoweri Museveni, invited Luis Moreno-Ocampo to investigate possible crimes against humanity being committed in the northern region of the country. A war between rebels and government-controlled forces had been raging there since Museveni had seized power in 1986.

Since 1966, when the national liberation hero Milton Obote suspended the constitution soon after taking power,

Uganda's history was a story of non-stop violence. Rebel war-lords (including the notorious Idi Amin) seized power one after the other, and although the country had rich natural resources, murderous sweeps through the rural territories had induced cycles of famine and starvation. The so-called Lord's Resistance Army was born in 1987 after the leader, Joseph Kony, climbed a hill to fast for several days before announcing that he would overthrow Museveni. Its origin was the Holy Spirit Movement, a cult led by a female priest who claimed that butter protected her warriors from bullets. Kony, her cousin, declared himself divinely ordained to create a Ugandan state based on the Ten Commandments; and in order to realize his utopia (which had no apparent political agenda), he and his rampaging gangs set out to destroy the local Acholi people in the north of the country. They abducted Acholi children between the ages of seven and fourteen to fill their soldierly ranks and sometimes forced them to murder their own par-ents. Thousands died. Two million people were displaced. The descendants of the nineteenth-century Christian missionaries must have quailed to see the result of their earnest teachings.

In July 2005, the ICC issued arrest warrants for five senior leaders of the Lord's Resistance Army, charging them with crimes against humanity, war crimes, intentionally directing an attack against a civilian population and the forced enlist-ment of children; and the following May, chilled by the prospect of arrest, Joseph Kony emerged from the bush to talk peace. "I am not a terrorist," he protested. "I am a rebel in military opposition. . . . If Museveni says [otherwise], then it means that all opposition leaders in Africa should also be taken to The Hague."[78]

In return for peace, Kony wanted all ICC charges against himself and his followers dropped, and Museveni, it seemed, was more than willing. He promised Kony that there would be no courtroom trials anywhere, including in Uganda. Not surprisingly, the Ugandan president's overtures angered the ICC prosecutor and the judges. "The position of the court . . . is that these warrants of arrest remain in force," said a spokesperson for the tribunal in July 2006. "The court has received assurances from the relevant countries that they will co-operate in effecting these warrants of arrest."

By then, a whole year had passed since the tribunal had issued its warrants. There had been no arrests, and a battle over amnesty versus justice was brewing. In July 2006 Moreno-Ocampo published a vague statement noting that the Ugandan minister for security had visited The Hague, and that it was the view of both the Office of the Prosecutor and the Ugandan government that "justice and peace have worked together thus far and can continue to work together."[79] This fooled no one, least of all Joseph Kony. The ICC seemed to be in trouble.

In September 2006, Luis Moreno-Ocampo reported on his activities over the last three years during meetings with the ICC States Parties and NGOs. He was pleased to observe that the international community had placed its trust in the International Criminal Court. The evidence lay in the many case referrals his office had received, including the all-important one from the United Nations Security Council concerning the crisis in Darfur. He described the criteria he followed in choosing which of the suggestions to investigate. Provided that the ICC had jurisdiction over a situation, cases were selected according to their "gravity," he said—a stipulation that was written into the Rome Statute. And because conditions on the ground were always difficult and sometimes dangerous for the investigative teams (they sought out witnesses who were frequently them-selves in danger), his office had decided to focus on the most serious crimes and the perpetrators who bore the greatest responsibility. He also said that the Office of the Prosecution hoped to complete two trials over the next two years.

There were questions and comments from the audience, but it was the troublesome business of securing a peace deal versus the need for justice that provoked the most discussion. Hlengiwe Mkhize, South Africa's ambassador to the Netherlands, recalled that her country had dealt with the aftermath of apartheid with a truth and reconciliation commission. "But there is no substitute for justice," she added. "Victims are entitled to peace *and* justice. . . . The prosecutor must pursue justice without undermining peace." (This, as everyone knew, was easier said than done.)

Gareth Evans, the former foreign minister of Australia (among other high-level positions) and now the president of the International Crisis Group, a well-regarded NGO that analyzes and seeks to prevent deadly conflict, probed the sticky issue with the greatest depth. "Dealing with impunity and pursuing peace are not necessarily incompatible objectives," he said, echoing Cherif Bassiouni. "They can unquestionably work in tandem, even in an ongoing conflict situation." He observed that the number of crimes committed by the LRA in northern Uganda had diminished drastically since the ICC arrest warrants were issued, likely because the leadership did not want to make things worse for themselves by multiplying atrocities. He also noted that the act of issuing the warrants seemed to have instigated the peace process. Joseph Kony may have believed that by coming to the table, he could trade off ending the insurgency for amnesty. "But only in the most exceptional cases . . . should serious consideration be given to discontinuing [judicial] investigations or granting formal amnesties," Evans continued.[80] "The risk of these situations is that the more the ICC's work is perceived as 'negotiable,' the more its role as a deterrent of atrocity crimes is undermined."

Gareth Evans didn't have to mention the need for accountability, the need for a historical record of what took place during a conflict or the need for long-term reconciliation: all these were part of the global understanding that justice is central to peace. His final point was a practical one. The ICC prosecutor's job is to prosecute, and he should get on with it, he advised. He should not be asked to adjudicate whether to give primacy to peace over justice. That is the job of those with the appropriate political responsibility, including the Security Council, which has the option to make that (short-term) choice under the Rome Statute, depending on the circumstances. "We are constantly wrestling with the tension between peace and justice," he concluded. "The international community needs to spend more time addressing [this] than it has so far."

The sly dealings of the Ugandan president Yoweri Museveni received only passing attention (what was said privately was another story), although it seemed obvious that he had solicited criminal indictments from the ICC in order to smoke LRA leader Joseph Kony out of the bush. Now Museveni wanted the ICC to withdraw altogether. He called the work of the tribunal "neo-colonialism." He pointed to South Africa's truth and reconciliation commission as a better alternative.

South Africa's TRC had served a purpose: among other things, it had created an authentic record of the apartheid years, thus preventing a narrative of denial from taking root. And, yes, it was the case that the white leaders of the National Party had refused to co-operate with possible courtroom trials, knowing they might be the first to be indicted for major crimes. But the circumstances in South Africa were different from those in Uganda. South Africa was in transition from white rule to a full civic democracy, with a new constitution and working institutions. Furthermore, the truth commission had the authority to transfer any perpetrator to the country's real law courts if certain conditions of the process were breached.[81] Uganda, by contrast, held none of this structural promise. One day, when there was stability in the country, a truth and reconciliation commission might be a useful addition to courtroom justice. But it was far too soon: the still-warring parties would be likely to use the new platform as a weapon against one another. In Uganda (as in Bosnia), fair trials for the perpetrators of massive atrocities had to come first; they would be the first necessary baby steps toward justice and durable peace.

Richard Goldstone, the first prosecutor of the International Criminal Tribunal for the former Yugoslavia, thought that dropping charges against Joseph Kony "would be fatally damaging to the credibility of the international court. I just don't accept that Museveni has any right to use the International Criminal Court like this. If you have a system of international justice, you've got to follow through on it. If in some cases that's going to make peace negotiations difficult, that may be the price that has to be paid. The international community must keep a firm line and say, Are we going to have a better world because of the international court or not?"[82]

In August 2006 Joseph Kony pleaded with the government of the Central African Republic (CAR) for asylum. CAR was a state party to the ICC. In February 2007 he was reported to have entered the country. (François Bozize, the president, claimed ignorance of this event.)

—

On March 17, 2006, the ICC announced that it had issued an arrest warrant for a suspected perpetrator from another conflict. Thomas Lubanga Dyilo was a citizen of the Democratic Republic of the Congo and the leader of a rebel movement called the Union of Congolese Patriots.

If Uganda's post-colonial hopes had been permanently sidetracked by its first leader, Milton Obote, the newly liberated DRC had also been ruined by internecine power struggles. As the American writer Adam Hochschild so vividly demonstrated in his 1998 book, *King Leopold's Ghost*, Belgium's misrule of the Congo was unequalled in the history of European colonization. Between 1885 and 1908 ten million Congolese (approximately half the population) died enslaved to the boundless greed of King Leopold II, the plunderer of the region's rubber resources, whose rule was enforced by legions of barbarous underlings who severed the limbs of workers who failed to meet the rubber extraction quotas (a practice later imitated by the brutalized Congolese). Faced with international opprobrium, the Belgian parliament took over the administration of the colony in 1908, but by the 1920s, national independence movements had undermined the passive acquiescence of the local populations there and all over the colonized world. By June 1960 the Belgian Congo was free. The new name for the country was the Republic of the Congo (later the Democratic Republic of the Congo, then Zaïre, then once again the DRC).

As in Uganda, an internecine power struggle immediately catapulted the country into a conflict from which it has effectively never recovered. The dream of settled democracy did not materialize.

Ironically, it was refugees fleeing the 1994 genocide in neighbouring Rwanda who touched off the most recent catastrophe. Among the escapees were Hutus who had participated in the massacres of the Tutsis. They formed militias in the refugee camps and mounted cross-border attacks on Rwanda, but also on a nearby Congolese community of ethnic Tutsis. The DRC president, Laurent Kabila, responded by training tribes of rural hunters and farmers to repel the Rwandan Hutus; in other words, he decided to wage war by creating millions of new "soldiers" without any overarching military leadership— with disastrous consequences.

The ensuing clash lasted until 2003, killing sixty thousand people, after which the Kabila-sponsored militias (who believed they had been insufficiently rewarded for their contribution and also hoped to control the mineral-rich province of Ituri) turned their sights on the government. One such group, the Mayi-Mayi guerrillas, were believed to hold mystical religious powers—and like the Lord's Resistance Army in Uganda, they hammered their "magic" into a weapon with which to terrorize the rural population and press children into their ranks. The humanitarian crisis exploded into the worst in the world: according to a 2006 UNICEF report, twelve hundred people, including six hundred children, were dying daily from violence, malnutrition and disease.[83] Ten million needed assistance.

In March 2004 President Joseph Kabila (his father, Laurent, was assassinated in 2001) asked the ICC to investigate the atrocities taking place in the northeastern province of Ituri, on the understanding that "complementarity" was not an option: the national courts of the DRC were, everyone agreed, incompetent to conduct major trials. A multinational team of ICC investigators heard testimony from victims and witnesses and identified several individuals who bore the most responsibility. Chief among these was Thomas Lubanga Dyilo. As luck had it, Lubanga was already in custody in Kinshasa. He had been jailed the previous year after investigations had linked him to the killings of nine Bangladeshi UN peacekeepers.

The ICC charges against him involved recruiting, or kidnapping, an estimated thirty thousand youngsters between the ages of seven and fourteen to serve in the myriad units of his armed guerrillas. Sometimes the children joined for food; sometimes to avenge their murdered families. No distinctions were drawn between soldiers and civilians.

Following the publication of his arrest warrant on March 17, 2006, Thomas Lubanga Dyilo was transferred to The Hague. And on March 20, 2006, he appeared before the tribunal's Pre-Trial Chamber, becoming the first person to sit in the dock of the new court.

It was a momentous occasion—but the complaints did not tarry. Although NGOs welcomed the arrest, as expected, they were concerned that the charges did not go far enough.[84] Lubanga and his movement were also responsible for rape, torture, mutilations and summary executions, they said. The people of the Democratic Republic of the Congo needed to know that these crimes would also be accounted for. In Ituri, people worried because only one leader, of one ethnic group, had been arrested. They thought this might actually exacerbate the conflict. The prosecutor replied that the "recruitment" charges against Lubanga were merely the start of his investigations.

Standing before his judges in a cold northern city far from home, Thomas Lubanga Dyilo was asked his profession. "I'm a politician," he replied. Given the long, sorry history of his country, one needn't have been surprised. Joseph Kony of Uganda had made the identical claim.

During our conversation in The Hague, the ICC prosecutor Luis Moreno-Ocampo had talked about "consensus," which he described as "the rules people live by, an agreement about justice and peace." But in places such as the Democratic Republic of the Congo and Uganda, there was no common accord. The defendants were poised for a collision with the rules of the international community. Their skewed understanding of politics, governance and law would be just one of the challenges facing the judges of the newborn International Criminal Court.[85]

Coda

———

On November 24, 2006, UN Secretary-General Kofi Annan sent a message to the representatives of the ICC States Parties, who were meeting in The Hague. The International Criminal Court has established itself "at the heart of a truly international system of criminal justice," he told the assembled members. "Few could have expected that by 2006, a fully operational entity would have initiated its first trials, an Office of the Prosecutor would be prosecuting or investigating multiple situations, there would be a Security Council referral, and the Court would have issued its first warrants of arrest."[1]

Kofi Annan did not exaggerate. The dramatic birth of the International Criminal Court and its early tentative successes suggest that the international community is moving slowly (if not unerringly) toward a regime of universal criminal justice:* the court already has the support of more than half the nations in the world. There is a practical reason for this success. Global society has shrunk so significantly that atrocities in one place have almost instant repercussions in another, as was made clear when the presence of genocidal war in Bosnia threatened its European neighbours. A respected system of international criminal justice is self-protection against others—and potentially against one's own.

The strongest countries will resist the longest because they believe themselves forceful enough to sustain old-style immunity for their elites. It is a fact that the United States, China, India and Russia are still not States Parties to the ICC. But if the examples of Augusto Pinochet, who was hounded by the threat of prosecution until the day he died, and Charles Taylor, who was extradicted to Liberia, then sent to The Hague for trial, are signs of things to come, the sleep of other dubious world leaders will become increasingly troubled as the years pass.

How and why this happened speaks to the personal drive of those who contributed to the creation of the court and the power of their commitment. Benjamin Ferencz, for one, never gave up: for sixty years he told whoever would listen that the missing link in the world order was accountability— international criminal justice. Cherif Bassiouni's long advocacy was recognized by a nomination for a Nobel Peace Prize. Simon Wiesenthal was still another. In his six-decade search for the fugitive perpetrators of the Nazi Holocaust, he acted

---

* By June 2007, the ICC had also issued arrest warrants for two suspected perpetrators of war crimes in Sudan (including the minister for humanitarian affairs) and opened an investigation in the Central African Republic.

on behalf of the millions whose voices were silenced by Hitler. But an utterly chance configuration of events also contributed to the re-emergence of international criminal justice during the 1990s. When the international community found itself helpless in the face of new genocides that it had failed to prevent, it reached for a solution: the courtroom trials of the perpetrators.

Beneath the better-known events of the past two centuries, there has coursed a second, parallel, history. It is a story of talk, as opposed to action—a tale of thousands of individuals, among them diplomats, policy-makers, philosophers and activists, who endeavoured to assign law to the chaos of the battlefield and to the treatment of prisoners and civilians. What elements might provide a sturdy foundation for peace after conflict, they asked; and what might constitute "justice." Among them, the enduring work of Socrates, the Athenian, still shines brightly. He characterized justice as equilibrium, or balance—what he called the "health" of an entity—whether a human being or a state. He argued that the *un*just person, or state, was destined to fail precisely because he, she or it, lacked such balance. Although few today read the ancient Greeks, Socrates' analysis informs our thinking in unnoticed ways. For the goals of international criminal justice—the deterrence of major crime, post-conflict reconciliation and long-term peace—are essentially those of social balance: the creation or *re*-creation of an environment where human beings can live in security under the protection of the rule of law.

This "justice," in the sense of balance, extends beyond the courtroom. It is present when compensation is paid to the surviving victims of major crimes against populations. It resides on the grassy knolls of present-day Rwanda, where tribal leaders sometimes complement the work of the International Criminal Tribunal for Rwanda by "prosecuting" local perpetrators before their communities. The idea of justice as restorative balance can be found in truth and reconciliation commissions designed to expose the irrefutable facts of a conflict, and to bring a perpetrator and his victim face to face.

At the root of all these efforts to define rights and to deprive high-placed criminals of their immunity before the law lies the tragedy of civilians who become trapped in the tangled web of violence. The right of ordinary people to protection from the consequences of wars they did not initiate was breached when the mighty Athenians enslaved the entire Melian population. It rose to the surface when the Allies spoke briefly of charging senior Turks for the indiscriminate massacre of their country's minority Armenians—before politics gained the upper hand and the matter was laid to rest. The mass murder of civilians underscored the trials of the top Nazis at Nuremberg. The inherent right to protection was written into the Universal Declaration of Human Rights, the founding document of the United Nations. It lies at the heart of the ICTY prosecutions for the former Yugoslavia, the ICTR prosecutions for Rwanda and the other designated courts currently hearing cases of crimes against humanity in places as diverse as Cambodia, Sierra Leone and Sarajevo. The survivors of atrocities are slated to play an even larger role at the International Criminal Court, which plans to focus on justice for the victims as well as the perpetrators, and to include the former in the proceedings of the tribunal itself. When Thomas Lubanga Dyilo of the Democratic Republic of the Congo becomes the first to sit in the ICC prisoner's dock, the evidence against him will highlight the tribunal's intent. Lubanga is accused of abusing children, the most vulnerable citizens of all.

Sadly, whatever help they receive, it is doubtful that civilian survivors can fully recover, or that justice, in whatever form it is offered, can fully satisfy. A memory of the past indelibly stains the future. As an example, I recently learned that at a residence for the elderly in Toronto, some Holocaust survivors who have lost their short-term memories can now remember nothing but the appalling torments that once consumed their bodies and minds.[2] All the same, the partial antidote of trial courts, truth and reconciliation commissions, symbolic compensation and other forms of support are of rare importance—and the permanence of the International Criminal Court is especially significant, for the global nature of criminal justice has the potential to redesign the international landscape in some small part.

The ICC is Robert H. Jackson's dream reborn. On December 20, 1945, the American chief prosecutor of the Nuremberg Tribunal recorded a message to be broadcast to the United States on Christmas Eve. He said, "The utter and irreparable collapse of the [Nazi] doctrine that might makes right is the most significant feature of the Nuremberg trials. . . . The world is proceeding on [the] basis that power and might are subject to moral responsibility."[3]

Sixty years later, Luis Moreno-Ocampo—Jackson's successor—stood at a podium in the modern metropolis of Nuremberg. "During the Nuremberg trials, those who committed massive crimes were held accountable before the international community," he reminded the delegates to an international conference on peace and justice. "For the first time, the victors of a conflict chose law to define responsibilities. But the world was not ready for a lasting institution. We would wait almost half a century and would again witness two genocides, first in the Former Yugoslavia and then in Rwanda, before the Security Council decided to create the ICTY and the ICTR, thus connecting peace and international justice once again.

"Today the issue is no longer whether or not we agree with the pursuit of justice in moral or practical terms. It is about the law that was created in the Rome Statute—law that built upon the lessons of decades of violence and atrocities.

For in the real world of 2007, no state has sufficient power to protect the lives and freedoms of its citizens. Only the rule of law can protect us."[4]

———

During the inauguration of the ICC in March 2003, a string ensemble performed Alexander Borodin's haunting Nocturne, from the String Quartet no. 2. There were many hundreds of us in the ancient Hall of Knights of the Netherlands that day— many who had striven for years to create the court, foreign diplomats representing their governments and observers like myself. The poignant music evoked the memory of those who had been lost and those who were saved. It reminded us that the new tribunal would confront the perpetrators of the world's most fearful crimes.

> *The dead read backwards,*
> *as in a mirror. They gather*
> *in the white field and look up,*
> *waiting for someone*
> *to write their names.*
>   —Anne Michaels, "What the Light Teaches,"
>   *The Weight of Oranges*

At the start of the twenty-first century, universal justice—the ancient dream of humanity—stands poised to greet the morning light.

NOTES

—

I. THE INAUGURATION

1. Genocide: Acts committed with the intent to destroy, in whole or in part, a national ethnic, racial, or religious group. Crimes against Humanity: Murder, enslavement, deportation, rape, and torture committed in a widespread and systematic attack against a civilian population, and persecutions on religious, racial or political grounds. War Crimes: Violations of the laws of war, such as the Geneva Convention of 1949 and the 1907 Hague Regulations on Land Warfare.

2. ROOTS AND TENDRILS

1. Thucydides, *History of the Peloponnesian War*, trans. Rex Warner, Penguin Books, Harmondsworth, Middlesex, England, 1954. 2, 40.
2. Ibid., 2, 37.
3. Sophocles, *Theban Plays*, trans. E.F. Watling, Penguin Classics, 1947.
4. "I did not think your edicts strong enough ... none of us can tell," unpublished translation by Thomas M. Robinson, 2006.

3. THE NEW WORLD ORDER

1. Alexander Kemos, "The Influence of Thucydides in the Modern World," *Point of Reference*, Harvard University, September 1997.
2. Ibid.
3. Ibid.
4. Elliott Abrams, Richard L. Armitage, William J. Bennett, Jeffrey Bergner, John Bolton, Paula Dobriansky, Francis Fukuyama, Robert Kagan, Zalmay Khalilzad, William Kristol, Richard Perle, Peter W. Rodman, Donald Rumsfeld, William Schneider, Jr., Vin Weber, Paul Wolfowitz, R. James Woolsey, Robert B. Zoellick, January 27, 1998.
5. *Neoconservatism*, edited by Irwin Stelzer (London: Atlantic Books, 2004).
6. Cited in *The New Statesman*, November 1, 2004.
7. Roland Paris, *At War's End: Building Peace after Civil Conflict* (Cambridge: Cambridge University Press, 2004). Paris uses case studies to argue that

345

instituting democratic elections too early in a post-conflict situation can lead to a resumption of hostilities, impeding reconstruction.

8. The first three conventions were passed many decades earlier, as we shall see. By summer 2006, the last holdout, Nauru, had signed the Fourth Convention. The US signed on August 12, 1949, but only ratified August 2, 1955. Israel signed on December 8, 1949, and ratified July 7, 1950. However, Israel claims that the convention applies only in the territory of a High Contracting Party and that the Occupied Territories essentially belonged to no one after the League of Nations mandates ended. (On July 9, 2004, the International Court of Justice ruled against the "high contracting parties" phrase on grounds that they ran against the convention's purpose, concluding that Israel's security barrier was a violation of the conventions.)

4. THE MAN AT THE STATE DEPARTMENT

1. Christopher Marquis, "Absent from the Korea Talks: Bush's Hard-Liner," *New York Times*, September 2, 2003.

2. Bolton couldn't take action against his superiors, but during the controversial hearings over his 2005 nomination as US ambassador to the United Nations, it was alleged by Alan Foley, a former CIA chief, that Bolton had visited CIA headquarters to demand that a senior intelligence analyst who disagreed with him on Cuba's biological warfare capabilities be removed.

3. Gabriel Espinosa Gonzales, "The Dubious Career of John Bolton: The Latest Mad Man at Foggy Bottom," *Counterpunch*, December 16, 2004.

4. Jeremy Rabkin, *The Case for Sovereignty: Why the World Should Welcome American Independence* (Washington, DC: AEI Press, 2004), 44–51.

5. See www.cia.gov/cia/reports/chile/#7.

6. Christopher Hitchens, *The Trial of Henry Kissinger*, Verso Books, New York, 2001.

7. Henry Kissinger, "The Pitfalls of Universal Jurisdiction: Risking Judicial Tyranny," *Foreign Affairs*, 80, no. 4 (July–August 2001): 86–96.

8. According to William Schabas, Article 98 of the Rome Statute was designed to ensure that established immunities, including diplomatic immunities, were not overridden by the obligation to transfer people to the court. (Should these immunities not be in place, no one would send ambassadors to another country.) When UN troops are involved, there is usually a treaty between the UN and the country called a Host State Agreement. In Schabas's opinion, the US distorted Article 98 by asking states to make agreements by which all Americans (and even some non-Americans who work with Americans) are protected. It would be as if they asked another state to recognize all their nationals as diplomats, and therefore the recipients of diplomatic immunity—technically possible, but a distortion of what

immunities stand for. In a speech to the Federalist Society on November 13, 2003, John Bolton defended the legitimacy of the Article 98 agreements, claiming that they were indeed coherent with the meaning of the Rome Statute. He blamed "EU officials" and "the presumptuously named civil society [groups]" for spreading false news.

9. Cited in Ian Traynor, "East Europeans Torn on the Rack by International Court Row," *Guardian* (London and Manchester), August 17, 2002.

10. Office of International Information Programs, US Department of State. www.state.gov.

11. American Non-Government Organizations Coalition for an International Criminal Court (AMICC) website: www.amicc.org.

12. Transitions Online, August 13–19, 2003.

13. Gary Solis, email correspondence with author, February 16, 2005.

14. Jeremy Rabkin, "The International Kangaroo Court," *Weekly Standard*, April 22, 2002.

15. Jeremy Rabkin, email correspondence with author, April 8, 2005.

16. Monroe Leigh, "The United States and the Statute of Rome," *American Journal of International Law* 95, no. 1 (January 2001): 124–31.

17. Monroe Leigh et al., memo to Chairman Hyde, House Committee on International Relations, February 21, 2001.

18. Leigh, "The United States and the Statute of Rome."

19. John Bolton, remarks to the Federalist Society, Washington, DC, November 14, 2002. Ignatieff recanted his support for the Iraq War in August 2007 ("Getting Iraq Wrong," *New York Times Magazine*, August 5, 2007), but he did not mention torture.

20. Nicolas Thompson, "John Bolton vs the World," *Salon*, July 16, 2003, www.salon.com.

21. President Bush appointed Bolton during a Congressional recess because the US Senate had refused to confirm his nomination. When Bolton was still unable to secure confirmation sixteen months later, he resigned.

22. Jeffrey T. Kuhner, "Balkan Justice Joust," *Washington Times*, October 24, 2004.

23. John Pilger, *Breaking the Silence*, ITV, September 22, 2003.

24. The Abu Ghraib scandal broke in April 2004; the interview with Bolton was conducted on November 5, 2004.

25. The Proxmire Act, 1987, and the War Crimes Act, 1996 (amended 1997). These acts drew directly, if incompletely (and with changes), from international legislation.

26. Many other countries had adapted their domestic laws to comply with the Rome Statute, in order to try persons accused of these crimes at home, thereby avoiding a possible ICC investigation.

27. Poll conducted by National Public Radio, the Kaiser Family Foundation and the Kennedy School of Government at Harvard, published as "Poll: Security Trumps Civil Liberties," at www.npr.org, November 30, 2001; cited in William Schulz, *Tainted Legacy: 9/11 and the Ruin of Human Rights* (New York: Nation Books, 2003), 7–8.

28. "How Far Americans Would Go to Fight Terror," *Christian Science Monitor,* November 14, 2001; Schulz, *Tainted Legacy,* 8.

29. "Poll: Security Trumps Civil Liberties."

5. THE ACTIVIST, THE UN ADVISER, THE WEST POINT PROF

1. The report of the Commission of Inquiry into the Actions of Canadian Officials in Relation to Maher Arar, September 18, 2006.

2. The US ratified the UN Convention against Torture in 1994.

3. White House Statement, November 13, 2001.

4. William Safire,"Seizing Dictatorial Power," *New York Times,* November 15, 2001.

5. William Safire,"Kangaroo Courts," *New York Times,* November 26, 2001.

6. *Turkmen et al. v. Ashcroft et al.*

7. Air Force Lieutenant General Randall Schmidt recommended that Army Major General Geoffrey Miller, the man who was in charge of detainee operations at Guantánamo Bay when the abuse occurred, be reprimanded.

8. www.aclu.org, April 25, 2007.

9. *The New Yorker,* May 24, 2004.

10. The Center for Constitutional Rights, www.ccr-ny.org.

11. In 1983 the Israeli Kahan Commission found that Sharon bore "personal responsibility" and recommended that he be dismissed from his post as minister of defence.

12. United Nations Economic and Social Council, "Advisory Services and Technological Cooperation in the Field of Human Rights," Report of the independent expert on the situation of human rights in Afghanistan, March 11, 2005.

13. *Democracy Now,* April 28,2005.

14. Chicago Public Radio, April 26, 2005.

15. Tim Golden, Ruhallah Khapalwak, Carlotta Gall and David Rohde, "Brutal Details of 2 Afghan Inmates' Deaths," *New York Times,* May 20, 2005.

16. Those citizens were Yaser E. Hamdi and José Padilla.

17. *Online News Hour,* PBS, May 3, 2004.

18. Habeas corpus tests whether a prisoner has been accorded due process according to the law. It is considered a safeguard against illegal imprisonment.

19. On May 8, 2002, José Padilla, an American citizen, arrived in the United States via a regular scheduled commercial airliner. It was alleged that he was

suspected of planning to explode a radioactive device or a "dirty bomb." On June 9, 2002, President Bush declared Padilla an "enemy combatant" and sent him to the prison at Guantánamo Bay. In April 2007, he was charged with "supporting a terrorist organization" and "conspiracy to murder, kidnap and maim." His trial in a federal court opened on May 14, 2007. He was found guilty on August 16, 2007.

20. The case against Donald Rumsfeld was dismissed on March 27, 2007. Chief Judge Thomas A. Hogan of the Federal District Court for the District of Columbia called the case "an indictment of the humanity with which the United States treats its detainees," but he agreed that US officials were immune from lawsuits stemming from actions taken "within the scope of their official duties." www.humanrightsfirst.org.

6. THE OLD SOLDIER

1. This was not an unreasonable assumption, since the United States had helped finance the (failed) French war to keep its colony in Indochina.

2. On March 31, 2005, the Security Council did refer the case of Darfur to the ICC, marking a historic advance in the recognition of the court. The United States agreed to abstain.

7. THE THINGS ROBERT MCNAMARA DIDN'T KNOW

1. Matthew McAllester, "Suspect unapologetic to end," Newsday.com, October 21, 2005.

2. The need to destroy the potential for compassion and empathy in new recruits may explain why the Pentagon's latest military training tool is a video game ("Full Spectrum Warrior"). When a toy can do the job, there is no need for simulators with hydraulics or wall-size screens. Besides, as a military spokesman pointed out, the kids taking the training grew up blowing off the heads of enemies in virtual videos.

3. Instructions for the Government of Armies of the United States in the Field (Lieber Code). April 24, 1863. Section 1. *Martial law—Military jurisdiction—Military necessity—Retaliation*, Art. 22.

4. Geoffrey Best, "Peace Conferences and the Century of Total War: The 1899 Hague Conference and What Came After," *International Affairs* (Royal Institute of International Affairs 1944–) 75, no. 3 (July 1999): 619–34.

5. Ibid. Toward the end of his life Carnegie came to believe that it was not enough to build institutions. "We have to change the way people think," he said.

6. See Nobelprize.org and Beatrix Kempf, *Woman for Peace: The Life of Bertha von Suttner* (Park Ridge, NJ: Noyes Press, 1973).

7. Andrew Dixon White, *The Autobiography of Andrew Dixon White*, vol. 2, chap. 47 (New York: The Century Company, 1905).

8. Geoffrey Best, "Peace Conferences and the Century of Total War," op. cit.
9. See www.haguepeace.org.
10. See www.theodoreroosevelt.org: Theodore Roosevelt Centennial CDRom: "Historical Documents," Mem. Ed. XX, 149; Nat. Ed. XVIII.
11. See www.peaceworkmagazine.org.
12. Laws of War: Laws and Customs of War on Land (Hague IV); October 18, 1907, Article 46.
13. See www.theodoreroosevelt.org: Theodore Roosevelt Centennial CDRom: "Historical Documents," Mem. Ed. XX, 281; Nat. Ed. XVIII, 241.
14. Cherif Bassiouni, "From Versailles to Rwanda in Seventy-Five Years: The Need to Establish a Permanent International Criminal Court," *Harvard Human Rights Journal* 10 (Spring 1997).
15. Wolfgang Schivelbusch, *The Culture of Defeat: On National Trauma, Mourning, and Recovery*, trans. Jefferson Chase (New York: Metropolitan Books, 2003).
16. Cited in Gerry Simpson, "The Trial of Saddam: Justice or Theatre?" BBC News, December 19, 2005.
17. William A. Schabas, *An Introduction to the International Criminal Court*, 5 (Cambridge: Cambridge University Press, 2001).
18. Michael Clodfelter, *Warfare and Armed Conflict: A Statistical Reference to Casualty and Other Figures, 1618–1999.* (Jefferson, NC: McFarland & Company, Inc., 1992).

8. BIRTH PANGS AT NUREMBERG

1. Telford Taylor, *The Anatomy of the Nuremberg Trials* (New York: Knopf, 1992), 539.
2. Cited in Richard Overy, "The Nuremberg Trials: International Law in the Making" in *From Nuremberg to The Hague*, ed. Philippe Sands (Cambridge: Cambridge University Press, 2003), 2.
3. Newly released records of Churchill's war cabinet, cited in *The New York Times*, January 22, 2006.
4. Richard Overy, op. cit., 3.
5. Harry Truman's Diary and Papers, www.trumanlibrary.org, July 25, 1945.
6. Crimes against humanity: murder, extermination, enslavement, deportation, and other inhumane acts committed against civilian populations, before or during the war; or persecutions on political, racial or religious grounds in execution of or in connection with any crime within the jurisdiction of the Tribunal, whether or not in violation of the domestic law of the country where perpetrated. *London Charter of the International Military Tribunal*, August 8, 1945, London, Article 6 (c). "Crimes against Peace" were also codified for the first time.

7. So-called positive law, based on legislation, treaties, precedents etc., gradually replaced natural law, although the latter continues to play a role, as Nuremburg demonstrated.

9. AGAINST IMPUNITY

1. "Rendering an area wholly homogeneous by using force or intimidation to remove persons of given groups from the area." The idea of "cleansing" a place of enemies was used extensively by the Nazis, with regard to the Jews. It also had an earlier Balkan pedigree going back to the 1940s.

2. Ljiljana Smajlović, "The Bad Guys Who Got Away," *Los Angeles Times*, January 23, 2006.

3. Erna Paris, *Long Shadows: Truth, Lies and History* (Toronto: Knopf, 2000). Erna Paris, *Duge Sjene: Istina, Laži i Povijest* (Zagreb: Prometej, 2003).

4. "War Crimes Trials in Serbia," Humanitarian Law Centre, Belgrade, January 11, 2007, www.b92.net/eng/insight/reports.php?yyyy=2007&mm =01&nav_id=39011.

5. Judith Armatta, "Expert Testifies Racak Not Staged," Coalition for International Justice, March 12, 2003.

6. For greater detail, see www.un.org/icty/cases-e/factsheets/achieve-e.htm.

7. See www.ohr.int.

10. RETURN TO BOSNIA

1. On November 30, 2005, Mittal Steel and former camp inmates announced that a memorial would be built at Omarska, but the company almost immediately put its plans on hold because opinion in the community was divided.

2. The United Nations and its 191 member states ignored sexual exploitation by peacekeepers and other field staff for decades and launched a crackdown only in 1994 after reports of abuse surfaced in West Africa and the Democratic Republic of the Congo.

3. *ICTY Prosecutor v. Momir Nikolić*, Case No. IT-02–60/1-S (Srebrenica).

4. On March 7, 2006, a United Nations Development Program poll revealed that almost 97 percent of all Bosnians believed the authorities in their country were corrupt. Agence France-Presse, March 7, 2006.

5. Case No. IT-02–60/1-S; Defence Ex. DS-17.

6. Reported by Emir Suljagić, IWPR, October 30, 2003.

7. "Statement of facts as set out by Dragan Obrenović" Case No. IT-02–60/2 Obrenović, May 20, 2003.

8. Judith Armatta, Coalition for International Justice (CIJ), October 31, 2003.

9. Krstić's appeal expanded the legal definition of genocide when his conviction was changed to "aiding and abetting genocide."

10. Ed Vulliamy, "Srebrenica: ten years on," *Guardian*, April 30, 2005. Vulliamy cited ICTY judge, Fouad Riad.

11. The Jews of Bosnia-Herzegovina are the descendants of Sephardic Jews expelled from Spain in 1492. The Ottoman Empire welcomed the exiles throughout its territory.

12. I am grateful to Dr. Francis Jones of the School of Modern Languages at Newcastle University, UK, for translating this verse for me. According to Dr. Jones, it is an excerpt from the poem "Uspavanka," which "almost certainly" appeared in the 1970 edition of *Kameni spavac* (Sarajevo: Veselin Maslesa).

13. On October 15, 2004, the Republika Srpska Commission on Srebrenica submitted to the Republika Srpska government a report concerning the 1995 events in Srebrenica and acknowledged for the first time that the Bosnian Serb Army had been responsible for the killing of more than seven thousand Bosniak men and boys. Republika Srpska authorities had previously claimed that only one hundred Bosniaks had been executed and that another nineteen hundred died in combat or from exhaustion (Human Rights Watch, World Report, 2005). In September 2007 there were 13,000 untried suspected war criminals according to BiH justice minister, Barisa Colak.

14. On November 20, 2005, a court in Banja Luka became the first in Republika Srpska to sentence three former members of the Bosnian Serb police for the murders of six Bosnian Muslims in Prijedor in March 1994.

15. "Srebrenica: Reconstruction, background, consequences and analysis of the fall of a safe area," Netherlands Institute for War Documentation, April 10, 2002.

16. *International Herald Tribune*, June 15, 2005.

17. The exact number of DNA matches was 11,600. See www.ic-mp.org.

18. In 2006, 892 suspected perpetrators named in the Republika Srpska report on Srebrenica were reported to be employed by governmental and municipal institutions.

19. The first case to be transferred from the ICTY to any Balkan country got off to a rocky start in Sarajevo on February 23, 2006. The defendant, Bosnian Serb Radovan Stanković, was charged with being in charge of a house where at least nine Muslim women and girls were subjected to repeated rape, torture and forced labour during the 1992–95 war. When asked by the judge to state his name, Stanković lambasted the court as incompetent to try his case. "War criminals such as you cannot try me!" he shouted. Agence France-Presse, February 23, 2006.

20. Nasir Orić was convicted on June 30, 2006, of "failing to take steps to prevent the murder and cruel treatment of a number of Serb prisoners in the former UN 'safe area'" and sentenced to two years. His light sentence

reflected the court's consideration of the "limited" nature of the crime. www.un.org/icty/pressreal/2006/p1094e=summary.htm

21. "Reconciliation for Realists," in *Dilemmas of Reconciliation: Cases and Concept*, Carol A. L. Prager and Trudy Govier, eds. (Waterloo, ON: Wilfrid Laurier University Press, 2003).

22.The Scholars' Initiative: Confronting the Yugoslav Controversies, 2001–2006," www.cla.purdue.edu/academic/history/facstaff/Ingrao/si/prospectus.pdf. For the results of their study see United States Institute of Peace, www.usip.org/newsmedia/releases/2006/0105_narrative.html

23. The Bosnia-Herzegovina War Crimes Chamber, a mixed tribunal composed of Bosnian and foreign judges, began its work in late 2005.

24. The Sarajevo court began its work after this meeting.

11. THE MAKING OF THE ICC

1. Principal sources: Cherif Bassiouni, "Negotiating the Treaty of Rome on the Establishment of an International Criminal Court," *Cornell International Law Journal* 32, no. 3 (1999); William A. Schabas, *An Introduction to the International Criminal Court* (Cambridge: Cambridge University Press, 2001); Roy Lee, ed., et al., "The International Criminal Court: The Making of the Rome Statute Issues, Negotiations, Results," *Kluwer Law International* (1999).

2. Carlos Difranchi Núñez Albornoz, lacasadejoe.com/biblioteca.

3. Statute of the Council of Europe, Chapter 1, Article 1. In May 2007, the Council was criticized for allowing Serbia to assume the chair of the organization without first delivering Ratko Mladić and Radovan Karadžić to the ICTY for trial.

4. "Securing Peace in Europe," *Symposium on the Political Relevance of the 1648 Peace of Westphalia*, Münster, November 12, 1998.

5. Speech at Humboldt University, Berlin, May 12, 2000.

6. See www.benferencz.org/arts/69.html.

7. Winston Churchill, *Never Give In! The Best of Winston Churchill's Speeches* (New York: Hyperion, 2003), pp. 299–300.

8. Raphael Lemkin, *Axis Rule in Occupied Europe: Laws of Occupation, Analysis of Government, Proposals for Redress* (Washington, DC: Carnegie Endowment for International Peace, 1944).

9. December 11, 1946; resolution 95(1). The first session opened January 10, 1946.

10. Email correspondence with author, September 19, 2006.

11. What constitutes "aggression" remains a legal quagmire; in 1998, the framers of the Rome Statute referred the subject to yet another working committee.

12. The Like-Minded states were mostly middle powers with no history of military or colonial aggression. They were later joined by developing states, some of whom had experience of the crimes defined in the Rome Statute, so had a strong interest in deterrence.

13. Telephone interview with author, April 25, 2006.

14. Omar represented the Southern African Development Community at the conference.

15. See http://www.dfait-maeci.gc.ca/ciw-cdm/caun/KirschWatt-en.asp.

16. Schabas, *An Introduction to the International Criminal Court*, 9.

17. The vote on "no action" for the US proposal was 113 in favour, 17 against and 25 abstentions. The "no action" vote on India's proposals was 114 in favour, 16 against and 20 abstentions.

12. HISTORY AND JUSTICE

1. The Assembly of States Parties comprised one representative from the eighty-eight countries that had already ratified the Rome Statute.

2. Paris, *Long Shadows*, Chapter 1.

3. The number of people killed in the still-controversial bombings of Dresden has been reassessed by British historian Frederick Taylor, *Dresden: Tuesday, Feb. 13, 1945* (New York: HarperCollins, 2004).

4. In May 2007, Justice Claude Jorda announced his resignation from the ICC for reasons of "permanent ill-health."

5. The question came from Athanasios Pafilis, a member of the Confederal Group of the European United Left—Nordic Green Left, March 16, 2006.

6. *Conversos* were Spanish Jews who converted to Christianity starting in 1391. Many converted to escape persecution by the Inquisition but continued to practise Judaism secretly, both in Spain and in the colonies. See Erna Paris, *The End of Days: A Story of Tolerance, Tyranny and the Expulsion of the Jews from Spain* (Toronto: Lester Publishing, 1995).

13. THE MORAL LANDSCAPE

1 Tony Judt, *Postwar: A History of Europe Since 1945* (New York: Penguin Books, 2005), 601.

2. Judge James Robertson, November 8, 2004. Cited in David Stout, "U.S. Judge Halts Military Trial of Qaeda Suspect at Guantánamo," *New York Times*, November 8, 2004.

3. United States Court of Appeals for the District of Columbia Circuit, [Salim Ahmed] *Hamdan v. Rumsfeld*, July 15, 2005.

4. CBS News, July 27, 2005.

5. Syndicated columnist Michelle Malkin, www.michellemalkin.com.

6. Senator John Warner, R-Va., Senator John McCain, R-Ariz., and Senator

Lindsey Graham, R-S.C. The support was bi-partisan, co-sponsored by
Lindsey Graham, Chuck Hagel, Gordon H. Smith, Susan M. Collins, Lamar
Alexander, Richard Durbin, Carl Levin, John Warner, Lincoln Chafee, John
E. Sununu and Ken Salazar. The unamended bill had already passed in the
House of Representatives.

7. Senate amendment 1977.

8. Lindsey Graham and Carl Levin amendment.

9. BBC News: December 25, 2005.

10. Email correspondence with the author, July 24, 2006.

11. R. Jeffrey Smith, "War Crimes Act Changes Would Reduce the Threat
of Prosecution," *Washington Post*, August 9, 2006.

12. PRNewswire, source: White House Press Office, September 28, 2006.

13. See leahy.senate/gov/press/200609/092806c.html.

14. The new act was cited by the Department of Justice on November 13, 2006.

15. The ICTY confirmed the universal prohibition against torture on
December 10, 1998, in its judgment in the case of Anto Furundzija,
which stated that no state or individual can authorize such acts. "In spite
of possible national authorization by legislative or judicial bodies to violate the principle banning torture, individuals remain bound to comply
with the principle. As the International Military Tribunal at Nuremberg
put it: 'individuals have international duties which transcend the
national obligations of obedience imposed by the individual state.'"
www.un.org/icty/furundzija/trialc2/judgment/index.htm

16. *Monitor*/TIPP poll, *Christian Science Monitor*, November 14, 2001, cited
in William Schulz, *Tainted Legacy: 9/11 and the Ruin of Human Rights* (New
York: Nation Books, 2003), 8.

17. Pew Center, survey of 2,006 adults, October 12–24, 2005.

18. The unreliablity of statements made under torture has been determined
by a multitude of studies, including those conducted on Chileans, Argentines
and other victims of abuse. While researching *Unhealed Wounds: France and
the Klaus Barbie Affair* (1985), I personally interviewed men and women who
were tortured forty years earlier by the Gestapo. To a person, they acknowledged that the need to stop excruciating pain made them admit to whatever
they were asked.

19. Alan Dershowitz promoted the use of legalized torture as early as
September 2002. CBS News, *Sixty Minutes*, September 20, 2002. Following
Dershowitz, Michael Ignatieff made a related case for torture as a "lesser
evil" in May 2004. "Lesser Evils," *New York Times Magazine*, May 2, 2004.

20. Graham's comments are cited in Peter J. Boyer, "The Big Tent: Billy
Graham, Franklin Graham and the Transformation of Evangelicism," *The
New Yorker*, August 22, 2005. Falwell's comments are cited in Alan

Cooperman, "Anti-Muslim remarks stir tempest," *Washington Post*, June 20, 2002. Vines's comments are cited in *Sixty Minutes*, CBS, October 6, 2002.

21. Mark Morford, "Ashcroft Sings, Nation Cringes: More proof positive that the United States Attorney General is quite possibly insane," *SF Gate*, March 8, 2002.

22. By late spring 2006 there had been forty-one suicide attempts since prisoners first began to arrive at the camp in January 2002. In June 2007, a fourth prisoner successfully took his own life.

23. BBC News, June 11, 2006.

24. Amnesty International Annual Report, 2005.

25. Richard W. Stevenson, "Bush hints he won't give in on Bolton documents," *New York Times*, published in *San Francisco Chronicle*, June 1, 2005.

26. Interview on *Larry King Live*, May 30, 2005.

27. William Branigin, "Rumsfeld decries Amnesty Rights Report," *Washington Post*, June 1, 2005.

28. Steve Tetreault, "Porter back from Guantánamo," *Las Vegas Review Journal*, August 3, 2005.

29. Richard W. Stevenson, "Bush Defends Detainee Treatment and Cites 'Stalling' on Bolton," *New York Times*, May 31, 2005.

30. By July 2007 only 375 detainees remained in the Guantánamo Bay prison, and in the face of a Congressional resolution requiring trial, release or transfer, as well as growing public opposition, the Bush administration seemed eager to close the camp. Eighty men were scheduled to be tried under the Military Commissions Act. Another thirty were scheduled for transfer to other countries. Human rights organizations reported that others had been returned to their countries of origin—places that were known to practise torture. Approximately 265 prisoners could not be charged with a crime and had nowhere to go.

31. By 2007, hundreds of detainees had been released from Guantánamo.

32. Judge David Trager published his decision on February 16, 2006. An appeal was launched in December 2006.

33. "Attorneys for Canadian Rendition Victim Vow to Keep Fighting Despite Ruling in Case," Center for Constitutional Rights, February 16, 2006.

34. "Commission of Inquiry into the Actions of Canadian Officials in Relation to Maher Arar," Ottawa, testimony of RCMP Superintendant Mike Cabana, cited in "RCMP shared intelligence with Syria, Arar inquiry told," CBC News. www.cbc.ca, June 30, 2005.

35. Ibid, June 29, 2005.

36. Previously censored documents released in August 2007 confirmed the knowledge and therefore the complicity of Canadian Security agents. "CSIS suspected US would deport Arar to be tortured," CBC News, August 9, 2007.

37. Bisher al-Rawi and Jamil el-Banna. George B. Mickum, *Independent* (London), March 16, 2006.

38. Downing Street memo, July 23, 2002, published in Walter Pincus, "British Intelligence Warned of Iraq War: Blair Was Told of White House's Determination to Use Military Against Hussein," *Washington Post*, May 13, 2005.

39. Richard Norton-Taylor and Clare Dyer, "Defence secretary calls for Geneva Conventions to be redrawn," *Guardian*, April 4, 2006.

40. Vikram Dodd and Carlene Bailey, "Terror Law an Affront to Justice-Judge," *Guardian*, April 13, 2006.

41. Jim Bronskill, "More than six dozen CIA-linked landings in Canada: declassified memos," Canadian Press, February 23, 2006. Beth Duff-Brown, "Memos Detail 74 CIA Landings in Canada," Associated Press, *USA Today*, February 23, 2006.

42. Ibid, *USA Today*.

43. The letter was from Stockwell Day, Minister of Public Safety and Emergency Preparedness.

44. Interview with author, January 31, 2007.

45. ec.europa.eu/commission_barroso/frattini/doc/2006/speech_24_01_06_en.pdf, "Statement by Vice-President Franco Frattini In Regard to the Information Memorandum Issued by Mr. Marty on "Alleged secret detentions in Council of Europe member states," Parliamentary Assembly, Council of Europe, January 24, 2006. On March 7, 2006, the British government admitted that aircraft suspected of being used by the CIA to transport detainees to secret interrogation centres had landed at British military airfields. *Guardian*, March 7, 2006.

46. Ibid. In his report of June 2007, Marty noted that Canada had acknowledged responsibility for the illegal rendition of the Canadian citizen Maher Arar.

47. Council of Europe, PACE, legal affairs, June 8, 2007. assembly.coe.int, Doc. 11302 rev. June 11, 2007.

48. Ibid., *Guardian*, March 7, 2006.

49. The three others were Muayyed Nureddin, Abdullah Almalki and Ahmad El Maati.

50. Graeme Smith, "From Canadian custody into cruel hands," *Globe and Mail*, April 23, 2007.

51. Alan Freeman, "ICC urged to probe transfer," *Globe and Mail*, April 25, 2007.

52. Michelle Shephard, "Some detainees are killers, Day says," *Toronto Star*, April 24, 2007.

53. The case opened on May 3, 2007. The new agreement was announced the same day.

54. Alan Freeman and Jeff Esau, "Hillier muzzles military over detainees," *Globe and Mail*, July 9, 2007

55. Senate bill number 4040. The senators neglected to review the title of their latter bill. They clearly did *not* wish to prosecute "effective terrorists."

56. Senate bill number S4081.

57. Ibid.

58. Associated Press, January 18, 2007.

59. Michael Sung, "Guantánamo detainee Hicks to serve most of 9-month sentence in Australia," *Jurist-Legal News and Research*, March 31, 2007.

60. Vikram Dodd, "Guantánamo man's family release 'torture' dossier," *Guardian*, August 11, 2007.

61. William Glaberson, "A Legal Debate In Guantánamo On Boy Fighters," *New York Times*, June 2, 2007.

62. www.trial-ch.org/en/trial-watch/profile/db/legal-procedures/omar-ahmed_khadr_455.html

63. June 12, 2007, www.lawyersagainstthewar.org. See also www.night-slantern.ca/law/omarkhadr13june07.htm

64. The others charged were former assistant attorney general Jay Bybee, former deputy assistant attorney general John Yoo, former counsel to the vice-president and current chief of staff David S. Addington, and general counsel of the Department of Defense William J. Haynes II.

65. *American Journal of International Law* 10, no. 33 (December 14, 2006).

66. Interview with author at ICC conference "All Roads Lead to Rome," Montreal, April 20–May 2, 2003.

67. Lomé Accord, the peace agreement between the government of Sierra Leone and the Revolutionary United Front of Sierra Leone, Article IX, July 7, 1999.

68. On March 17, 2006, the new Liberian leader, Ellen Johnson-Sirleaf, demanded Taylor's arrest and return for trial. Nigeria claimed ignorance of his whereabouts, but located him after international pressure was applied. Taylor and his trial were later transferred to The Hague for security reasons.

69. Email correspondence with author, January 23, 2007.

70. See www.icc-cpi.int.

71. Pursuant to Security Council Resolution 1564 of September 18, 2004. Report tabled in Geneva, January 5, 2005.

72. Algeria, Brazil and China also abstained.

73. See www.worldpublicopinion.org.

74. Jess Bravin, "US Warms to Hague Tribunal," *Wall Street Journal*, June 14, 2006.

75. Stephanie Hanson, "Africa and the International Criminal Court," www.cfr.org/publication/12048. Hanson cited a Stimson Center report

available at stimson.org/fopo/pdf/US_Military_and_the_ICC_FINAL_
website.pdf.

76. Bantz J. Craddock, "Statement before the Senate Armed Services
Committee," Combat Commander's Military Strategy and Operational
Requirements in Review of the Fiscal Year 2007 Defense Budget, March 14,
2006, www.iccnow.org/documents/CICCFS-CommentsUSofficials_BIA-
ASPA.

77. The ICC received complaints concerning suspected war crimes committed during the Iraq war. These were rejected by the prosecutor on grounds of
non-jurisdiction. Iraq was not a State Party to the Rome Statute, nor had it
accepted the jurisdiction of the court. Without a Security Council referral,
the conflict there was out of bounds. For further information, see
www.icccpi.int/library/organs/otp/OTP_letter_to_senders_re_Iraq_9_
February_2006.pdf.

78. Agence France-Presse, May 24, 2006.

79. "Statement by the Chief Prosecutor Luis Moreno-Ocampo," International
Criminal Court, July 12, 2006.

80. Evans added that Sudan, which was being investigated by the prosecutor,
was not a case where trading away justice was likely to provide direct benefits to peace.

81. For a fuller discussion of South Africa's Truth and Reconciliation
Commission and its impact on society see Paris, *Long Shadows*, Chapter 5.

82. *Mail & Guardian* (Johannesburg, South Africa), January 9, 2007.

83. See www.unicef.org/childalert/drc/content/Child_Alert_DRC_en.pdf,
July 2006.

84. Human Rights Watch took the lead.

85. Lubanga Dyilo's trial was scheduled to open in 2008.

CODA

1. UN News Service, November 24, 2006.

2. Baycrest Centre for Geriatric Care, Toronto.

3. I thank Ewen Allison and Professor John Q. Barrett, St. John's University
School of Law, New York City, for bringing this speech to my attention.

4. Nuremberg Conference on Peace and Justice, June 25–27, 2007.
www.jordanembassy.de/nuremberg_conference_on_peace_an.htm. Edited
by the author. Approved by Luis Moreno-Ocampo.

—

The following selection of English-language books may be of interest to the general reader.

Arendt, Hannah (the Literary Estate of). *Responsibility and Judgment*, Schoken Books, 2003.

Axworthy, Lloyd. *Navigating a New World: Canada's Global Future*, Knopf Canada, 2003.

Byers, Michael. *War Law: Understanding International Law and Armed Conflict*, Douglas & McIntyre, 2005.

Falk, Richard A. *Human Rights Horizons: The Pursuit of Justice in a Globalizing World*, Routledge, 2002

Goldstone, Richard J. *For Humanity: Reflections of a War Crimes Investigator*, Yale University Press, 2000.

Gutman, Roy and Rieff David (eds.). *Crimes of War: What the Public Should Know*, Crimes of War Project, W.W. Norton, 1999.

Hagan, John. *Justice in the Balkans: Prosecuting War Crimes in the Hague Tribunal*, University of Chicago Press, 2003.

Hazan, Pierre. *La Justice face à la guerre: de Nuremberg a La Haye*, Stock, 2000. *Justice In A Time Of War: The True Story Behind The International Criminal Tribunal For The Former Yugoslavia*, tr. by James Thomas Snyder, Texas A&M University Press, 2004

Hersh, Seymour M. *Chain of Command: The Road from 9/11 to Abu Ghraib*, Harper Collins, 2004.

ICC in 2006: Year One: Legal and Political Issues Surrounding the International Criminal Court, International Justice Tribune, Series-No.1, Justice Memo, 2006.

Minow, Martha. *Between Vengeance and Forgiveness: Facing History after Genocide and Mass Violence*, Beacon Press, 1998.

Neier, Aryeh. *War Crimes: Brutality, Genocide, Terror, and the Struggle for Justice*, Times Books, 1998.

Neuffer, Elizabeth. *The Key to my Neighbor's House: Seeking Justice in Bosnia and Rwanda*, Picador, 2001.

Nye, Joseph, S. *The Paradox of American Power: Why The World's Only Superpower Can't Go It Alone*, Oxford University Press, 2002.

Paris, Erna. *Long Shadows: Truth, Lies and History*, Knopf, 2000.

Rabkin, Jeremy A. *The Case for Sovereignty: Why The World Should Welcome American Independence*, The AEI Press, 2004.

Ratner, Michael and Ray, Ellen. *Guantanamo, What The World Should Know*, Chelsea Green Publishing, 2004.

Robertson, Geoffrey. *Crimes Against Humanity: The Struggle for Global Justice*, The New Press, 1999.

Sands, Philippe. *Lawless World: America and the Making and Breaking of Global Rules*, Penguin Books, 2005.

Sands, Philippe (ed.). *From Nuremberg to The Hague: The Future of International Criminal Justice*, Cambridge University Press, 2003.

Schabas, William A. *An Introduction to the International Criminal Court*, Cambridge University Press, 3rd edition, 2007.

———. *The UN International Criminal Tribunals*, Cambridge University Press, 2006.

Schulz, William. *Tainted Legacy: 9/11 and the Ruin of Human Rights*, Nation Books, 2003.

Sewall, Sarah B. and Kaysen, Carl. *The United States and the International Criminal Court: National Security and International Law*, Rowman and Littlefield, 2000.

Taylor, Telford. *The Anatomy of the Nuremberg Trials: A Personal Memoir*, Little Brown & Co (paperback), 1993.

Zompetti, Suzette; Zompetti, Joseph P.; Driscoll, William (eds.). *The International Criminal Court: Global Politics and the Quest for Justice (Idea Sourcebooks in Contemporary Controversies)*, International Debate Education Association, 2004.

—